BEING WITH OLDER PEOPLE

Other titles in the
Systemic Thinking and Practice Series:
edited by David Campbell and Ros Draper
published and distributed by Karnac

Asen, E., Neil Dawson, N., & Mchugh, B. *Multiple Family Therapy:
The Marlborough Model and Its Wider Applications*
Baum, S., & Lynggaard, H. (Eds.) *Intellectual Disabilities: A Systemic
Approach*
Bentovim, A. *Trauma-Organized Systems. Systemic Understanding of Family
Violence: Physical and Sexual Abuse*
Boscolo, L., & Bertrando, P. *Systemic Therapy with Individuals*
Burck, C., & Daniel, G. *Gender and Family Therapy*
Campbell, D., Draper, R., & Huffington, C. *Second Thoughts on the Theory
and Practice of the Milan Approach to Family Therapy*
Campbell, D., Draper, R., & Huffington, C. *Teaching Systemic Thinking*
Campbell, D., & Mason, B. (Eds.) *Perspectives on Supervision*
Cecchin, G., Lane, G., & Ray, W. A. *The Cybernetics of Prejudices in the
Practice of Psychotherapy*
Cecchin, G., Lane, G., & Ray, W. A. *Irreverence: A Strategy for Therapists'
Survival*
Dallos, R. Interacting Stories: *Narratives, Family Beliefs, and Therapy*
Draper, R., Gower, M., & Huffington, C. *Teaching Family Therapy*
Farmer, C. *Psychodrama and Systemic Therapy*
Flaskas, C., Mason, B., & Perlesz, A. *The Space Between: Experience,
Context, and Process in the Therapeutic Relationship*
Flaskas, C., & Perlesz, A. (Eds.) *The Therapeutic Relationship in Systemic
Therapy*
Fredman, G. *Death Talk: Conversations with Children and Families*
Groen, M., & van Lawick, J. *Intimate Warfare: Regarding the Fragility
of Family Relations*
Hildebrand, J. *Bridging the Gap: A Training Module in Personal and
Professional Development*
Hoffman, L. *Exchanging Voices: A Collaborative Approach to Family Therapy*
Jones, E. *Working with Adult Survivors of Child Sexual Abuse*
Jones, E., & Asen, E. *Systemic Couple Therapy and Depression*
Krause, I.-B. *Culture and System in Family Therapy*
Mason, B., & Sawyerr, A. (Eds.) *Exploring the Unsaid: Creativity, Risks, and
Dilemmas in Working Cross-Culturally*
Robinson, M. *Divorce as Family Transition: When Private Sorrow Becomes a
Public Matter*
Seikkula, J., & Arnkil, T. E. *Dialogical Meetings in Social Networks*
Smith, G. *Systemic Approaches to Training in Child Protection*
Wilson, J. *Child-Focused Practice: A Collaborative Systemic Approach*

Credit card orders, Tel: +44(0) 20-7431-1075; Fax: +44(0) 20 7435 9076
Email: shop@karnacbooks.com

BEING WITH OLDER PEOPLE

A Systemic Approach

edited by
Glenda Fredman, Eleanor Anderson,
and Joshua Stott

Systemic Thinking and Practice Series:

Series Editors
David Campbell & Ros Draper

KARNAC

First published in 2010 by
Karnac Books Ltd
118 Finchley Road, London NW3 5HT

British Library Cataloguing in Publication Data

A C.I.P. for this book is available from the British Library

ISBN: 978 1 85575 582 6

Edited, designed and produced by The Studio Publishing Services Ltd
www.publishingservicesuk.co.uk
e-mail: studio@publishingservicesuk.co.uk

www.karnacbooks.com

CONTENTS

ACKNOWLEDGEMENTS

Although we take full responsibility for the written words in this book, we authors cannot take full credit for the ideas and the thinking that inform them, since these have been developed and formed in so many conversations with very many people. We are indebted to the older people, their families, our colleagues, trainees, and supervisees with whom we created the material for this book. Our families and friends gave generously of their time and encouragement to support our writing the several drafts and redrafts that went towards forming this book. There are far too many people who have inspired us and generously shared their stories with us for us to be able to name them all. Therefore, we have decided to dedicate this book to our "elders", whose contribution past and present continue to guide us.

Tom Andersen, Bert Barnes, Charlie Bird, Elma Bird, Lionel Bird, Quentin Blake, Leslie Burke, Violet Burke, David Campbell, Gianfranco Cecchin, Joyce Chitrin, Ronald Coleman, Lloyd Colwell, Mable Colwell, Minnie May Colwell, Vernon Cronen, Mona Cupido, Isla Currie, Ella Davis, Ros Draper, Pamela Ekdawi, Mounir Ekdawi, Jane Fior, Stukkie Fox, Gus Fredman, Sheila Fredman, Jack Galvin, Emmah Gumede, Maria Hansen-Thirifay, Hilda Holyrood, Amelie

Johnson, Arthur Johnson, David Johnson, Sylvia Johnson, Bertha King, Max King, Peter Lang, Barbara Martin, Jack Martin, Minnie Mary Martin, Kate Mcalman, John Messent, Rosa Messent, Lily Miller, Barbara Milton, John Milton, Lillian Morgan, Andry Moustras, Henriette Neiertz, Barnett Pearce, Edith Potter, Charles Potter, Alan Reid, Marion Belle Reid, Vair Reid, Emil Sazdanic, Olga Sazdanic, Momir Pejin, Drenka Pejin, Katica Pejin, Andrija Petronic, Zivana Petronic, Philippa Seligman, John Shotter, Paul Sitsha, George Stonehouse, Lily Stonehouse, Helen Stott, Bill Stott, Janet Stott, Oci Stott, Robin Stott, Rosie Tanner, Eve Toop, Arthur Toop, Margerie Whipp.

Eleanor Anderson was a highly specialist systemic psychotherapist in the older adults mental health service at St Charles Hospital in London, where she pioneered systemic approaches with older adults for eleven years. She is now semi-retired, supervises and consults to other systemic practitioners, works voluntarily with the Bereavement Network at the Peace Hospice in Watford, and enjoys grandparenting and gardening.

Isabelle Ekdawi is a consultant clinical psychologist and accredited systemic psychotherapist. She worked in Camden and Islington older people's services for eight years as joint head of psychology for older people. She is now head of complex needs psychology in Lambeth. Isabelle contributed to systemic training in Camden and Islington and organized the systemic sub-unit for the doctoral clinical psychology training course at University College London. She is co-author of *Whose Reality Is It Anyway: Putting Social Constructionist Philosophy Into Everyday Clinical Practice*, and a freelance consultant and supervisor.

Glenda Fredman is a consultant clinical psychologist and accredited systemic psychotherapist. She is director of foundation and intermediate training courses in systemic psychotherapy with Camden and Islington NHS Foundation Trust. Glenda is committed to sharing systemic approaches with people using and working in public services and values working in the Camden and Islington Older Adults Systemic Project with colleagues who share that enthusiasm. She is tutor/trainer with KCC Foundation, freelance trainer and author of *Death Talk: Conversations with Children and Families* and *Transforming Emotion: Conversations in Counselling and Psychotherapy*.

Esther Hansen is a clinical psychologist working within a range of physical health services for older people in Camden and in surgery at the Royal Free Hospital. She has been working with older people for over five years. She greatly enjoys being part of innovative services for older people. She has completed foundation level accredited training in systemic psychotherapy and uses a systemic approach in much of her work with services and people using them.

Sarah Johnson is a clinical psychologist working within stroke, physical rehabilitation, and mental health services for older people in Camden and Islington NHS Foundation Trust. She is about to complete her intermediate level training in systemic psychotherapy and is interested in applying systemic approaches across different settings with older people who use these services, their families, and carers, and with multi-disciplinary teams.

Eleanor Martin is a consultant clinical psychologist and accredited systemic psychotherapist. She is deputy head of Psychology for Older People in Camden and Islington NHS Foundation Trust. Eleanor is tutor on the foundation course in systemic psychother-apy and has presented and published her work with older people in residential care nationally. Eleanor is dedicated to working with older people, their families, and systems.

Alison Milton is consultant clinical psychologist and head of psy-chology for older people in Camden and Islington. She is also an accredited systemic psychotherapist. Alison contributes to the sys-temic training programme in Camden and Islington and to other teaching and training events nationally. As well as leading the service, Alison's clinical work is in a community mental health team providing mental health care to older people. She has worked with older people for over twelve years.

Goran Petronic was born in Sombor, a small town in former Yugoslavia. He is a clinical psychologist. He is currently working in South East Barnet community mental health team with people suffering from severe and enduring mental health problems. He has published research using "memory work" qualitative research methodology. Goran has a postgraduate certificate in systemic psychotherapy at intermediate level.

Penny Rapaport is a clinical psychologist working with older people in Camden and Islington. She is committed to working systemically with older people, their families and wider systems, and is interested in ways of working which value the knowledge, resources, and experiences that older people bring to a therapeutic context. Penny has completed foundation level accredited training in systemic psychotherapy.

Joshua Stott is a clinical psychologist working with older people in Camden and Islington. He has completed foundation level accredited training in systemic psychotherapy and is committed to systemic practice with older adults and their systems. He is also clinical tutor on the clinical psychology doctorate at University College London, where he is joint co-ordinator of the curriculum as it relates to work with older people. He supervises trainee clinical psychologists in their research.

David Campbell

As I was thumbing through the newspaper recently during one of the coffee breaks that punctuated my writing of this foreword, I came across a newspaper article exclaiming that, for the first time in recorded history , the population the UK over age sixty-five was larger than those under sixteen. If one extends this trend into the future, we will all be faced with major changes in the structure, values, and very fabric of our society. Clearly, the "grey vote" will influence new legislation that reflects the rights and values of older people. Greater purchasing power will mean a new range of products and services for the elderly. But perhaps the area of interest for most of the readership of this book is about the increasing demand on health services, and, most particularly, the mental health services.

Other books in this field focus on the systemic understanding of ageing in the family or community; structural issues that must be addressed in setting up services and some of the technical and personal aspects of providing psychotherapy or supervision of other workers. But this book takes a different direction from the outset. The focus of the book is on the challenge of building relationships with older adults. The assumption of the book is that if we can build relationships that are genuinely reciprocal, these will provide the platform for any interventions or services developed for the elderly.

From the very title, the reader knows that something is afoot. Why should a book aimed at professionals providing mental health services for the elderly be titled *Being with Older People* rather than "working with older people"? I believe the answer to this emphasizes that working with older people is more a state of mind than a series of techniques, and the state of mind requires each person, client, or worker simply to *be* . . . to be themselves, and, thereby, get closer to the being of the other.

In the early chapters the authors contribute to a unique exercise that breathes new life into the practices of social constructionism. They begin by emphasizing the paramount value that memory plays in the lives of older people. It is woven into their identities and provides the groundwork for making relationships with others. In order to prepare a therapist or consultant to become a conversational partner, they are asked in various ways to explore their own memories, or particularly experiences they have had with older people. These personal experiences are shared in the more familiar structure of the reflecting team, who comments and acts as a kind of witness group for the therapists' own memories. In one fell swoop, the authors have utilized many systemic concepts, particularly self-reflexivity, in the service of constructing conversations with older people.

One can easily see how this model would be applied to supervision and consultation to those working with an older age population. The work would focus less on the older person as an "other", and more upon the meaning that memory and conversation with older people have for the carer and her/his evolving relationship with the older person, and how an understanding of this co-constructed conversation can move both participants to new positions.

As one ages, or, shall we say, "becomes an older person", there is always the risk that society will consign this population to a new social category called "older people" that leads to a polarization between us and them: the "us" of the non-older people and the "them" of the older people. This distinction is important in some areas, such as developing services for the appropriate group of service users, but polarizing people in this way also makes it more difficult to make the connections across the different positions, since each position is imbued with its own connotations, values, and emotions. It is important to polarize in order to achieve certain ends, but, as this happens, it is crucial to be aware that we are part of the process of polarizing and be aware of the risks and consequences. We are citizens of the society creating these distinctions. What I have enjoyed about this volume from the start is that it recognizes the complexity of this polarization, but also, in a playful, yet subtle way, it offers the reader ways of thinking and exercises to match that carry one's thinking beyond the polarized positions towards a greater connectedness between the "older" and the "non-older".

The book also practises what it preaches in terms of inviting the reader into a relationship with the authors, each of whom presents his or herself personally and professionally through their memories and reflections of their "being with" older people. The text makes one stop and think twice about possible meanings. For example, they make a distinction between "working with" and "being with" people, and they talk about trying to "speak the theory" in their writing. Many of the sharp, concise sentences kept me a bit off balance as a reader, and I was aware of being taken into new areas of thinking. Throughout, I was aware that the material presented in this book came from personal and professional experiences that had been thoroughly considered, with humility and honesty as the essential building blocks for relationships with older people.

David Campbell
March, 2010

WHO ARE WE IN THIS WORK?

We are a group of ten clinical psychologists and / or systemic family psychotherapists working with older people in inner London. To introduce ourselves to you, our reader, we interviewed each other about "Why we work with older people?"; "What engages us in this work?"; and "What sustains our commitment to working with older people in public services?" Each of us then wrote down our responses to these questions. Three of us (Glenda Fredman, Sarah Johnson, and Penny Rapaport) read all the written responses of the group and drew out the following themes (illustrated with quotes in our own words) that connect us with each other and with our enthusiasm for this work.

What drew us to our work with older people?

Some of us chose to work with older people because we were energized by the variety of the work. Working with older people also offered a good fit with our values and overall view, which made it possible for us to put our systemic principles and skills into practice.

"I have in the past told myself that I 'fell into' work with older people, but actually I think that this is not the case. I think I was initially drawn to it because of the variety of the work. What initially attracted me was that older people came to a service because they are over sixty-five, not because they fall within a particular 'presenting problem' type, and this meant that 'anyone' could walk through the door."

"I also chose it because I liked working with networks of people. When you work with older people, you are nearly always linked into a network of people, both families and professionals. I had finished my systemic training, and this service enabled me to put into practice some of my emerging skills."

"I have always been keen to work with marginalized groups (always had awareness of discrimination and wish to see 'fairness') and see older people as a group with little voice."

Many of us described feeling motivated by positive formative experiences of older family members dating back to when we were children. For example, we grew up with older people with whom we developed special personal connections. Positive images of these older relatives have stayed with us and continue to engage us with the work. They seemed to transcend ageist stereotypes of old age and inspired us with what is possible.

"I remember the story about my great uncle driving around Europe on a motor bike with my Mum on the back. It never occurred to me that he would have been young at the time—I always imagined him being the same age! This image stayed with me and has made me think of the possibilities that are there."

"The 'older people' in my family have never seemed particularly 'old' to me. It was and is their uniqueness and vitality that I value, their experience of life, how they approach the present, their stories of the past, and what got them through difficult times."

"My maternal grandfather lived next door to us until he died at ninety-six. As a small girl I think I saw him as my friend—he was often "silly" (according to my grandmother), which for me meant willing to enter into wonderful worlds of make-believe with me. I had a sense from about the age of ten (when my grandmother died) that our affection for, and interest in, my grandfather kept him going."

"I was partially brought up by my maternal grandmother and came to associate older women with strength and resilience."

Some of us described wanting, through our work, to "make good" or "give back" to our older relatives.

"In retrospect we are now aware in my family that dementia started to take our father away from us probably ten years before he died. . . . Working in this area now reconnects me with my father's experience—it was too hard for me at the time to stay with what was happening to him (and our family) for too long and my youth helped me to put it aside and focus on getting on with building my life. Working with older people now draws me back to those times and I feel I am able to revisit my family experience and draw from it to inform our work with families going through similar experiences."

"I believe what drew me to this work is my love and respect towards my grandparents and a great grandmother who looked after me when I was small. Working with older adults gives me the experience of giving back care and respect to my grandparents."

"I hear my grandmother's voice and think about what she would say about my work."

"Reminding myself of my mother's experiences of ageism—she was so hurt by the way she was treated in hospital when she had surgery at eighty-five—helps me to hold on to these values."

Some of us described experiences of good practice in the care we witnessed older relatives receiving, which inspired us in our future careers:

"It reminds me of the pioneering dementia ward my Granny was on—all patients and staff ate at a central table together and lively conversation always seemed to happen. Each patient had one glass of sherry or wine if they wanted. The patients were treated as people and their histories and practices were respected. It is important for me to recreate that in my work."

Some of us noticed an absence of older people in our lives when growing up and wanted to redress this in our work.

"While I like older people, there have not been many in my life for a long time as all my grandparents had died by the time I was about fifteen. I wonder if this was something that I missed."

Many of us were inspired by our early work experience with older people. We were surprised at how much we enjoyed it. We were also deeply touched by the effects of ageism and discrimination that affected the older people's care.

"I remember volunteering on a holiday for older people, which I really loved—to my surprise (and it wasn't the exotic location—we went to Bracknell in Berkshire!!!)."

"I was surprised on placement working with older people by how much I enjoyed it—I hadn't been looking forward to it—it challenged my stereotypes"

"I would never have chosen to work with older people if I had not had a placement with older people during my training to be a clinical psychologist. It was my second placement and my supervisor encouraged me to listen and not 'do'. This somehow freed up my thinking so that I could hear people talk differently. Through this listening and hearing differently I realized the stories that older people told were rich, complex and often very interesting."

"I am reminded of when I worked as a 'home carer' as a teenager and everyday I would support an older woman called Edna. She seemed to have chosen an unconventional path in her life and as she had grown older she had been labelled as 'eccentric' and 'difficult to engage'. Over time, Edna was felt to be unsafe at home and moved to a nursing home for people with dementia. When I visited her, her wayward hair had been brushed and her red bobble hat removed, her clothes did not seem to be what she would have chosen and the sparkle had gone from her eyes. Although she was extremely well cared for, I couldn't help feeling that the person I knew had been overlooked, and there had been nobody around to advocate on her behalf."

What engages us with this work?

Many of us recounted feeling inspired, energized, and driven by the resourcefulness, resilience, strength, and courage of older people we work with.

"I am inspired by seeing people with very little still laughing, sharing and fighting back."

"I have been moved by watching how people respond to the difficulties they face, either brought on or exacerbated by ageing bodies, minds, and a society that can be indifferent to what they are facing."

"What inspires me is talking with older people who make changes and do things that challenge our assumptions, for example Ev, who is eighty-four and walks down the canal every day giving every boat a free paper. She also alters her grandson's and his friends' trousers so they are really tight. She has had a stroke and depression is in and out of her life. Her resilience inspires me."

"I also love the way this work surprises me—to work with a woman who has never had a sexual relationship who, at seventy-five, says 'now I am ready' and three weeks later finds her 'first lover' can only happen in this field of work."

For us working with older people is a privilege. We see our relationship with them as reciprocal. We learn so much from them, which affects many aspects of our lives both within and outside work. Many of us see our older clients as helping us prepare for our own futures.

"My relationships with older people also seemed more reciprocal—I was learning as I was listening. I got ideas about how I want to live now; I started to appreciate things I had taken for granted so far. I also heard comforting things about how being older can be OK."

"Older people give us small immaterial gifts without realizing it."

"It is a privilege to talk to people who have years of experience of life—to find out what has been important to them, what has enabled them to come through difficulties or what has held them back, what has made them who they are. They link into history, connect to past generations and the values of those times . . . I am now getting older myself, and find people's stories of resilience are inspirational for me. With some of the people I see, it is like having personal mentors for the time ahead."

We appreciate being audience to the rich, complex and interesting stories of older people.

> "I really value hearing the stories of the older people. It is such a privilege to share histories that go back sometimes ninety or one hundred years. I can travel the world, entering different cultures and times without moving from my chair—that is something very special."

> "It is a privilege to work with and hear stories of people who have lived through such a massive period of social, cultural, and political change."

What keeps us going?

Being able to make a valuable contribution to the lives of older people, to work with them to create better futures, sustains us.

> "It is rewarding when together you can find something that helps people find a way out of difficulties or helps people connect with their spirit again. For example, in a network meeting, a woman living in a residential home, whom staff were finding very demanding, articulately expressed for the first time how lonely she felt without her husband and how she wanted more company."

> "What excites and inspires me is how small (systemic) changes can make such big differences. I am reminded of the times when systemic work was first introduced in the 1970s and it seemed like 'magic'! I witness many episodes like that in our work. But now we know this is not magic, but that working holistically, honouring people's dignity, and creating respectful contexts for talk with all significant people involved can create powerful changes."

Our shared values and commitments engage us with this work and keep us going. They include: taking a person-centred approach; addressing and countering discrimination and social inequalities; privileging respect and dignity; and creating connections between people.

> "I am committed to putting the person at the centre of conversations that are happening in our team, to stop them from losing the

person. I have also become aware of my challenge in continuously trying to improve social connections with older people. This connects with my concern about loneliness and its often negative effects."

"I value the opportunity to make older people's lives and experiences more visible to others. It is important to me that older people are included and treated fairly. It is important for me to be respectful, thoughtful, encouraging, and friendly to the people I work with (not just the older people)."

"It is important to me that I take a stance to mental health that is non-discriminatory and is resource- rather than problem-orientated—and situates problems in relationship as opposed to within individuals."

"It is important for me to challenge my prejudices. I grew up in a political regime that discriminated against people because of their race. This touched me deeply and I have—for as long as I can remember—had a commitment to challenge discrimination."

Many of us described feeling sustained by our colleagues and managers (and of course our clients) who inspire us with stamina, commitment, and vision, and by our family and friends who value our work.

"Team members (as well as the clients) help me to hold on to values. Staff in older people's services are very committed. Services for older people are often poorly resourced—staff 'band together'."

"Colleagues and the work have enabled me to reflect upon and challenge my own assumptions".

"My colleagues inspire me with their stamina, commitment, and vision."

". . . that this work also is valued by and appreciated by people I work with and my friends and family."

"My managers also make it possible with their 'up-for-it' stance . . ."

Many of us also spoke of being fuelled by the shared values emerging in our ongoing work together. Working and writing together has made an important contribution to sustaining our optimism and keeping our dreams alive.

> "The Older People's Project has become something of an 'internalized' supervisor. I like that I can contact group members to ask questions and seek ideas. It has also been a source to stimulate my curiosity and offer ideas, opening my mind. It has helped me become more explicit and clear about my intentions and convictions."

> "The group and writing the book have given me a way of theorizing what is important to me—helped me understand why I do what I do. It has helped me develop a language as to what it is about older people that holds my attention."

Our hopes and dreams for the future

This project was inspired by our hopes for developing and providing services that promote respect, dignity, and opportunity for older people and the practitioners who work with them and us. We all wanted our services to be accessible and welcoming to older people, regardless of their ethnicity and physical health status.

> "My hopes are that our service is fair and inclusive and welcoming and more widely available and accessible (in a community sense). I hope that we continue to be a place where people want to work and feel that their opinion and view is valuable and listened to whatever their experience. I hope we can keep this up. I hope that people will look at our service and want to share some of the things we have."

> "This connects to my hopes and dreams of the service providing non-discriminatory services to older people that promote good mental health and provide a rehabilitation model as opposed to symptom based treatment."

> "I am sure that my political and personal commitments fuel my hopes for a service that engages with older people with respect and honours their dignity."

> "I hope that services do not replicate wider societal prejudices and can positively contribute to the older person's life . . . that older persons are thought of as more than just the 'illness' or 'problem'."

We are dreaming of enabling wider changes in our communities that extend beyond the individual older person. Some of us saw these visions as somewhat fanciful or idealistic, yet inspiring us with positive images toward which to strive.

"I have dreams—perhaps fanciful—like setting up 'positive ageing' (Gergen & Gergen, 2008) groups in primary care or developing 'adopt an elder' services for older people to have regular (weekly) contact with one family."

"I hope the service can link older people together—something like the 'Council of the Experienced' for people's voices to be heard both by each other and by other professionals."

"It also connects to my rather more fanciful ideas that the service is a force for thinking about communities that promote mental health rather than focusing solely on individuals with mental health problems. For example, thinking about schemes such as LETS (Croall, 1997) or time banking (Cahn, 1999) that promote 'social capital'."

"Some call it humanistic optimism, whereas I feel it is very natural."

"These hopes are possibly idealistic, although this does not make them a bad thing."

Our work with older people has also sensitized us to ageism and the potential loneliness and invisibility of older people. Since working in this field, we tend to notice older people more and make conscious efforts to respond respectfully and warmly.

"One of the biggest effects of this work on me is how it has sensitized me to ageism and age discrimination. I see it everywhere now—not only in the wider culture but also institutional ageism, which is insidious and not even (yet) named."

"I am more aware of the loneliness and the sense of invisibility that older people experience—I also notice older people more—and I choose consciously to respond respectfully and warmly. I smile at older people crossing the road, get up for them on buses, and engage in conversations in supermarket queues."

References

Cahn, E. (1999). Time dollars, work and community: from "why?" to "why not?" *Futures*, 31: 499.

Croall, J. (1997). *LETS Act Locally*. New York: Calouste Gulbenkian Foundation.

Gergen, M., & Gergen, K. (2008). *Positive Ageing Newsletter*. www.taosinstitute.net/resources/pa/ (accessed 24 November).

CHAPTER ONE

Introduction: being with older people—a systemic approach

Glenda Fredman

I t is a cold, wet, winter's day and we are meeting in a "multi-purpose room" in a day centre for older people in Camden, North London. Some of us are moving furniture, including a television, overhead projector, and small tables, to the back of the rectangular room so that we can arrange the heavy chairs with high backs and plastic mock leather seats along the sides of the walls to help us see each other when we are seated. We are careful not to disturb the lines of white masking tape laid down on the floor for a game of carpet bowls. The scores of the last game still remain on the flipchart: Amy, 6; Angus, 7; and Duncan, 3.

We are all pleased to see each other. For about four years, we have been working together in small teams with older people, their families, and caring networks. Over the years, the group has grown, and today, after a few minutes of debriefing about impossible battles with public transport and the challenges of cycling through the inclement weather, twelve of us practitioners trained as clinical psychologists and/or systemic family psychotherapists settle down to our task for the hour. We have come together to plan the outline of the book we intend to write about our work with older people and their significant systems of carers and families. This is a precious hour. Everyone will be "giving back" time at the end of the day to compensate for the hour lost from clinical practice or the ever-increasing demands of paperwork. I am poised with marker pen in hand next to the flipchart as we begin to brainstorm possible chapter topics. I try to write fast as the words come quickly from the group: "Dementia . . . depression . . . anxiety . . . physical health . . . psychosis . . . death and dying". Then the group falls silent, as if the ideas have dried up. I feel disappointed and disorientated and wonder to myself, "Is this what we have been doing in our work with older people over the past four years?" I ask, "Where do these chapter titles come from? How do they connect with what we have been doing together in our work with older people?" Some group members note that these topics reflect the sorts of headings we might find in "standard psychology textbooks on older people". Others note that the titles all address problems coherent with medical diagnosis. There is some exchange of opinions, such as, "People will expect to find 'dementia' in a book on older people", and "I think we should share our approaches that our older clients, their families, and our colleagues have found useful." We all agree with the view that "we need to write about what we, ourselves, are doing, our practice with older people—not what others have already done or said we should be doing". A working title for the book emerges, "Being With Older People", and we plan to meet again to share stories of our current practice as a way of helping us "reconnect with practice—what we actually do".

This is my memory of our first book-planning meeting. At first, I thought I should check back with all the authors you will meet in this book to agree that the memory is correct, that I have recalled it as it really happened so that I can be sure to tell you, our reader, the "truth" of what happened and not my own fantasy. However, in this book, we authors acknowledge that we construct our memories in conversations with others and in many different contexts. Therefore, there could be as many different versions of the past as there are contexts and people to tell them, with no one version being more accurate, real, or true than another. In this book, we authors have shared our memories of working with older people, first with each other and now with you, our reader, recognizing that remembering "changes what is remembered in ways that enhance and transform it according to the present circumstances" (Middleton & Edwards, 1990, p. 6). We have used our group conversations as the context from which to transform and enhance our memories so that they can make a useful and creative contribution to our future practice with older people. It is this process of remembering, telling, and retelling our memories that has created this book.

How this book came about

About eight years ago, my manager, Dr John Cape, suggested I join the clinical psychologists working with older people's services in Camden and Islington, London, to support systemic practice with older people and their significant networks of family and carers. Over a period of about four years, Isabelle Ekdawi, Alison Milton, Eleanor Martin, and I, all clinical psychologists and systemic psychotherapists, met fortnightly to work with older people. Over that time, Alison Pearce, Philippa Hyman, Louise Crocker, and Sarah Scott, also clinical psychologists who have since left our older people's service, joined with us as we worked in teams with older people and their families in their own homes, in hospital wards, day centres, and in outpatient settings.

Bringing together older people with their networks of families, carers, and practitioners created opportunities for significant changes for the people with whom we worked. We were able to facilitate communication between older people and family members and open space for practitioners to co-ordinate plans, not only with each other, but also to include their older patients and family members in the decision-making. Because of the positive outcomes that followed our meetings with older people, their families, and carers, Isabelle, Alison, and Eleanor went on to set up regular systemic clinics for older people within their psychology services, where they offered systemic couple and family therapy (see Chapter Nine). By this time, Josh Stott, Penny Rapaport, Sarah Johnson, and, later, Esther Hansen were also part of the clinical psychology service. Having witnessed the positive outcomes of this work, John Cape invited me to join the group in writing up the approach we were using. He said, "This work is innovative . . . I think people could learn from what you are doing." We invited Eleanor Anderson to join our group, and she brought with her a wealth of experience and memories from her work as a systemic family therapist at St Charles Hospital in West London.

All of us work in the inner city of London. The older people with whom we work represent London's rich multi-ethnic population. Many of the people we see live on their own; some reside in supported housing or residential homes. We also work with people in nursing homes and hospital medical and psychiatric wards. Many of the older people using our services have been given mental health diagnoses that carry stigma, as Bob reflects when he tells Esther Hansen, in Chapter Six, that he has no hopes for their work together since "you have probably already read my notes—they say I have a paranoid personality disorder." The older people we see also commonly experience discrimination because of their age and health status, and possibly also their race, culture, or physical or cognitive disability. In our search for literature to inform our work with these situations, we found no books that specifically addressed therapeutic practice with older people in the contexts of power and discrimination in relation to gender, race, sexuality, physical and cognitive ability, and, of course, age. Therefore, we authors of this book joined together with enthusiasm to write up our work with a view to sharing the principles and practices of the systemic approach we were using to work with older adults and their significant systems of family, carers, and practitioners. We hoped to offer a practical approach to the challenges facing practitioners and the older people with whom they work.

We have tried to write this book in a style accessible to a range of practitioners interested in making their encounters with older people more therapeutic. This book is, therefore, intended for practitioners working with older adults across a range of contexts and disciplines: for example, nurses, psychotherapists, residential workers, managers of care homes, psychologists, social workers, doctors, and occupational therapists. It could also be of use to older people, their families, and carers to create openings for potentially challenging conversations.

How we created this book

Following our first planning meeting, our group convened fortnightly to share memories of our practice. Since some of our group wanted to make sure our memories reflected "key themes found in standard textbooks", we chose some of these themes like "dementia", "death and dying", "delusions and hearing voices" and "physical health" as triggers to our memories.

At first we told our memory stories spontaneously to the group. Our stories touched us in profound ways and some of us were moved to tears as well as deeply inspired by the stories. After the story-telling, four or five of us would reflect in front of the group, talking to each other in a small circle about the connections and differences we noted between the memories. We considered themes that might pull these connections together. A second small group of four or five then connected with the themes discussed in the first group and reflected on connections with the theory and literature we had read. Everyone was very excited by this process of telling and re-telling, and telling about the re-telling. It brought our work alive. We were staying close to the experience we were recounting and also we were learning so much, not only from each other, but also from the telling of our own experiences. Seeing potential for learning from practice in this process, many of us began to bring trainees to the meetings. At this point, we began to call ourselves the "Older People's Project" and agreed that a personal or professional memory was "currency" to participate in the project.

It was at this stage that Goran Petronic joined our group as a trainee clinical psychologist. What we were doing immediately resonated for Goran with the memory work methodology (Haug, 1987) he had used in his own previous research (Petronic, 2001). There was a wish in the group to start recording our "tellings" and "retellings" in written form so as not to lose "the richness". I re-engaged with the memory work approach of Crawford, Kippax, Onyx, Gault, and Benton (1992), which helped us to organize our reporting and recording. Therefore, we agreed to bring written versions of our memories to future meetings. I go on below to invite you into the process of how we generated the material for this book from writing and telling our memories of "striking moments" (Shotter, 2004) with older people to finding and sharing possibility stories that point to ways to go on.

We began by sharing memories of our work with older people across a range of contexts, including mental and physical health and residential care. Some of us shared personal memories relating to our families, friends, and members of our communities. We all listened as each person read to the group their own memory, triggered by the same topic. We each expressed our ideas about each memory in turn, naming what struck us, what touched or moved us, and what inspired us. Then we drew out themes that connected our memories and connected these themes to questions and dilemmas in our practice. These questions and dilemmas pointed us towards recollecting other stories from our practice and professional literature, thereby orienting ourselves to new possibilities for our work with older people. In this way, we were involved in a recursive, spiral-like process of five phases, the first phase being our writing and telling memories from experience and the second phase involving reflecting on and connecting the memories. The possibility stories generated from this process of ours of remembering, telling, and retelling, and then telling about the re-telling, offered new memories from which we could find new themes, patterns, and connections that opened space for further new ways to go on with older people (Figure 1.1). You may prefer to skip the next section, in which I unpack this process with more detailed examples, and return to it later once you have immersed yourself in the stories and practices we present in the book. In this case you might move on to our "Guiding principles", which begin with our acknowledgement that "Age is just a number" (p. 15).

Writing and telling our memories (Phase one)

We continued to use our original topics, such as "dementia" and "death and dying" to trigger our written memories. We wrote our memories on our own, and then read them aloud in the presence of the whole group. It did not matter how accurate the memory was, as we were trying to capture the meanings of an event for each of us. We wanted the memories to reflect striking moments from our experience. For example, we sought moments where we felt absorbed in the conversation, where our curiosity was sparked, where we learnt something, or moments that inspired or moved us. To help newcomers connect with what we were doing, we prepared guidelines for writing memories. These guidelines evolved over time (see Figure 1.2). The approach and practices we present in this book emerged from these memories and, thus, are grounded in experience and in practice.

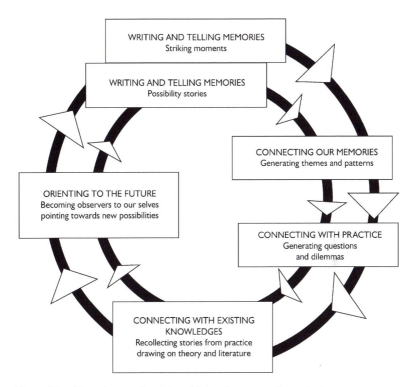

Figure 1.1.   Five phases of writing this book: a recursive spiral.

This was a new way of writing for many people in the group. As professionals, and especially for those of us trained within the discipline of psychology, we had been taught to write as external observers to ourselves and to those with whom we work. Shotter (2004, p. 164) calls this "monological–retrospective–objective" writing or "aboutness writing", which is intended to address professionals and academics. We, however, wanted to write our memories, not as detached observers, but as participants involved in the ongoing process; we wanted to write "from within" the "living moment", to immerse ourselves in what Shotter calls "withness writing". To help us do this, we freeze-framed a moment we had shared with older people and then visited and revisited that moment, each time searching for new facets of the moment we may not have noticed. We wrote about concrete details, quoted the spoken words, and used metaphors, making comparisons. We often

---

1. Write a memory of a particular moment that involves [trigger word, e.g., Dementia]
Choose a moment where you were touched or moved or struck, or inspired with wonder. Share a moment that you have experienced as emotionally rich or as wisdom.
We are not looking for ideal examples but rather examples that raise questions, illustrate dilemmas, spark our curiosity, or inspire or move us—John Shotter calls these "striking moments"; Peter Lang calls them "moments of wonder".
2. Write the description in the third person (e.g., Glenda was standing next to her father. They were both facing the mirror. She could see her reflection as well as his . . .) or the first person (e.g., "I was standing next to my father. We were both . . .")
Choose to write in the person position that is most generative of the memory.
You may choose to write first from one person position and then from another to thicken your telling of the memory.
3. Describe as much detail as possible. Include even inconsequential or trivial detail, paying attention to sounds, smells, what is happening around you as if you are inviting the reader to live the moment with you—like a video-replay of the episode.
4. Describe without interpretation, explanation or theory.
We are trying to avoid retrospective judgements. We can include thoughts or judgements made in the course of the remembered episode.

Figure 1.2.   Guidelines for writing memories.

wrote the memory twice, using different person positions, for example in the third person and then in the first person to thicken our telling of the memory.

Throughout this book, we will share with you, our reader, a selection of the wealth of moving memories we produced, such as the following, which are samples of the memories we generated from the trigger "dementia".

> We are standing in front of the mirror. My left arm is linked under my father's right arm, my hand holding him around his dwindling waist. He holds his right arm around me in a similar manner. He is leaning slightly to the right. Suddenly he raises his left hand above his head and waves, at the same time calling out loudly, "Hello!" When I ask him, "Who are you waving at Dad?"; he replies, "Who is that old man over there waving at me—standing there with that pretty young girl?" I laugh. We laugh together. [Glenda and her father, seventy-four]

Golda sits with her arms crossed, an angry look on her face as she tells Steven yet again how useless he is, how she has never asked to be "a carer", how she "cannot be doing with all this". [Eleanor Anderson with Steven, seventy-four, and Golda, seventy]

She asked me, "How is the little one?" and "How did you get here?" I said, "I walked around Granny", and she replied, "Oh, I thought you came in your little red aeroplane." I started laughing but at the same time felt wrong for doing so. [Eleanor Martin with her grandmother, eighty-eight]

Tom, whom I care co-ordinate, is sitting opposite his wife, Annette. He is smiling, his bright eyes hidden from me by the angled light hitting his glasses. I, sitting on a sofa, drinking a cup of the previously proffered orange juice and thinking it would have been impossible and offensive to refuse, wonder aloud what it would be useful for us to talk about today. Annette says that perhaps the most important thing she has to discuss is how to do all the things she has to do, wrangling with the builders, attending her own frequent hospital appointments, dealing with her own semi-blindness and mobility, while simultaneously looking after her husband. Tom has, she says, become "even more like a baby . . . just like a baby, no use any more", and her hand is shaking. I look towards her husband and, although I still cannot see his eyes, I can see that he is not smiling any more and I wonder how much he understands. [Josh with Annette, eighty-one, and Tom, eighty-six]

The point of writing our memories from within the living moment was to help us open space for new ways of perceiving our experience with older people. Therefore, we used the methods of memory work to help us, not to discover new facts, but to change our way of looking at things (Shotter, 2008). We have drawn from, not replicated, the memory work methods of Haug (1987) and Crawford, Kippax, Onyx, Gault, and Benton (1992) and developed them to fit our purpose. Thus, the process of our inquiry was emergent from our practice and our choice of methods were driven by the questions that emerged from our practice. In this way, we were involved in a process of "practical enquiry".

Connecting our memories (Phase two)

When we had heard all the memories for a particular trigger topic, we engaged in a series of reflecting conversations in response to the memory sharing. Subgroups of four or five people formed a small circle and talked together, while the rest of the group listened to their conversation. The subgroups followed on from each other, talking together, reflecting on the previous conversation, and building on each other's reflections. Thus, we used a series of reflecting conversations to explore first similarities and differences between the memories, what was not written in the memories that we expected might be included, and aspects or events that did not appear amenable to comparison. Second, we noted continuous elements, recurring themes, and common patterns between the memories, also identifying cultural imperatives or popular conceptions that were emerging. For example, in relation to the dementia memories, the themes of "setting up meetings", "identity", "impact on roles and relations with carers" and "our personal and professional relationship with dementia" emerged.

The new "carers" theme that emerged from the dementia memories generated further memories, such as Eleanor Martin's memory of Henrietta, and my memory of a conversation with my mother, which follow.

> Henrietta replied, "Oh, he has been fine. It's me who has a problem. I thought we would ride off into the sunset together when we retired, not him ride off in an ambulance to a day centre every morning. It makes me so sad." [Eleanor M with Henrietta, aged seventy]

> I asked, "Did you talk to anyone about Dad when you noticed those early signs [of dementia] . . . in those early days?" My mother replied, "I never said a word to anyone." I asked, "Why not?" My mother stared ahead for quite some time, as if she was looking out of the window for the answer. Then she turned to me, frowning, and replied, "I don't know." She paused again and looked ahead once more as if still searching before asking, "Do you think I could have been ashamed?" [Glenda with her mother, aged eighty-four]

We contributed these memories to a new pool of carers' memories. Later, we included "diversity", "loneliness", "gender", "sexuality", and "spirituality" as further triggers for memories.

Starting from practice was a very different approach for many psychologists in the group, who were trained to use theory to lead their practice. Some group members complained that this approach to writing the book was "too slow", and queried, "Why don't we just write it?" Other group members responded with, "And if we 'just write' how will we write . . . what will we write?" Most of the group were inspired by the approach, which was enabling us to "stay client centred", "ground our approach in practice", and "generate richer accounts", and so we agreed to continue.

Connecting with practice: generating dilemmas and questions (Phase three)

Having generated connecting themes from our memories, we moved on to ask ourselves, "What questions about practice do these themes (from our memories) bring forth? Do they highlight, or point us to, any dilemmas?" Our exploration of the dementia topic generated questions such as: how do we set up therapy sessions with people with cognitive impairment? How would people affected by dementia like to be described; what stories would they like told about them? How do we incorporate some of the laughter and lightness that we see in personal relationships into our professional relationship with dementia? How do we manage feelings of helplessness and strong personal emotions? How can we make power imbalances clear and address these? How can we attend to our prejudices and assumptions? How might we manage different roles, such as "identifying risk", "being positioned to do an assessment to stop medication", "care co-ordinating" and "addressing the emotional impact of changes"?

We documented the practice questions we generated for each trigger topic. As we repeated this process with different topics, for example, "loneliness", "diversity", "physical health", we found some new and many similar themes and practice questions emerging, and it was these connecting and recurring themes and questions that we used to form chapter titles and subheadings that became this book.

Connecting with our existing knowledges (Phase four)

Having generated a range of practice questions and dilemmas, we revisited our practice with older people. Using reflecting conversations, we shared recollections from our experience of useful practices evoked by the themes, questions, and dilemmas. Then we built on the ideas generated by keeping in mind questions such as, "how might our existing theories account for what we have experienced and learnt here?" Thus, each subgroup revisited the memories, new stories, and ideas from practice told in previous reflecting conversations in the context of a range of theories that they drew from the professional literature. In this way, the issues and practices presented in this book emerge from experience, and theory was constructed from practice.

Orienting to the future (Phase five)

Writing and sharing our memories offered us the opportunity to create new meanings, directions and practices for working with older people. Engaging with our memories, having a conversation with them, responding to them "as another responds to oneself" (Crawford, Kippax, Onyx, Gault, & Benton, 1992, p. 39) already offered us two or more perspectives on our experience and, therefore, new ways of relating to our situations. By reflecting on the connections between our memories, thereby looking at them from multiple perspectives, we were engaging in what Andersen (1995) called "reflecting processes". Generating themes, dilemmas, and questions, and then reviewing our practice experience and professional theories to shed further light on these dilemmas, pointed us towards new practices.

Like Crawford and colleagues, we also found that we engaged in a sort of "consciousness raising" through this process. By examining our own memories, we were exploring our own participation in the process of our socialization as professionals in our fields. Our memories enabled us to explore how we have become professionally socialized; how our professional identities have been formed. For example, the memories that follow invited not only Penny, Eleanor Martin, and Eleanor Anderson, who wrote those memories, but all of us, hearing their memories, to examine our assumptions, prejudices, and pre-understandings in relation to age and sexuality.

> When Kirsten, a Danish woman, told me that she was appreciating men again in a way she had not for a long time, I asked her what effect this new appreciation had on her relationships with, for

example, her sons. She laughed and said, "I love your English-ness—only an Englishwoman could ask about sons, not lovers." [Eleanor M with Kirsten, aged seventy-four]

Brian laughed dryly and said, "Being seen anywhere in public with you would be like being babysat." I imagined myself in the betting shop or pub that Brian wanted to get back to and could not help wondering what Brian was making of me—this young woman visiting his home fortnightly to offer cognitive behavioural therapy for his fear of leaving the house. [Penny with Brian, aged seventy-three]

My younger and very attractive female colleague had not been able to work with Arnold because he constantly made risqué jokes. She had complained that he was "unable to talk about what really mattered". Not long after we met, Arnold told me how much he missed his "physical relationship" with his wife since he had started taking the antidepressants. I wondered if the fact that I was older, not so "sexy", made it easier for Arnold to talk with me. But then a small part of me felt sad that I was no longer so young and "sexy". [Eleanor A with Arnold, aged seventy-five]

Reflecting on these memories sensitized us to the discourses and power imbalances that shape and form who we are and how we act as professionals. By discourse, we mean interrelated ideas, prac-tices, assumptions, rules, and institutional structures that share common values and both reflect and construct a specific worldview (Burr, 1995; Hare Mustin, 1994). Thus, our telling, re-telling, and reflecting on the tellings of our memories enabled us to become observers to our selves and to our discourses, and, thus, to question the ethics of our practice. In this way, we were enabled to find new ways of looking that oriented our future practice so that we found new ways to go on.

Thus, we used the questions and dilemmas to orient us, asking ourselves, "Where do they point us?" "What can we find in our experience to shed light on these dilemmas?" By looking at our experience, rather than just thinking in general terms, we began to respond to our current situations in terms of their particular details rather than general or abstract pre-formed theories. We acted in response to what we saw, experienced, and felt, and not just what we thought. Thus, this process prepared us for how to go on by orienting us to our situations in a new way.

As we continued, we began to share more of what we went on to call "possibility stories" that pointed to further new ways of working with older people. For example, in Chapter Ten, Josh discusses how loneliness and isolation brought despondency upon both Ron, seventy-five, and himself, when they began to address ending their contact. Josh shows how Eleanor Martin's story of "Martha and the Mother Book" lifted his own despondency and inspired him with hope and possibilities to approach the ending with Ron.

Writing this book

Throughout this book, we have tried to privilege the voices of the people with whom we work, the older people, their carers, families, and practitioners. Therefore, we have offered detailed descriptions of memories of "arresting moments" (Shotter & Katz, 1998, p. 81) in practice, verbatim quotes of words or phrases people used in the course of conversation as well as transcripts of conversations. Recognizing that writing always involves interpreting, our writing of this book aims not to "explain" but to "portray", that is, to sketch a picture that "brings alive the qualities of the phenomenon", the "living moments" (*ibid.*). By "tacking back-and-forth" (Geertz, 1983, p. 33) between our portrayals of striking moments from practice, the emergent themes and patterns we identified, and our accounts of connections with practice, we have developed the multi-layered practical theories we present in this book. Thus, as theory emerged from practice and practice became theory, we have been able to elaborate further repertoires, thus increasing the choice of moves available to practitioners working with older people.

We wrote this book as a team over several years. The ten of us, with Philippa Hyman, Sarah Scott, and Harriet Conniff, all contributed to our collection of well over a hundred memories. We documented the themes we identified and recorded the questions and dilemmas that emerged in writing. We transcribed from tape recordings our recollections of practice stories and possibility stories that we generated. We also made notes of the ideas we contributed from professional theories and literature, including resources we might continue to use. We all used these writings of ours as our resource materials. Therefore, although specific authors took responsibility for writing the chapters, this book is a co-creation of all those who participated in the Older People's Project. What emerged through our writing was how we "work with" and especially how we "be with" older people. The titles of our chapters, which reflect the themes emerging from our practice, therefore point not only to what we do in our systemic practice, but also to the ethics and aesthetics of our approach. Thus, throughout this book, we use a practical theory, intending our presentation of personal stories, transcripts of conversations, and case vignettes, wherever possible, to "speak" the theory. In order to ensure that the people presented cannot be recognized by others, we have changed their names and other potentially identifying characteristics. In some situations, we have merged examples or combined the experiences or reports of different people to construct one composite "profile". This approach is intended to protect anonymity further.

This book offers a practical approach to how we relate and interact with people in all sorts of contexts, not just therapy. We offer a repertoire of possibilities, a practical theory, to use in different contexts, not a manualized therapy. Thus, we invite you, our reader, to take what fits for you. Our ethics and practices are intricately interwoven into what Lang, Little, and Cronen (1990) call the "aesthetics" of systemic practice. I will go on to outline the beliefs, values, and principles guiding us towards these aesthetic practices. To whet your appetite, I share some examples of how we authors have used these guiding principles in the chapters that follow.

Age is just a number

Seventeen-year-old Jasper told seventy-two-year-old Simon, "Age is just a number" when Simon playfully asked Jasper and another teenager, "Can I join your football team?" This older man and the two young men were users of our mental health services. We had invited them to participate in a group of "experience consultants" (Epston, White, & "Ben", 1995; Katz, Conant, Inui, Baron, & Bor, 2000; Walnum, 2007; see also Chapter Ten) comprising six adults, older adults, and young people whom we were consulting to help us improve our work with clients using our mental health services. About fifty clinical psychologists working with children, adults, people with intellectual disabilities, and with older adults in our Camden and Islington clinical psychology service witnessed this conversation. They laughed, albeit "with" Simon, when he put himself forward for the football team.

Although our services identify "older people" as "over sixty-five years", we approach age in this book in much the same way as Jasper's wise words suggest, as a social construction (Gergen, 1999). Central to this perspective is the notion that we construct our realities in conversations and relationships with others, and that these realities are constituted through language and maintained through narratives. Hence, there is no essential truth, but only knowledge that arises within communities of knowers (Freedman & Combs, 1996). In this sense, then, "old" is not an objective phenomenon, but is a construction, a label given to certain actions and observations, which consequently constitutes the identities of some people within a culture. (This is not to say that these constructions do not have real effects.) Therefore, we recognize that meanings of "old age" change over time, as Gracie succinctly suggested on her seventieth birthday, when she exclaimed, "Old is the new young!" We also acknowledge that the meanings of age and "old" are informed by how they are used in particular contexts and shape our sense of ourselves, as my ninety-three-year-old friend, Rachel, shows with her comment, "I had never thought of myself as old . . . well, not in that way anyway . . . but people are constantly reminding me that I am old . . . they say, 'What do you expect at your age?' when I complain that I cannot walk now and that my health does not get better."

We also recognize that changing historical, political, and social contexts continually modify how and whom we identify as "old" and the language we use to describe older people (Gergen & Gergen, 2000). Gracie also told me, "I feel different when I think of myself as senior citizen—it makes me feel important, like I have finally reached the top class . . . 'Pensioner' makes me feel I am over the hill and no one is interested in what I have to say . . .." Making distinctions between people with language is never neutral. As Rachel shows, we do not always have the power to choose our own self-descriptions and labels: "old", "elderly", "senior citizen", and "pensioner" are commonly attributed by people holding most power.

Attention to language

Throughout this book, therefore, we pay careful attention to the language we use. Believing that how we talk about people influences what they and we become, we try to talk about the people with whom we work respectfully at all times, even when they are not with us. Chapter Two shows how naming requests from other practitioners for our involvement as "gracious invitations" helps us avoid connoting referrals as "demands" or "obligations" and, thus, helps us position ourselves respectfully with referrers and colleagues. Chapters Six, Seven and Eight give examples of how attributing a label or causal description to people's problems can invite blaming or negative self-descriptions which, at worst, can speak to our older clients not only of who they are, but who they can become. Chapter Seven describes how using externalizing language to separate the person from the problem can open space for positive aspects of identity to be expressed.

Mindful that a word or phrase can enhance the identity of a member of one generation while diminishing the identity of a member from a different generation, Chapter Six shows how the authors check with older clients what words they prefer to describe their ethnicity and clarify the meanings they give to words such as "black", or "people of colour". Therefore, throughout this book, we approach the meanings of words as uniquely related to the people we are talking with and pay attention to communication, taking care how we construct and co-ordinate our meanings with older people and their network of family and carers.

Communication

Attention to communication is central to our systemic constructionist approach. In interaction, it is taken that all behaviour is communication. Chapters Four and Five suggest how we might facilitate the process of communication by adjusting the pace and style of our talks so that family members, including the older person, can listen and talk to one another and feel able to express their opinions. Throughout this book, we try to stay close to the client's language, modifying our own language and resisting the temptation to attribute meanings according to our own ideas and biases, allowing time for the older people to give their own mean-ing in their own time. Chapters Four and Five offer useful pointers as to how we might tailor our talk to the older person's compre-hension and communication abilities, so that people with cognitive or physical impairment or communication difficulties may be engaged in a systemic process and helped to have a voice that others can hear.

Not knowing too quickly

Recognizing that the meaning of the message is given as much by the receiver as the sender (Maturana & Varela, 1980), we take time to join with people's logic of meaning, trying to connect with how they understand the "message" we offer. In Chapter Four, Agnes, aged eighty-three, shows us that when practitioners assume we "know already" what people mean we are at risk of disconnecting from the people we are talking with, as we become more involved in our relationships with what we know than with the people we are intending to help. Intending to "know from" the other, on the other hand, positions us to connect with them in a collaborative conversation. Therefore, Chapter Four offers relational practices towards creating contexts for talking and listening with older people where they feel comfortable and respected, which include "talking about talking", co-creating a contract and focus for the work, and adopting a "learned not knowing" and "curious" stance.

Assuming that clients are the best judges of what is useful, Chapter Four suggests how we might refer to clients' expertise on their experience. The authors ask about the effects of their practices and modify what they do according to clients' responses to ensure that their efforts have the intended empowering effects, rather than unintended disempowering effects. Informed by this ethos, we never assume that people meeting with us want, or even expect, to talk. In Chapters Two and Five, therefore, we carefully frame our invitations to older people and their networks in terms of how "useful" we can be rather than how "helpful", since we have found the idea of taking help less likely to engage older clients. We also explore with curiosity rather than assume that we have found a suitable time for talking and take into account whether we have sufficiently created the sort of relationship that can enable a conversation in the way people want to have it, if at all. The use of relationship questions, rather than statements or suggestions, is central to the systemic method (Tomm, 1988) we use in this book. Therefore, we ask questions about relationships between people and between versions of one's self. We also ask questions about the difference between people's views and between contexts. News of difference is intended to introduce new information (Bateson, 1979) to the interviewee and, thereby, to create opportunities for new meanings to emerge and for possibilities of change. The choice of language and the juxtaposition of certain questions also introduce new information into our conversations and enable clients and practitioners to make new connections. It is intended that clients become observers to their own thinking, actions, and contexts in the process of considering their answers to systemic questions. Chapter Nine shows how questions that address the effects or consequences of beliefs on actions or relationships, or of relationships on actions or beliefs, have invited practitioners to look at themselves, their older clients and patients, and their situations from different perspectives.

Multiple perspectives and many stories

Rather than giving advice or interpretations informed by our own preferred theories or beliefs, therefore, we ask questions that closely follow the clients' feedback in an attempt to explore their preferred theses and explanations, thus generating multiple views from which to formulate ways to go on. In this respect, we are influenced by the systemic approach as described by Boscolo, Cecchin, Hoffman, and Penn (1987). That is, we are not trying to predict the behaviour of clients, recognizing that human biological systems are more complex than machines. Rather, we intend to engage clients in the exploration of "hypotheses" from a position of curiosity (Cecchin, 1987) so as to introduce difference and open space for change. In Chapters Two and Ten we show how systemic hypothesizing helps us to generate a repertoire of ideas that the therapist can use to facilitate the therapeutic relationship. Hypothesizing also helps us to become aware of our own beliefs and prejudices and of how the discourses informing them might affect our interactions with people in meetings (Chapter Three). By sharing systemic hypotheses with other practitioners, the authors of Chapter Nine create contexts where different ways of seeing can be welcomed, thereby introducing systemic perspectives into their services.

Many of the authors of this book use versions of reflecting teams to present and value multiple perspectives. The lead practitioner interviews the clients, who may be any combination of individuals, couples, families, care staff, or significant professionals. The team listens to the interview while they talk. At a time agreed with those being interviewed, the team talks about what they have heard while the lead practitioner and those who were interviewed listen. This creates an opportunity for the team to offer multiple perspectives, for the family to hear different conversations and to enable more egalitarian relationships between clients and practitioners. Using the language of the clients, the team talks tentatively and respectfully about what has been said (not what is not said) and offers differences that are not too unusual (Andersen, 1987; Lax, 1995).

Recognizing that no one story is the final story, we invite multiple perspectives and look for different understandings that can create opportunities to reformulate the most generative and life-enhancing story for the older person. The use of the word "story" here does not suggest that people are living a fantasy, or that the stories people construct are whimsical. Rather, it implies that narratives are constructed to make sense of experience and that the meanings these stories hold provide a framework for interpreting further experiences and for influencing actions. Chapter Seven addresses how negative stories about old age can hide stories of hope and ability. The authors suggest how we might resurrect former life-enhancing stories while also respectfully witnessing challenges facing older people. Chapter Eight suggests how we can navigate a way through the different professional discourses which may be contradictory to, or conflicting with, our preferred discourse. Coherent with the systemic approach informing our practice in this book, we approach discourses not as right or wrong, but more or less useful to the situation. Thus, in Chapters Three, Six and Eight, we suggest how we might become reflexive to our discourses and use them as a resource towards collaborative practice with the practitioners and older people with whom we work.

Collaboration

With a systemic approach we are mindful that since people are connected in relationship, what one person does has an effect on other people in the system as well as on relationships. Therefore, we pay careful attention to relationships with clients, referrers, carers, family, and community. Working to facilitate connections for older people, our intention is to enable movement from a relationship pattern in which the individual identified "as" or "with" the problem is isolated or alienated by shifting the focus from an individual problem to a joint achievement. Therefore, we are always looking for people in the system who potentially could be a collaborative resource. In Chapter Two, therefore, we ask relationship (circular) questions to explore the connections between people, thereby also drawing the attention of those involved to how they are interconnected, how each person's feelings and actions are influenced by, and influence, the actions and feelings of the other. Chapter Five demonstrates the value of engaging the collaboration of the wider system, including not only the immediate and extended family but also carers, professionals, and wider networks of significant people.

In Chapter Five, the authors create contexts in which the older person and their significant network can all participate in more rewarding interactions, thereby diminishing a sense of isolation. They work with immediate and extended family, direct care staff, managers, and other professionals, depending on whom the person and their immediate system see as influential to the problem. They have found that involving different parts of the system in this collaborative work has effected change in the wider system. For example, through participating in open dialogue with their older clients, care staff and family have been enabled to look beyond the problem towards noticing the abilities of the older person.

Therefore, we are committed to including all voices of people involved, actively listening out for the experiences and perspectives of marginalized people. Mindful of the power differential inherent in all systems, we are intent on offering choice to people, taking into account their preferred views, and are careful to invite narratives of competence, ability, and resources with people whose identities are commonly constructed from dominating discourses of incompetence and inability.

Resources and competence

An emphasis on collaboration honours the expertise of all people involved, clients as experts on their experience and practitioners as having expertise in their specialism.

Therefore, we work to build a foundation of competence, connection, and hope that could contribute to resolving difficulties rather than focusing on problems and weaknesses. None of the authors in this book takes a problem-focused approach that emphasizes dysfunction. We aim to facilitate the process of change by attending to people's strengths, resources, and abilities. In Chapter Three, the authors reflect on how our training as clinical psychologists has focused our eyes on problems, limitations, and deficits, with the risk of blinding us to clients' abilities and resources. Chapter Seven notes that stories describing older people as weak and lacking abilities are often so powerful and prevalent that it may be difficult for these people and those of us working with them to construct, live, and circulate alternative stories of competence and hope. The authors share examples of narrative practices that enable the empowerment of older people marginalized by diminishing discourses. With its focus on resurrecting and discovering people's abilities and resources rather than diagnosing pathology, they show how a narrative approach can offer an antidote to labelling, diagnosing, and stigmatizing, whereby problems have been located inside the person, overshadowing or obscuring their abilities or competencies.

Recognizing that older people affected by physical or intellectual impairment or ill health have less (if any) power than others to choose and construct their identities, we authors of this book take care not to reproduce in practice with older people the oppression many may have experienced. Hence, we are committed to including all voices of people involved, especially the voice of the older person, and to focus on resources rather than weaknesses.

Power and choice

Working in collaboration with people as co-participants rather than expert advisers implies appreciation of people's rights to choose.

Throughout this book, we demonstrate our belief in clients' abilities by offering choice in how we work together. For example, we check the older person's preference with questions such as "Is that something that suits you?" Chapter Five offers creative ways to ensure we include and hear the voice of the older person in large network meetings set up to make decisions about future care.

However, inviting multiple perspectives and collaborative practice does not mean we take a position of moral relativism, whereby all perspectives are seen as equally desirable. Since each discourse shapes our experience and, thereby, enables and constrains what we feel, think, and do, we acknowledge that we might differentially affect people's sense of belonging and self-worth if we privilege one discourse over another. Therefore, we propose that we evaluate, reflect on, and take responsibility for the consequences of adopting different positions or practices for our selves, for others, and for our relationships. For example, in Chapter Six, Isabelle explains why she takes a clear position against an older person's racial abuse of a member of staff within an institution and in Chapter Eight Goran transparently lays out his professional responsibility to inform his older client's doctor about risk of self-harm.

We authors of this book are well aware that moral relativism can deny differences in the power and opportunity of older people disadvantaged by cognitive or physical disability or ill health, or discriminated against on the basis of their race, culture, class, or mental health status. Recognizing that the inequalities of power affecting older people are related to wider cultural patterns of inequality has led us to constantly question whether many of the problems facing older people identified with mental health problems are a consequence of exclusion, discrimination, or humiliation by society. We have found that systemic constructionist and narrative approaches offer us possibilities of enabling and empowering the people we work with to access their rights to independence, choice, inclusion, respect, and accessibility.

Chapters Four and Six acknowledge that practitioners are powerful within the therapeutic relationship. Therefore, Chapter Four points out the importance of co-creating a clear contract that includes clarifying how we work and addressing the power differential to create a context where the older person can feel comfortable and respected. The authors of Chapter Six see it as their responsibility to initiate talk about discrimination or oppressive practices in case the client does not feel entitled to do so.

We are also constantly mindful of the effects of values within institutions, society, and the wider culture on the lives and relationships of older people. Therefore, we are continually negotiating the tension between adopting respectful postures of curiosity and appreciation with people in therapeutic conversations on the one hand, and taking into account safety and protection from risk for the older person as well as our need to work alongside colleagues responsible for their diagnosis and medical treatment on the other. Atten ding to how power is created in the system, we consider our rights, duties, and responsibilities in relation to each other, with a view to enabling people to share and participate safely and ethically (Chapter Eight).

Attending to multiple contexts

Attention to context particularly distinguishes the systemic approach. Since context gives meaning to our actions, we always make sense of behaviour and beliefs within the contexts in which they arise. Therefore, throughout this book, we attend to the social and cultural contexts that shape the actions and beliefs of the older person, their family and practitioners, and ourselves. We pay specific attention to the relationship contexts of the older person, that is, their family, their work, their group home, their day centre, and recognize that these contexts are informed by the contexts of their culture, ethnicity, race, age, physical and intellectual ability, health, sexuality, and gender. Burnham (1993) suggests the acronym (social) GRRAACCES to help us stay mindful of the contexts of Gender, Race, Religion, Age, Ability, Culture, Class, Ethnicity, and Sexuality. Chapter Two addresses the older person's relationship to help in the contexts of the culture of their generation, gender, ethnicity, and class to facilitate a positive therapeutic relationship. In Chapter Nine, the authors show how contextualizing older clients' symptoms offers new meanings to their colleagues and opens space for more empowering and fruitful conversations between older people and practitioners.

Including ourselves in the system

Situating ourselves in our personal and professional contexts, we identify and question our own assumptions. We consider how we act and the effects of our actions on people's lives. Eleanor Martin and Josh consider the "pre-understandings" they draw from the cultures of their gender, family, and age (Chapter Three); Isabelle and Esther address their prejudices in relation to age, race, culture, and sexuality (Chapter Six), and Sarah, Goran, and I highlight how we are shaped by the discourses of our professional contexts (Chapter Eight). From a position of transparency, we try to share our assumptions with clients and practitioners to invite them into a more collaborative relationship. Acknowledging that we construct the world through our personal, subjective lenses, we attend to how our personal beliefs and prejudices contribute to our work with clients (Cecchin, Lane, & Ray, 1994) and use our self-reflexivity as a potential resource for change (Chapters Three and Six).

Acknowledging that the practitioner cannot stand outside the client system and gain an objective view of the situation, we all see ourselves as a part of the "helping" system. Therefore, in Chapter Two, we include ourselves in the relationship map of the clients' system from the start. We also address how we might prepare ourselves for conversations with clients by reflecting on the "emotional postures" we might expect to meet and might ourselves carry into the therapeutic relationship (Chapters Two and Three). Chapter Three addresses how we can work with ourselves as a resource in sessions with older people; for example, through transparency, self- and relational-reflexivity and sharing different versions of our selves.

We address the approaches we present in this book from different positions, including those of professionals and clients. We also take different personal positions in relation to the material. Therefore, at times, we speak with the voices of our family and culture. At other times, we narrate with our professional voices as helper, trainer, supervisor, or consultant. Thus, we move between references to "clients", "carers", "professionals", "people", "patients", "colleagues", and "participants" in an attempt to reflect the relationship that has emerged in the course of a particular episode of communication. You, our reader, may choose to take different positions during your reading of this book. For example, you may elect to read from the perspective of a family member of an older person, a colleague, a carer, or an older person yourself. You may also choose to read from the position of a practitioner or person offering training or receiving supervision. This book is, therefore, intended for people who work with older people as well as for those interested in exploring their own ageing or extending their repertoire of abilities to talk about or be with older people.

Working aesthetically with older people

I have outlined the principles guiding our practice with older people and their networks. Informed by systemic constructionist and narrative approaches, working aesthetically, for us, involves joining people in their contexts, locating expertise within the persons seeking help and maintaining a sense of respect for the people with whom we are engaged. Therefore, we pay careful attention to people's language and communication.

What engages us with the systemic approach is the emphasis on pattern and process and, hence, the recognition that the whole is much more than the sum of its parts. What we particularly appreciate is the focus on context, relationships, communication, and interaction: that is, what is happening between people rather than within people, since this moves us away from pathologizing individuals and towards viewing symptoms as interpersonal. In our practice, therefore, we move away from organizing events into linear sequences that could provide us with neat cause-and-effect explanations of problems towards identifying circular patterns that connect symptoms with relationships and communication (Watzlawick, Beavin Bavelas, & Jackson, 1967). We try not to assume too quickly, and welcome as many perspectives as there are people available to give them.

Informed by this approach, in this book we share with you, our reader, how we work with older people from how we begin (Chapter Two) to how we end (Chapter Ten). We use ourselves as resources to our practice (Chapter Three) throughout the book to enable us to create contexts for talking and listening where older people can feel comfortable and respected (Chapter Four). We offer practices for meeting with families and networks (Chapter Five), and for talking with older people about difference and discrimination (Chapter Six), and we address the challenges and opportunities of a focus on strengths and resources to enabling older people to move from problems to possibilities (Chapter Seven). Recognizing the challenge of holding on to the ethics of systemic constructionist and narrative approaches within public services, we share how we have sustained the ethics of our approach when working with risk, diagnosis, and limited resources (Chapter Eight) and how we have introduced systemic approaches into our services (Chapter Nine).

We present the ideas and practices that follow as offerings and invitations to you. It is not our intention to put forward here a picture of how things are, or a recipe for how they should be done. Therefore, we will not be providing an inventory of problems facing older people or techniques designed to manage them. Instead, we present a range of theories and stories intended to offer openings to conversations and ways to go on. We anticipate that you, our reader, will be further elaborating the practices presented here as you use them creatively in your different contexts.

References

Andersen, T. (1987). The reflecting team: dialogue and meta-dialogue in clinical work. *Family Process, 26*: 415–428.

Andersen, T. (1995). Reflecting processes; acts of informing and forming: You can borrow my eyes, but you must not take them away from me! In: S. Friedman (Ed.), *The Reflecting Team in Action. Collaborative Practice in Family Therapy.* (pp. 11–37). New York: Guilford.

Bateson, G. (1979). *Mind and Nature.* London: Wildwood Press.

Boscolo, L., Cecchin, G., Hoffman, L., & Penn, P. (1987). *Milan Systemic Family Therapy.* New York: Basic Books.

Burnham, J. (1993). Systemic supervision: the evolution of reflexivity in the context of the supervisory relationship. *Human Systems: The Journal of Systemic Consultation and Management, 4* (Special Issue, 3 & 4): 349–381.

Burr, V. (1995). *An Introduction to Social Construction.* London: Routledge.

Cecchin, G. (1987). Hypothesising, circularity and neutrality revisited: an invitation to curiosity. *Family Process, 26*: 404–413.

Cecchin, G., Lane, G., & Ray, W. A. (1994). *The Cybernetics of Prejudices in the Practice of Psychotherapy.* London: Karnac.

Crawford, J., Kippax, S., Onyx, J., Gault, U., & Benton, P. (1992). *Emotion and Gender. Constructing Meaning from Memory.* London: Sage.

Epston, D., White, M., & "Ben" (1995). Consulting your consultants: a means to co-construction of alternative knowledges. In: S. Friedman (Ed.), *The Reflecting Team in Action. Collaborative Practice in Family Therapy* (pp. 277–313). New York: Guilford Press.

Freedman, J., & Combs, G. (1996). *Narrative Therapy and the Social Construction of Preferred Realities*: New York: Norton.

Geertz, C. (1983). *Local Knowledge: Further Essays in Interpretive Anthropology.* New York: Basic Books.

Gergen, K. (1999). *An Invitation to Social Construction.* London: Sage.

Gergen, K., & Gergen, M. (2000). The new aging: self construction and social values. In: K. W. Schaie & J. Hendricks (Eds.), *The Evolution of the Aging Self.* New York: Springer.

Hare Mustin, R. T. (1994). Discourses in the mirrored room: a post-modern analysis of therapy. *Family Process, 33*: 19–35.

Haug, F. (1987). *Female Sexualisation: A Collective Work of Memory,* E. Carter (Trans.). London: Verso.

Katz, A. M., Conant, L., Inui, T. S., Baron, D., & Bor, D. (2000). A council of elders: creating a multi-voiced dialogue in a community of care. *Social Science and Medicine, 50*: 851–860.

Lang, P., Little, M., & Cronen, V. E. (1990). The systemic professional domains of action and the question of neutrality. *Human Systems: The Journal of Systemic Consultation & Management, 1*(1): 32–46.

Lax, W. D. (1995). Offering reflections: some theoretical and practical considerations. In: S. Friedman (Ed.), *The Reflecting Team in Action: Collaborative Practice in Family Therapy* (pp. 145–166). New York: Guilford Press.

Maturana, H., & Varela, F. (1980). *Autopoesis and Cognition: The Realization of Living.* Boston, MA: Reidel.

Middleton, D., & Edwards, D. (Eds.) (1990). *Collective Remembering.* London: Sage.

Petronic, G. (2001). What is understood by "dominance"? An interpretation through memories. In: C. Willig, *Introducing Qualitative Research in Psychology: Adventures in Theory and Method* (pp. 154–170). Buckingham: Open University Press.

Shotter, J. (2004). Getting it: withness-thinking and the dialogical in practice. London: KCC Publications.

Shotter, J. (2008). *Conversational Realities Revisited: Life, Language, Body and World*. Chagrin Falls, OH: Taos Institute Publications.

Shotter, J., & Katz, A. (1998). "Living moments" in dialogical exchanges. *Human Systems. The Journal of Systemic Consultation & Management, 9*: 81–93.

Tomm, K. (1988). Interventive interviewing. Part III: Intending to ask lineal, circular, strategic or reflexive questions. *Family Process, 27*: 1–15.

Walnum, E. (2007). Sharing stories: the work of an experience consultant. *International Journal of Narrative Therapy and Community Work, 2*: 3–9.

Watzlawick, P., Beavin Bavelas, J., & Jackson, D. D. (1967). *Pragmatics of Human Communication: A Study of Interactional Patterns, Pathologies and Paradoxes*. New York: Norton.

CHAPTER TWO

How do we begin? Working with older people and their significant systems

Glenda Fredman and Penny Rapaport

he nurses asked Sarah, a clinical psychologist, to see Norman, aged eighty-one, because the noise from his singing at night was creating problems on the ward. When Sarah first met Norman, he was sitting in an armchair in the day room, singing. His daughter, Susan, sitting beside him, explained that Norman always sat in the same chair. She pointed out that it was next to a mantelpiece with a table to the left, a similar arrangement to Norman's favourite seating at home. Norman looked happy and the singing sounded joyful to Sarah's ear. He did not join in the conversation with Sarah and Susan, but did not appear to mind their sitting with him. Susan explained that he was a very quiet man. He used to work back stage at the opera house and enjoyed hearing others sing, even though he did not sing himself. Norman fell asleep during Sarah's conversation with Susan.

The psychiatrist asked Philippa Hyman, a clinical psychologist, to assess Olive's memory because her family was concerned about her. Philippa arrived at Olive's house on a cold autumn day. Olive opened the door to Philippa, smiled, and invited her in. She said that she had forgotten that Philippa was coming but she was welcome. Philippa followed Olive up a small staircase to the living room. They sat at a large oak dining room table and began to talk. Philippa could hear a vacuum cleaner start and stop downstairs as a cleaner performed her job. When Philippa asked if she had any concerns about her memory, Olive said, "No . . . I have become slightly more forgetful . . . it's just normal ageing . . . but my daughter Kathleen is worried about how I will manage at home."

We begin before we start

In this chapter, we describe our approach to beginnings, highlighting the steps we take from receiving a request for help to preparing for a first meeting. Our intention is to begin in a manner that enhances our opportunity to work ethically with the older person and with those involved and concerned about their well-being, holding that "well begun, half done" (Lang & McAdam, 1990) is a useful principle.

We start long before we meet with the older person or their family, since our first contact is usually with a practitioner or a family member other than the older person identified with the problem. It was the nurses who spoke to Sarah about Norman, and it was the psychiatrist who asked Philippa to "assess Olive's memory". How we respond to the person asking for our help has consequences for the older person and their significant system, whether or not we accept the request to be involved. Therefore, we see ourselves as having an effect on the people connected to the identified problem from the moment we are asked to be involved.

The decision about whether or not we get involved with the older person depends upon how the request fits with our professional duties and responsibilities as well as the task and referral criteria of our agency or service. We may have particular obligations or constraints that affect how we respond to requests for our service. As the ward psychologist, Sarah had a duty to respond to referrals from the nurses. Philippa had the responsibility, as the clinical psychologist in a mental health team, to offer cognitive assessment to older people if there were concerns about memory difficulties. Both these practitioners were obligated to accept the referral from their colleagues and were expected to respond to their requests for help. However, when Sarah went to see Norman, at the request of the nurses, she felt uncomfortable. She had interpreted the nurses' request to mean that she should stop Norman singing, which she perceived could undermine this older man, for whom singing appeared to be a great pleasure. Believing that older people have the right to informed consent regarding memory assessment placed Philippa in a similar dilemma with Olive. From the start, therefore, we consider how we can create a context for working together with people so that all involved, practitioners and clients, feel heard, included, and respected. In our busy working environments, where resources are limited and requests complex, this is not always easy to achieve. As Sarah and Philippa show us, sometimes we experience requests for our involvement as demands, or unwanted obligations. We have found that relating to requests as "gracious invitations" (Lang & McAdam, 1990) rather than demands or obligations helps us to engage with the referrer and the task in a respectful way.

Requests as invitations

Approaching a request for our involvement as an invitation generally slows us down so that we are able to reflect on who is inviting us to do what. In this way we can begin to take a relational perspective, broadening our view to include other people in the older person's system. "Who" questions come to our minds, such as, "Who is asking for our help?" and "Who else is affected by this problem?", so that we want to engage further with the people making the invitation. Thus, Sarah went back to ask the nurses more questions when she approached their request as an invitation, and Philippa asked Olive, "Who is worried about your memory?" and "How does their worry affect things [relationships] between you all?"

When Sarah approached the nurses' request for her to see Norman as an invitation, she reflected on what they were inviting her to do. Were they inviting her to join them in their work with Norman, or to take the problem away, or to solve it? Mindful that any request for our involvement requires a practitioner to expose the work they have been doing at a time when they may feel it is not going so well, Sarah wondered what it was like for the nurses to ask for her help. She also wondered what ideas they had about the situation and what they had tried. Viewing the psychiatrist's request for her to assess Olive's memory as an invitation helped Philippa to adopt a position of curiosity (Cecchin, 1987) in relation to the different people involved with Olive. Hence, she began to wonder what had led the psychiatrist to make this invitation. Assuming that the invitation arose out of Olive's family's genuine concerns about her well-being, Philippa began to wonder what the family wanted to happen and whether Olive knew about their request. Thus, Philippa began to take a relational perspective on this request and no longer felt pressured to respond to her assumption of a demand for memory testing or assessment of a possible dementia. This opened space for Philippa to learn that Olive's daughter Kathleen was worried about her mother's ability to manage on her own at home, whereas Olive was not concerned about her memory.

I (Penny) work as a clinical psychologist in a multi-disciplinary mental health care team for older people where requests for my help usually come via conversations with our team members. Colleagues have come to expect that I will ask more questions as part of the process of getting started. Asking for help from another professional can sometimes feel exposing, since asking for help involves a move from a private to a public arena whereby our work becomes open to scrutiny (Lang & McAdam, 1990). When requests come from within the same team or agency, this effect may be magnified. I was recently reminded of this when a community psychiatric nurse, new to our team, asked me to get involved with a family with whom she was working.

> Denise, the community psychiatric nurse, asked me to meet with the family of her patient, Mr Jacobs. Forgetting that Denise was new to the team and this was the first time she had invited me to join her, I immediately launched into asking her questions about her request. It was only when Denise asked if her response to my question was "right" that I stopped and clarified the intentions informing my questions. The nurse said she felt reassured. She had found it unusual that I had been asking questions and had been wondering whether she had "got it wrong" or made an "inappropriate referral".

Therefore, we always take care to acknowledge referrers' expertise, recognizing that they have an understanding of the older person's situation from their experience of working with him or her. We often thank our colleagues for inviting us to be involved and then ask them if we can ask some questions to help us work out how we can best take things forward. After Sarah had met briefly with Norman and his daughter Susan, she returned to the nurses, saying, "Thanks for asking me to help with the concerns about Norman. I would appreciate your helping me work out the best way to take this forward. Would you mind if I asked you some questions so I can draw on your experience with Norman so far? That would help me get more of a picture of the situation and where to go from here."

With whom do we talk first?

Once we have accepted an invitation to become involved, we address the question "With whom do we talk first?" or "To whom do we initially respond?" Older people like Norman and Olive are commonly referred for help to our service by a concerned practitioner or family member. Rarely, in our experience, has the older person him or herself been the first person to identify the problem. Often, they do not perceive a need for, or want, our help, and at times have not known that people hold concerns about them or that we were asked to help. Therefore, we do not assume that those referred for our help are even aware that a referral has been made. When older people are aware of the referral, we do not assume that they see the issue of concern as a problem, that they themselves are asking for help, or that they want to talk to us. Consequently, we consider questions such as: "Who is asking for what for whom?", "Who is this a problem for?", and "Who is concerned?"

Norman was an inpatient on a physical health ward. He had been given a diagnosis of dementia. The nurses were asking for help with the "noise"; they were concerned that it might disturb the other patients. The singing seemed to offer Norman comfort and familiarity in a strange situation; his daughter understood it within the context of his working life and Sarah heard the joy in the singing. In this situation, it is the nurses who are asking for help. They are concerned about the effects of Norman's singing on other patients in the night. Addressing the question "Who is asking for what for whom?" on receipt of a request for our involvement can enable us to move from an individual perspective of the "problem" to a more relational perspective. That is, rather than locating the problem within Norman (Norman's singing) or seeing it as part of Norman's identity (Norman is noisy, or Norman has dementia), we move to a more relational perspective. In this way, we begin to see the "problem" involving and affecting not only the referred person, Norman, but also others involved, concerned, or connected, for example, the nurses and other patients. Therefore, we do not think about problems as located within individuals or within families. Instead, we think of problems in relationship with people. That is, we think in terms of "Who is connected to the problem?", or "Who is concerned about the problem?", or "Who is affected by the problem?" To help us answer these questions, we draw a relationship map (Marriott, 2000; McGoldrick & Gerson, 1986), which helps us to take the next step towards deciding whom to invite or whom to meet in order to move forward.

Mapping the system of relationships

When we create a relationship map, we include who is concerned, affected, and connected to the request and to the identified problem. We also consider who else is significant or involved. In particular, we are interested in who offers resources to the problem and who has an opinion about the problem. We also include ourselves on the map, thereby making explicit how we are already connected to the situation and how the resources we may be able to offer fit with the resources of other people in the system. Including ourselves on the map enables us to consider what position we are being invited into, who is asking or expecting what of us, and who can enable or support the work. We may need to have further conversations with those inviting our involvement to help us generate a useful map.

The nurses helped Sarah to generate a relationship map of Norman's system. As well as Norman, they included specific nurses and doctors who were involved and Sarah, to whom they had referred. They discussed "Who is most concerned about the situation?", which prompted them to add a couple of patients on the ward. When Sarah asked, "Who has helped with the situation?", and "Who could offer resources to the situation?", they added Norman's daughter Susan, as well as one of his home carers who had visited him in hospital. After some discussion, they added the warden at his sheltered accommodation (see Figure 2.1).

The consultant psychiatrist who invited Philippa to assess Olive's memory helped Philippa create a relationship map for her work with Olive. Philippa asked questions such as "Who else is involved/connected with this situation?", "What views do they have about the situation?", "Who is most/least concerned?", "Who else would it be useful to talk with about this?", and "Who else might have a view?"

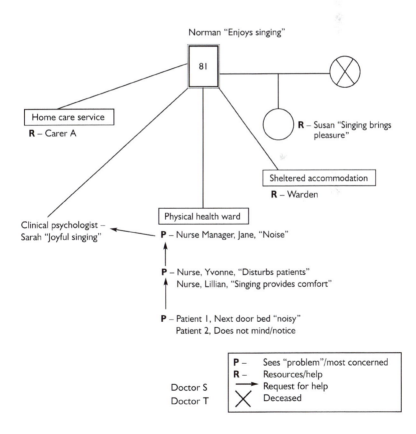

Figure 2.1.   Norman's relationship map.

The consultant psychiatrist told Philippa that Olive had two daughters, Kathleen, who lived locally, and Margaret, who lived with her family outside London. Kathleen had attended the initial assessment with her mother and seemed very concerned about her mother's memory and her ability to cope with living on her own. Kathleen had explained that her sister, Margaret, who had less contact with their mother, did not share the same level of concern. During Philippa's meeting with Olive, the cleaner, Sandra, was downstairs. Olive told Philippa that although she had known Sandra for many years and found her to be "an enormous help", she sometimes felt that she was "spying on me . . . I heard her talking to Kathleen on the telephone about me only last week." Olive also told Philippa that there were a number of "ladies" living in her apartment block: they "often laugh together about growing old . . . we are all forgetful these days . . . they don't think I'm any different from the lot of them."

Figure 2.2 is a relationship map for Olive's system of concern and involvement. By including herself on the relationship map, Philippa notices "Who is asking for what for whom?" and how their expectations fit with her professional duties and responsibilities. A relationship map can help us bring into relief the people who

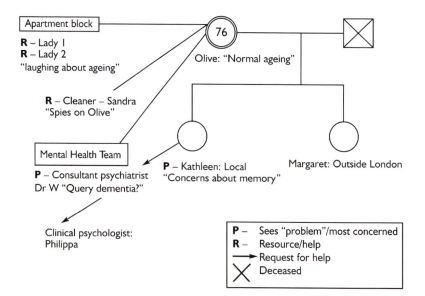

Figure 2.2. Olive's relationship map.

are in communication about the problem. This can help us decide whom we invite to a first meeting.

Whom do we invite?

Norman was singing at night. The patient in the bed next to him complained to a nurse that he could not sleep. The nurse discussed the complaint with her nurse manager who suggested referring Norman to Sarah, the psychologist.

In this situation, Norman's singing has been identified as the "problem". The people in communication about the "problem" are the other patient who complained, the nurses, and Sarah. We think about problems as created between people in language. That is, a problem can only be what somebody communicates and is brought into existence through talking about it with others. Therefore, the "problem" (Norman's singing) exists because the other patient signals distress or complains about what Norman is doing. Implied in this communication is that this is a problem that must change. The problem is brought forth into existence when someone (the nurses) designates it as a problem and someone accepts this designation. Thus, the problem is determined by those in communication about the problem, the "problem-organizing system" (Anderson, Goolishian, & Windermand, 1986), who could include an individual, couple, family, staff group, or any combination of people who are communicating about, and organized around, a shared problem.

It is not uncommon in our work with older people that someone concerned about the older person identifies a problem but other involved people do not accept this as a problem. For example, Olive's daughter, Kathleen, expressed concern about her mother's "memory" and the psychiatrist, accepting this distinction of the problem, queried "dementia". On the other hand, Olive's younger daughter, Margaret did not share this concern and Olive offered an alternative explanation of "normal ageing". Therefore, it is not necessarily the case that there is consensus around the definition of the problem in the problem-organizing system, or that a single problem is identified. There can be as many problem definitions as there are members of a system involved with each other around the problem. The meaning and nature of the problem is dependent on who is talking with whom about the problem at any given moment and the definition of the problem is likely to change as the membership of the "problem-organizing system" changes. When Sarah joined Norman and his daughter, Susan, in the dayroom, the "problem" seemed to disappear as Norman sang sweetly and Sarah experienced the joy in his singing. In conversation with the nurses, Sarah was introduced to a different version of the singing as "noise" that "disturbed the patients". Philippa's conversation with Olive about her memory brought forth amusing stories about "normal ageing" shared between Olive and the "ladies" in her block of flats, whereas talking with the psychiatrist (who had been in conversation with Olive's daughter, Kathleen) brought forth concerns about "dementia".

We think of those involved, connected with, and engaged in constructing a problem as having the potential to "dis-solve the problem" (Anderson & Goolishian, 1988) if enabled to talk and think differently together about the situation. Therefore, our intention is to bring together those people in communication about the problem and to facilitate a conversation, which opens space for new possibilities to emerge. In this way we can think of these people as participating in "problem dis-solving" conversations (ibid.). As well as inviting "who is concerned", "who defines the problem", "who is talking with whom about the problem", and "who needs/wants to have a conversation with whom about the problem", we also tune in to "who might offer potential resources" to dis-solving the problem. Working from an assumption that we could accomplish more within a network of collaborative relationships than each on our own, we work towards co-creating a "resource-full" community (Fredman, 2007) whereby we might pool the abilities of people involved in the older person's care.

> Recognizing that Norman's daughter, Susan, and the nurses could offer resources to the situation, Sarah invited them to meet together to help her address "the concerns about Norman's singing at night". After the nurses heard Susan's story about the pleasure singing brought her father, one nurse noted that some patients did not seem to mind or notice Norman's singing. She wondered if it would make a difference if they moved him nearer the patients who could not hear or did not

notice. Another nurse noticed that the singing seemed to provide Norman with comfort and familiarity in a strange situation and the nurses began to wonder what else they could offer him to create familiarity and comfort.

During her initial conversation with the consultant psychiatrist, Philippa asked questions such as "Who sees Olive as able to manage in certain ways?"; "What do they notice?"; "Who helps or supports Olive to carry on or cope?"; "What helps Olive's daughter, Kathleen, to manage her concerns?"; "How have Olive and Kathleen been able to manage the situation?" By asking "resource generating" questions of the consultant who referred the "problem", Philippa learned of potential resources towards dis-solving the problem. For example, Kathleen worried less knowing that Olive had regular contact with neighbours, and that Olive was happy to receive assistance from the cleaner, Sandra, whom she had known many years. Hence, Philippa began to consider whether the "ladies" and the cleaner might make a useful contribution to a first meeting.

Relationship to help

At eighty-three, Faye was taking care of her eighty-eight-year-old husband, Tom, who was severely disabled by Parkinson's disease. For at least six years, Faye had been helping Tom to bathe and dress. Only when Faye injured her shoulder did their GP realize that Faye, a small woman, had been lifting her six-foot tall husband several times a day for years. The GP then arranged for an occupational therapist to visit their home to assess for a hoist to support with lifting. A social worker was also present at this assessment, following which Faye was allocated a carer's financial allowance on the basis that she was "full-time carer" for her disabled husband. When Fay received her first payment, she called the social security department to explain that they had "overestimated" her allowance. Having done her sums, she concluded that she was "not full-time carer but only part-time carer as two thirds of what I do are part of my normal responsibilities as a wife . . . I have been doing that for years . . . any wife would expect to do that anyway." Faye was intending to "give back two-thirds of the money . . .". Her telephone conversation with the official answering the phone did not go well. At first, he suggested she send her "complaint" in writing. Then he explained that she would have to be reassessed if she was "asking for further assistance". When the official finally understood that Faye wanted to "give back" some of the money, he explained, "That is not possible . . . we don't have a form for that . . ." Later that evening, Faye phoned her son to ask him to help her with this "upsetting" situation. She was distraught that she had been "accused of complaining" and insisted that this money was "not rightly" hers. Her son tried to clarify, "This is your right . . . you and Dad paid taxes for fifty years . . . you aren't taking this money, you earned it." The next day, Faye, whose income was modest, set up a standing order to a charity supporting Parkinson's disease for the sum of her estimated "overpaid" carer's allowance.

Whether we are a client or a practitioner, we hold beliefs about giving and receiving help. These beliefs are informed by our past experiences of help and helping, and by the stories we tell and are told about giving and receiving help in the cultures of our families, gender, age or generation, ethnicity, class, and our professional training. Therefore, we act out of and into many different contexts, which inform our "relationship to help" (Reder & Fredman, 1996). These include the values we ascribe and rules we make about whether and how we give or receive help.

Different contexts over time informed both Faye's and her son's relationship to (financial) help. Faye was in her thirties before the National Health Service was set up to offer free health care in Britain. When she was growing up in a family with ten children, "a visit to the doctor was costly; we only went if things were desperate . . ." Therefore, Faye, like many of the older people we meet, viewed free health care as a privilege. Her son, on the other hand, had never known a time when medical treatment was not free. He was born ten years after the creation of the National Health Service and saw free health care as a right. It seems that a similar view informed the actions of the GP, occupational therapist, and social worker, who assumed that Faye would want her full "entitlement to help". The social security official, unaware of Faye's story about "health care as privilege", was quite unable to make sense of Faye's request to pay back the financial support. The context of Faye's age also informed her view that "younger people deserve it more", thereby reflecting ageist societal discourses that devalue the worth or entitlement of older people, who are perceived as less likely to make a financial contribution to society or are viewed as a burden on public services.

> Dan, seventy-two, had diabetes. His daughter, home-help, and district nurse were concerned that he was not taking his medication or eating regularly and that they would find him "in a diabetic coma" if they did not constantly phone or visit him. Dan, on the other hand, felt he was "managing just fine", and did "not want them interfering, thank you very much". The district nurse appealed to Eleanor Anderson, the family therapist, for "help with Dan".

Having mapped the "problem-organizing" system with the district nurse, Eleanor learnt that Dan's management of the diabetes was a problem for his daughter and home-help. They had approached the district nurse in the hope that she could help resolve the problem by giving Dan some advice. They saw Dan's participation as necessary for resolving the problem, defined as his "poor management of diabetes". Dan's daughter, home-help, and nurse were willing to attend a meeting with Eleanor; however, they doubted Dan would be prepared to come along. Dan had always been "polite" to the nurse, who complained to Eleanor, "But what can I do if my patient won't accept the help I offer?"

Informed by her professional training, the district nurse felt obligated to monitor Dan's health and responsible for ensuring he maintained a safe blood sugar level. However, believing that Dan had a right to accept or refuse her help, she did not know how to go on when he would not accept the help she offered. Informed by her systemic training, Eleanor brought to this "helping relation-ship" with Dan the belief that people are more likely to change when they feel respected and affirmed in the relationship with the practitioner. She was also mindful that offering unsolicited help could imply that the client has a weakness or lacks some ability, and that the practitioner is more competent in this respect. Eleanor, therefore, explored how she might be of "use" to Dan, his family, and carers rather than how she could be of "help" (Cecchin, Lane, & Ray, 1994).

How do we frame the invitation?

Like Dan and Faye, many of the older people with whom we work insist that they do not want or need our help. Therefore, we rarely frame our invitation to a first meeting in terms of help. That is, we do not begin by offering help or enquiring how we might be helpful. First, we consider people's "relationship to help" (Reder & Fredman, 1996): for example, "What is their previous experience of help?", "What are the stories of help they take from the cultures of their family, age, gender, ethnicity, and so on?", "What are their experience, expectation, and understanding of our service?"

If the social worker had explored Faye's relationship to help, she might have learnt that Faye believed it was "wrong" to accept payment for the "normal responsibilities of a wife". Before talking with Dan about attending the meeting with the nurse, home-help, and his daughter, Eleanor did reflect on Dan's relationship to help. She had already learnt that Dan had said he was "managing just fine" and that he had framed the nurse, home-help, and daughter's offers of help as "interfering". Therefore, Eleanor wondered what it was like for Dan to have three younger women, including his daughter, "checking up" to see if he was all right. She wondered how, as a man of his generation, he experienced help from women.

> When Eleanor spoke with Dan, she was clear to locate the concern with his daughter, nurse, and home-help. She explained that they had asked her to help them with "their worries". She asked Dan for his opinion on their request. Dan told Eleanor that he had "always looked after (his) own health" as well as that of his family, and he had "never had to rely on hospitals". Dan was clear that he did not want his daughter to "worry" about him, and agreed to help Eleanor with the worries of his daughter, the home-help, and the district nurse. At first, Dan was unsure if he wanted to be at the meeting, so Eleanor offered to feed back to him. In the end, he did attend the meeting in his own home, where Eleanor took care to focus on the concerns of the "carer team", constantly requesting Dan's help with his carers' worries.

By talking to Dan before arranging a meeting with the family, Eleanor began to develop an understanding of Dan's "relationship to help"; that he had never had to rely on services before and that this did not feel comfortable for him. She went on to develop an hypothesis that this older man, who had always taken care of other family members, was experiencing their help as undermining his position in his family. Hence, Eleanor framed her invitation to Dan in terms of finding a way that he could support his daughter with her worries, in order to show respect for his view that he was "managing just fine". Being transparent with Dan about the nature of the request, having the meeting at Dan's home, and inviting him to join if he wanted, may also have avoided Dan's feeling that he was being perceived as a problem or a burden, or was being excluded from the situation.

Therefore, on receiving a request for help, we attempt to take a position of curiosity (Cecchin, 1987) in relation to invitations to become involved, not automatically assuming that the older people being positioned as in need of help want or need this help. We start to wonder or hypothesize (Selvini Palazzoli, Boscolo, Cecchin, & Prata, 1980b) about why clients and practitioners may or may not want help, and what are people's stories, expectations, and beliefs about help, which may be informing their decisions. Thus, we hypothesize about clients' and referrers' relationship to help to enable us to frame the invitation in a way that fits for all involved. Since many of the older people we are invited to see do not necessarily see themselves as having a problem, we frame invitations to meet with us in terms of finding out whether or not we might have something useful to offer. We make explicit that we are interested in hearing about the ways the older people and those connected to them have found to manage a situation, positioning them as experts on their own experiences. We also ask if they would like to have other people with them when we meet. Often, we invite the referred older person to bring with them those who may have something useful to offer the situation, intending to give them choice and control over who attends an initial meeting. Philippa learnt that Olive was not concerned about her memory, but was concerned about her daughter's concerns that she could not manage on her own. Therefore, Philippa asked whom Olive might like to invite to a meeting to help address her daughter's concerns. As well as her daughter, Kathleen, Olive suggested Sandra, the cleaner, and one of her friends from the group of "ladies" in her apartment block. She wanted Philippa to invite her younger daughter, Margaret, as well, although she assumed "she won't make it . . . it really is too far for her to come."

Who issues the invitation?

Considering who should issue the invitation and how to do this for each person invited can make a difference to the meeting's progress when it finally convenes. Dan's daughter suggested that Eleanor invite Dan to the meeting, since "You are a fresh face—I think the rest of us have got ourselves off on the wrong foot now . . ."

If we make an invitation by letter, we think carefully about how we word it. We always clarify our relationship to those defining the problem, the problem-organizing system, by explaining who has asked us to be involved and naming how we are all connected. For example, unable to contact Olive's daughter, Margaret, on the phone, Philippa wrote to invite her to their meeting. She clarified, "In discussion with your mother I have agreed to convene a meeting to discuss some concerns about her memory and to plan a way forward. Your sister Kathleen contacted the psychiatrist in our team for help with these matters. The psychiatrist, Dr W, asked me to meet with your mother since I work with older people where there are concerns about memory. Your mother has asked me to invite you to the meeting so you are kept in the picture. She asked me to be clear that she would like you to come but she also understands if you cannot make it since you live a long way away and have small children."

We also name who is asking for what from this meeting. We tend to avoid offering help in a letter, preferring phrases such as "We are hoping you can join us to discuss ways forward for your mother"; "We are inviting you to meet with us to see whether we can offer something useful to . . ."; or "We want to hear all that you think it is important for us to understand". We also identify and affirm how the people we invite can offer a potential resource to the situation; for example, "As one of the people in the family whom she respects and trusts, we are hoping you can help us . . .".

Addressing practical challenges to participation

We often seek referrers' ideas about how we might invite the referred people to meet with us in a way that they feel comfortable and respected by us. This includes addressing some of the practical challenges to getting involved that older people may experience, for example, where would be the best place to meet and whether any sensory or physical impairments might affect our talking together.

How we decide where to meet depends on practicalities, such as how mobile people are, who is attending, and the size of room needed. The resources available often limit us in our places of work. If circumstances allow a choice, we prefer to ask our older clients where they would be most comfortable, and, if possible, to accommodate this. Some people prefer to meet in their own home, or have to meet there due to immobility; others prefer to come to our consulting rooms. If we do meet in someone's home, we ask our clients to help us make the setting one where we can listen to them easily. For example, if the television is on, we ask if it can be turned off to enable us to listen without distraction; if the seating is too far apart or is in a straight line, we ask if we can move it enough to be able to see and hear each other well. If we meet in our own consulting rooms, we check with the client or referrer how many people will be coming, and consider where different people sit. Sometimes, we talk with clients before a meeting about where they would like to sit and who sits next to them (Fredman, 2007). We find that a room without a table, with seating in a circle that allows people to see and hear each other, works best.

When a person has hearing difficulties, we experiment with the volume and pitch of our voices, to see what best enables hearing. We may comment on how increasing the volume of our voices could come across as harsh or shouting, clarifying that this is not our intention. In the meeting with Dan and his carers, aware that Dan's hearing was impaired, Eleanor asked, "Dan, people often tell me I talk with a quiet voice. Am I talking loud enough for you to hear me well? I can turn the volume up much louder (raising her voice) like this. Which is better for you?" When Dan said, "That is much better," Eleanor went on, "Good. You can hear me well. But sometimes my loud voice can sound a bit strong—as if I am shouting. Can you let me know if it sounds like I am shouting— because I don't mean to shout . . ." If the person with hearing difficulties finds it easier for one person to do most of the speaking with them, we invite him or her to choose who relates what other people are saying.

We also check on who can and wants to see what and whom in the room, and try to arrange seating accordingly. We allow extra time in our scheduling for people who may have slower mobility to get from a waiting room to the meeting room, arrange for seats that are high enough for older people who have mobility difficulties, and, of course, try to find meeting rooms that have access for wheelchairs. Attention to these sorts of practical details makes a difference to facilitating everyone's participation.

How we begin: an example

So far, we have addressed how we respond to requests for our involvement from the point of receiving the request to deciding with whom to talk and then, when appropriate, whom to invite to a meeting and how best to do this. Our intention throughout this process is to engage and join with people who can contribute to the older person's resource-full community and towards dis-solving the identified "problems" through useful conversations. Below, Penny describes how she approached the psychiatrist's request for help with eighty-three-year-old Alfred's family. We see how Penny used the principles we describe above to help her consider with whom to talk first, whom to invite to a meeting, and how to frame her invitation to that meeting. We then go on to outline other practices we can use to help us prepare before we actually meet with people, including pre-session systemic hypothesizing and preparing ourselves emotionally for the meeting.

> The consultant psychiatrist in a mental health care team for older people asked me (Penny) to meet with Phil and Lorraine, Alfred's son and daughter. Alfred had been known to the mental health team for five years. He had experienced anxiety and emotional distress for many years, even before he was referred to the team. The worry and distress had got the better of Alfred, who was living with Lorraine. He did not want to be at home on his own when she was at work, so had taken to spending all day out on buses or walking the streets. His children were concerned about his physical well-being and vulnerability. Alfred had also been phoning Lorraine repeatedly when she went out in the evening. He was calling his GP and frequently attending the local hospital emergency department, complaining that he could not breathe at night when he was unable to sleep. The psychiatrist said that Alfred

had always been described as "of nervous disposition . . . he has never been motivated to change and is not likely to do so now." She asked me to offer Alfred's children, Phil and Lorraine, "strategies to manage their father's behaviour" since they were finding it very difficult to cope with his symptoms.

Approaching the request as an invitation, I asked the psychiatrist to clarify "Who is asking for what for whom?" I was also interested to learn more about "Who Alfred's symptoms were a problem for?", and "Who was most affected by and concerned about the problem?" I incorporated what the psychiatrist told me into a *relationship map* (see Figure 2.3).

Alfred had been married to Mabel for fifty years. Mabel had died seven years before, at which time Alfred had moved to live with his daughter, Lorraine, and her daughter. His son, Phil, who lived some distance away with his wife and children, had asked the psychiatrist for "psychological help" for himself and his sister to help them "cope with father's behaviour".

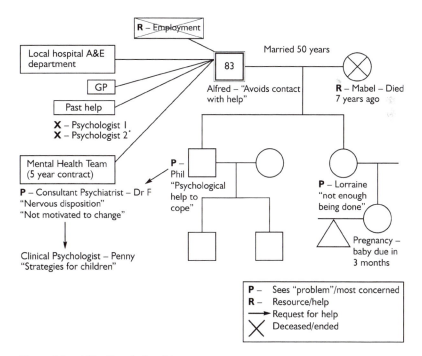

Figure 2.3. Alfred's relationship map.

In order to help me work out *whom to invite to a meeting* and *how to frame the invitation* so that I might engage them, I asked the psychiatrist, "Who sees this as a problem?"; "Who is talking with whom about the problem?"; "Who wants to have a conversation with whom about the problem?" Thus, I was beginning to learn about the family's *relationship to help*.

> Alfred and his children had had contact with a series of psychologists over the past seven years, primarily to help Alfred manage his over-whelming feelings of worry. However, Alfred had "gone to great lengths to avoid having to see psychologists and psychiatrists". Therefore, for the past nine months, only his children had had contact with the mental health service. Phil and Lorraine seemed to hold differ-ent views about what the mental health service could and should be offering their father. Whereas Phil was asking for "psychological help" to enable both of them to "cope", Lorraine had, at times, become angry and frustrated with professionals, and complained that "not enough was being done".

In order to *explore the resources* available to the situation, I asked the psychiatrist, "When has Alfred/his family managed the worries better?"; "Who notices when he is managing OK?"; "Who offers support or resources to this family?"

> Alfred had found ways to manage the symptoms so that they did not get the better of him and his family while his wife was alive and he was working. He was currently living with Lorraine and her daughter, who was pregnant. The psychiatrist was not sure how Alfred got on with his granddaughter, as "no one has mentioned any problems there."

I was unsure whom to invite to a first meeting. I had been told that both Phil and Lorraine identified their father as the problem, so, from this perspective, the *relationship in focus* seemed to be Alfred and his children. However, the psychiatrist had explained that Alfred had always been described as "of nervous disposition . . . he had never been motivated to change and was not likely to do so now" and that he had "gone to great lengths to avoid having to see psychologists and psychiatrists." Therefore, it seemed that Alfred was not asking for any help from professionals, nor was he willing to meet with any psychologist or psychiatrist. I did not know whether Alfred saw the anxiety or worries as a problem, but, since he had told both his children that he did not want to come to any meetings with our service, I decided to invite both Phil and Lorraine to an initial meeting "to discuss whether we might make a useful contribution to addressing the concerns you have discussed with [the psychiatrist] about your father." However, I was mindful that it was the psychiatrist who had approached me for help, and that the family had had contact with the mental health team for five years. Therefore, I began to wonder whether Lorraine, who had apparently at times "complained that not enough was being done", might want to have a conversation with the psychiatrist and whether the relationship in focus was Alfred's children and the mental health team. Because of this, I also invited the psychiatrist to attend the first meeting with Phil and Lorraine to offer her psychiatric perspective.

Preparing for an initial meeting

We allow time before meeting with people to prepare. Where possible, we do this with other colleagues who go on to join us in the session as our team. We find this sort of preparation useful even when we work on our own without a team, in which case we ask a colleague or a supervisor to think with us prior to the meeting. Working on my own, I (Penny) invited a colleague to help me prepare for the meeting with Alfred's family a few days before I met with them.

We start with reviewing what we have already learned about the clients and their system, perhaps from a referral letter, a phone call with the clients, or a conversation with an involved professional. We usually add to the relationship map of the client's system that we have been drawing from the start, and include the referrer in the picture (Reder & Fredman, 1996; Selvini Palazzoli, Boscolo, Cecchin & Prata, 1980a). This helps us to organize all we have learnt about the different perspectives on the "problem". I (Penny) shared with my colleague what I had learnt about Alfred's family situation, clarifying whom I had invited and how I had framed the invitation.

Preparing for the therapeutic relationship

Before the meeting, we generate a repertoire of ideas that the practitioner can use to facilitate the conversation with people in the first meeting through 'pre-session hypothesising' (Hedges, 2005; Lang & McAdam, 1995; Selvini Palazzoli, Boscolo, Cecchin, & Prata, 1980b). Figure 2.4 offers a (heuristic) map that we hold in mind to guide the process of our pre-session hypothesizing. It helps us to keep in mind the relationships between different parts of the system.

Our first step is to reflect on "Who most and least wants this meeting?"; "What they might want/not want from this meeting?"; "What they might be anticipating will happen?" To help us do this, we begin by hypothesizing about the relationship between the clients and the referrer (Figure 2.4a). For example, we may wonder whether the clients are very attached to the referrer or disappointed with the referrer. We wonder whether it was the clients or the referrer who suggested they attend, what they thought, and how they understood this suggestion or recommendation (Selvini Palazzoli, Boscolo, Cecchin, & Prata, 1980a). We also reflect on our own (service's) relationship with the referrer (Figure 2.4b). For example,

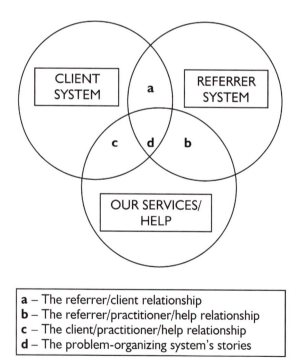

| a – The referrer/client relationship |
| b – The referrer/practitioner/help relationship |
| c – The client/practitioner/help relationship |
| d – The problem-organizing system's stories |

Figure 2.4. Guiding map for hypothesizing.

we wonder what the referrer has told the clients about our service/who we are/this meeting. We also revisit what we have learnt from the referrer about "Who wants what for whom?", "Who is asking for what for whom?", "What are clients' experience of giving and receiving help?" (Figure, 2.4c). Thus, my colleague and I (Penny) reflected upon Phil and Lorraine's "relationship to help".

> We were curious about how Phil and Lorraine had experienced past support offered. Had Lorraine or Phil felt let down by mental health professionals, since, despite practitioners' repeated attempts to intervene, their father's situation appeared to have deteriorated and Lorraine was complaining that "not enough was being done"? We also wondered if Lorraine really wanted this meeting, since it was Phil who had asked for help. Mindful that Lorraine was caring for their father at home and that her daughter, also living at home, was about to have a baby, we wondered if Lorraine was hoping someone would recognize the burden of responsibility she was shouldering. Perhaps she was thinking about alternative accommodation for Alfred? Perhaps Phil had a different opinion? I also wondered about the relational, practical, and emotional resources available to this family, including the resources Alfred could contribute.

Thus, Penny and her colleague were offering different perspectives towards generating a "systemic hypothesis". We can see how they gather together a repertoire of ideas that the practitioner, in this case Penny, can then go on to use to guide the therapeutic conversation in a meeting with clients. In this way we develop hypotheses that are intended to be not right or wrong, "neither true nor false but rather, more or less useful" (Selvini Palazzoli, Boscolo, Cecchin, & Prata, 1980b, p. 5). At this point, Penny and her colleague were taking the perspectives of different people in the problem-organizing/problem dis-solving system. The idea is to collect as many different perspectives as possible from which we can draw out themes that can inform the questions we go on to ask in the session.

From the theme—people, especially Phil and Lorraine, might have "different views about the meeting", Penny developed questions to explore whose idea the meeting had been; what people thought about this idea; what they thought people wanted from the meeting; who most/least wanted this meeting. Curious about Phil and Lorraine's "experience of past support", Penny planned to ask them what they had found more or less helpful. Wondering about the "differences between Phil and Lorraine", Penny also wanted to explore a focus for the meeting that included both of their perspectives. Since systemic hypotheses should be about relationships and include all members in the system (Stratton, Preston-Shoot, & Hanks, 1990), the pre-session hypothesizing prepared Penny to keep the psychiatrist in the conversation throughout the session, as well as Alfred, even if he was not physically present.

As well as hypothesizing about the client's relationship to therapy and help, the contexts the clients are acting out of, the stories the client might bring, the client's relationship to the practitioner, how clients might be feeling or what they might be expecting when they arrive, we also reflect upon our own relationship to help and the personal and professional contexts that we may bring to our contact with older people and their system (Reder & Fredman, 1996). Thus, we are making explicit the assumptions, prejudices (Cecchin, Lane, & Ray, 1994), or pre-understandings (Andersen, 1995) we bring to our work and which inform our approach to invitations to get involved. By making explicit the stories informing our own relationship to help, we are able to consider how our stories fit with the older person and others in their system. Below, Penny shows how she is able to use her beliefs as a resource to her work with Alfred's system.

> I (Penny) noted my discomfort at being positioned as an "expert" to "provide coping strategies to Lorraine and Phil". Drawing out the theme of "expertise", my colleague and I went on to reflect on the inability of experts to help Alfred and his family in the past and began to wonder how Alfred and his children had been coping all these years. We hypothesized that they had developed multiple strategies of their own and wondered whether their expertise had been recognized by professionals. Thus, we became curious about how the abilities of each family member, including Alfred, might contribute to the situation. At this point, I began to find myself taking a rather oppositional and unhelpful stance towards the psychiatrist's request for help. I was seeing Alfred's voice as silenced and his contribution undermined. My colleague helped me to recognize that my "prejudice" that "older people should not be marginalized or discriminated against because of age" was undermining my ability to remain curious about everyone in the system. Hence, I wondered if Alfred wanted a voice, whether he

would say he was being marginalized, or whether those involved, including Alfred himself, may have found a way of functioning which suited them and which fitted with their own family, cultural, and personal stories.

Pre-session hypothesizing can help us become aware of our own beliefs and prejudices and of how the discourses informing them might affect our interaction with people in the forthcoming meeting. In this way, we intend to be more mindful of the effects of differential power on the therapeutic relationship. Here, we see how Penny notices her beliefs getting in the way of her ability to hold in mind the different priorities, needs, and perspectives of others connected to the older person's situation. With her colleague, she was able to make use of her beliefs and prejudices as a resource (Cecchin, Lane, & Ray, 1994; Fredman, 1997; Martin & Stott, Chapter Three of this volume) to further inform their hypotheses.

Preparing our emotions

We have experienced times when practitioners have strong beliefs or feelings about a person or a situation, which could affect the sort of relationship they might create with the client or another practitioner. For example, we have heard practitioners say, "John is so cold and unfeeling; I wish my client had another key worker", or "Jean, my client, is so difficult. All she thinks about is herself. She is so manipulative." These beliefs and feelings of ours show not only in our speech, but also in our body language, our "emotional postures" (Griffith & Elliot Griffith, 1994).

The emotional postures in which we meet people affect how we relate with each other and the quality of the relationship we go on to create with professionals and clients in a meeting. Therefore, we have found it useful to prepare ourselves for the session by reflecting on the emotional postures we might expect to meet and might ourselves carry into the session through the ritual of "emotional presupposing" (Fredman, 2004, 2007). This ritual involves practitioners anticipating the likely emotional flow within the forthcoming therapeutic conversation. By becoming aware of our own emotional postures, and thinking about those of our clients and our colleagues, we can reflect on the postures we want to adopt in order to enable a respectful, safe, and collaborative meeting (Fredman, 2007). Eleanor Anderson invited her team to prepare their emotional postures in relation to Mr W and his family.

> Mr W, aged seventy-two, was originally from Nigeria. He had been admitted involuntarily to the psychiatric ward. The mental health team described his family as "difficult". They asked Eleanor to convene a meeting, including Mr W's daughter, who was "angry about the admission" and his son-in-law, who was " distrustful about the medication".

Before the meeting, Eleanor invited her team to presuppose what postures they might expect to meet in the session. Some questions we ask ourselves to help anticipate the emotional postures of the people we have invited to meet with us are: "How are they likely to feel on arrival at the meeting?"; "How might they express this either verbally or non-verbally?"; "Are they likely to be relaxed and open to different views, or wary, watching out for threat or blame?"; "What might they want us to appreciate about them?"; "What is their story of what is happening here between us?"

> The team wondered if the family wanted this meeting. They discussed how Mr W's daughter had been caring for him for many years. Perhaps she felt that they thought she had not done a good enough job? They were curious about the family's story of the admission, how different it was from their own, and wondered if the family might perceive the team as inflexible. They wondered if Mr W's son-in-law was aware of the evidence of over-diagnosis and over-medicating of black men in the British mental health system (Mind, 2008). Perhaps he felt obligated to protect his father-in-law from (institutional) racist practices? They were aware that Mr W's daughter and son-in-law had requested a separate meeting without Mr W at first. Eleanor shared that Nancy Boyd-Franklin (1989), a black person herself, had taught her about the "need to establish credibility" when "joining" with a black family, in order to build a relationship (*ibid.*, p. 95).

The team went on to anticipate the possible emotional postures that they, themselves, might hold in the forthcoming meeting with questions such as "What feelings will we be taking into this meeting?"; "How might this show in our bodies?" They reflected on whether these were preferred postures, and contemplated the postures they preferred to create by exploring the possible implications of the different postures with questions such as "How would

we prefer to feel or to be towards the daughter and son-in-law?";
"What effect could these feelings or actions have on the daugh-
ter/son-in-law?"; "Will it affect how they might be listening to us
or what they say to us?"; "How might we respond to them to help
them feel relaxed and listened to?"

> Emotional postures varied in the team. One doctor was aware that he
> "became angry in response to angry relatives". One of the nurses said
> she felt "intimidated". They all agreed that they wanted to establish a
> "good working relationship with this family". Eleanor wondered how
> they could enable the family to feel "comfortable and respected" in
> their meeting. They decided that Eleanor should begin the meeting by
> thanking the family for coming and clarifying their intentions for the
> meeting with something like, "We are so pleased you were able to
> come, as meeting with you can help us. You probably have things you
> would like to ask us about. And we want to understand your concerns
> and to hear what you think is important for us to know. This helps us
> all to be clearer about how to find a way forward." The team's by now
> genuinely curious, non-defensive position opened space for the family
> to talk about their fears that the team did not understand Mr W's
> culture and, therefore, had misunderstood his behaviour. This process
> thus enabled the team and family to begin a dialogue.

Emotional presupposing is intended to help practitioners prepare for co-ordinating emotional postures with people in therapeutic conversations. The task is to consider in which emotional posture one should approach the other and to extend the interviewers'
repertoires of positions they might adopt in the conversation.
Practitioners reflect on the postures they might carry into the conversation, anticipate how their own postures might fit with those of
the people they are meeting and the implications for choosing to
adopt one posture or another. Thus, practitioners might transform
emotional postures deemed unwanted or unhelpful towards postures intended to open space for conversations in which people are
most likely to feel safe and respected.

Beginning as we would like to go on

In this chapter, we offer a repertoire of practices to begin our work
with older people and their significant systems. We have found that

spending more time on beginnings greatly enhances how we are able to go on with both clients and practitioners, saving us more time in the long run. For example, we find that approaching requests for our involvement as invitations increases our chances of engaging referrers and other practitioners in collaborative working, so that we are not left working alone with an isolated older person. Mapping the older person's system, including "who is concerned" and "who can offer resources to the situation" can help us join with a resource-full community towards dis-solving the identified problems. Using our understanding of people's "relationship to help" to inform "whom we talk with first", "whom we invite", and "how we frame the invitation" to meet with us, enhances the possibilities of our meeting with the relevant people, engaging the older person ethically, and connecting with people who can offer a resource to the situation. Preparing our emotions and hypothesizing about people's relationship to help facilitates the therapeutic relationship.

The constraints of time and limited resources can challenge our abilities to engage with all these practices. However, not every situation with which we work requires our using all the practices or the extended forms of these practices as we have described them here. Reflecting on a few of the questions, such as "Who wants help for what for whom?"; "Who offers resources to the situation?"; "How do we respond?"; "How do we position ourselves in the work?"; "What might (clients) want us to appreciate about them?", can usefully orient us to beginning as we would like to go on.

References

Andersen, T. (1995). Reflecting processes; acts of informing and forming: You can borrow my eyes, but you must not take them away from me! In: S. Friedman (Ed.), *The Reflecting Team in Action. Collaborative Practice in Family Therapy.* (pp. 11–37). New York: Guilford.

Anderson, H., & Goolishian, H. (1988). Human systems as linguistic systems: preliminary and evolving ideas about the implications for clinical theory. *Family Process, 27*: 371–392.

Anderson, H., Goolishian, H., & Windermand, L. (1986). Problem determined systems: towards transformation in family therapy. *Journal of Strategic and Systemic Therapies, 5*: 1–13.

Boyd-Franklin, N. (1989). *Black Families in Therapy: A Multi-Systems Approach*. New York: Guildford Press.

Cecchin, G. (1987). Hypothesising, circularity and neutrality revisited: an invitation to curiosity. *Family Process*, 26: 404–413.

Cecchin, G., Lane, G., & Ray, W. A. (1994). *The Cybernetics of Prejudices in the Practice of Psychotherapy*. London: Karnac.

Fredman, G. (1997). *Death Talk: Conversations with Children and Families*. London: Karnac.

Fredman, G. (2004). *Transforming Emotion: Conversations in Counselling and Psychotherapy*. London: Whurr/Wiley.

Fredman, G. (2007). Preparing our selves for the therapeutic relationship. Revisiting "hypothesizing revisited". *Human Systems: The Journal of Systemic Consultation & Management*, 18: 44–59.

Griffith, J. L., & Elliott Griffith, M. (1994). *The Body Speaks. Therapeutic Dialogues for Mind–Body Problems*. New York: Basic Books.

Lang, P., & McAdam, E. (1990). Referrals, referrers and the system of concern. Unpublished manuscript. Kensington Consultation Centre, London.

Lang, P., & McAdam, E. (1995). Stories, giving accounts and systemic descriptions. Perspectives and positions in conversations. Feeding and fanning the winds of creative imagination. *Human Systems: the Journal of Systemic Consultation & Management*, 6: 71–103.

Marriott, A. (2000). The family tree: a way of gathering information. *Family Therapy with Older Adults and their Families*. London: Winslow Press.

McGoldrick, M., & Gerson, R. (1986). *Genograms in Family Assessment*. New York: Norton.

Mind (2008). *Race and Mental Health*. www.mind.org.uk/News+policy+and+campaigns/Policy/RMH.html (accessed 17 April).

Reder, P., & Fredman, G. (1996). The relationship to help: interacting beliefs about the treatment process. *Clinical Child Psychology and Psychiatry*, 1: 457–467.

Selvini Palazzoli, M., Boscolo, L., Cecchin, G., & Prata, G. (1980a). The problem of the referring person. *Journal of Marital and Family Therapy*, 6: 3–9.

Selvini Palazzoli, M., Boscolo, L., Cecchin, G., & Prata, G. (1980b). Hypothesising, circularity and neutrality: three guidelines for the conductor of the session. *Family Process*, 19: 3–12.

Stratton, P., Preston-Shoot, M., & Hanks, H. (1990). *Family Therapy. Training and Practice*. Birmingham: Venture Press.

CHAPTER THREE

Using our selves in work with older people

Eleanor Martin and Joshua Stott

The other evening I (Eleanor) was telling a friend that I am co-writing a chapter on "Using our selves in our work with older people". The friend looked confused, and asked, "Why do you include your personal self in a book about therapy with older people? Shouldn't you be interested in the patient, not yourself? My therapist never gives anything away."

We often face dilemmas about how best to make use of our selves in our work. By this, we mean how to use our life experiences, our emotions, and what goes through our minds when we are with people in therapeutic conversation. We make judgements about whether to share, what to share, how much to share, how best to do this, and what it means to the older person if we choose to share or not. In this chapter, we suggest that a consideration of both our professional and personal lives can make a valuable contribution to our work with older people. We would, therefore, like to introduce ourselves to you, the reader, from some of the personal and professional contexts that inform and shape our actions and interactions with the older people with whom we work (Cronen & Pearce, 1980). When we refer to "contexts", we mean the many different backgrounds and circumstances informing our lives, such as our gender, religion, sexuality, and age, to name a few. These contexts also inform the perspectives we present in this chapter.

> I am Eleanor Martin, a thirty-five-year-old woman. I define myself as a white, English, able-bodied woman. Having been born and grown up in Sheffield and attended university in Leeds, I identify myself as Northern English, particularly since I have been living in London. I am in a long-term heterosexual relationship, and am a mother of two young children. I am a daughter to my mother and father, an older sister, and, until recently, a granddaughter. I am the first woman in my family to go to university. I define myself as middle class, because of my educational background, my lifestyle, and my financial circumstances. I work as a clinical psychologist with older people in the public health service.

> I am Josh Stott, a thirty-year-old man. I define myself as white and as British. My mother's family trace their roots several generations back in Britain. My father's family would also define themselves as white and British, although they have strong connections with Africa as well. My father was born and lived in Kenya until he was thirteen years old, and his first language is Swahili. I also lived in Zimbabwe for three of my first seven years, and still see Southern Africa as part of my identity. I define myself as coming from a middle-class background: my father comes from a line of seven medical doctors, who all attended the same university. My mother's family are scientists going back three generations. Thus, having a profession and going to university were important goals in my family. Politically, my family and I have connections with socialism and value diversity and multi-culturalism. I attended an inner city comprehensive school and live in an inner city urban area. I am in a heterosexual relationship, and have no children. Professionally, I work as a clinical psychologist in the public health service.

To help us address the friend's question "Why do you include your personal self in a book about work with older people? Shouldn't you be interested in the patient, not yourself?" we will begin by introducing you to Greta, and then to Gillian.

Greta, sixty-eight, had been diagnosed with depression. Since she was involved in a road traffic accident, she has struggled to go out of her home, resulting in her getting very little exercise. As a consequence she had gained significant weight, which had restricted her mobility.

I (Eleanor) was talking with Greta in her lounge. She sat on the chair and I sat on the sofa. Her brother had hung photographs that I had never seen before, including one of her late husband, about whom we had spoken often. I asked if the photo on the mantlepiece was of the two of them. She ushered me to get up and look. I felt interested as I approached the photo to see what they both looked like. I felt surprised at how young and beautiful Greta looked in the photo, and was not sure if I wanted her to know that. To avoid commenting on how different she looked, I asked her when and where the photo was taken. She told me it was on holiday, but then asked me, "How do you think I looked when I was younger?" I blurted out, "Greta you looked amazing!" She burst into tears, and once the tears slowed, she spoke. She told me that the hardest part of growing old was that her looks had changed. She said, "I long to look young, thin, and beautiful again". Hearing this made me feel tearful and guilty, as I was indeed younger and thinner. I was stuck for what to say.

We are connected in relationship

As the therapist, I (Eleanor) am not outside of this relationship with Greta, acting upon it, but I am part of it, collaborating with her and moved by what I say and hear. The words I choose to use and how I express them have an effect on Greta and they also affect me. For example, my initial reluctance to comment on Greta's appearance may have left her more curious about what I thought, and therefore influenced her direct question, "How do you think I looked when I was younger?" Thus, my not commenting was, in itself, a response. Indeed, we cannot *not* respond. What we say and do, as well as what we do not say or do, always have an effect on the other and ourselves. Greta's response, her asking me the direct question, surprised me, and in turn I blurted out, "You looked amazing". This affected her response, which was to cry, and hence my experience of feeling tearful and guilty, and so on. Since our words and actions influence and affect ourselves and the other recursively, as practitioners we pay attention to ourselves in our interactions with our clients. We see the fact we are always affected by the other person as an opportunity in our work rather than an obstacle.

We act out of and into contexts

In every interaction, we act out of our own contexts and into the contexts of the other (Cronen & Pearce, 1980). I (Eleanor) was approaching my conversation with Greta as a younger, able-bodied woman, and professionally as a psychologist working in a mental health setting. These contexts of age, ability, gender, and profession affected how I acted and interacted with Greta and the meanings I gave to both of our actions and interactions (Cronen & Pearce, 1985). For example, as a younger, slimmer, and more able-bodied woman, I felt conscious of the difference between us and I felt uncomfortable commenting on how Greta had looked in the photograph. Hence, I avoided commenting until directly questioned. Not only was I acting out of contexts such as age, gender, and ability, but also I was acting into the contexts that informed Greta. For example, from previous conversations with Greta, I was aware she had an idea that for a woman "appearance was everything". Therefore, my concern about responding was also based on my knowing from Greta that this issue was important to her as a woman. In this way, I was acting into her context of gender.

Our pre-understandings inform our actions and relationships

We come to any situation or interaction with pre-understandings (Andersen, 1995). We choose to use Andersen's word, "pre-understandings", here rather than Cecchin, Lane, and Ray's (1994) "prejudices", since the term prejudice can mean "injustice" or "intolerance", and, therefore, carries a negative connotation. Equally, we prefer "pre-understandings" to "beliefs" or "cognitions", as we find these terms can imply something internal, non-relational, and divorced from their context.

We see our pre-understandings as the assumptions we hold, which we often take for granted and may not necessarily be aware of. The contexts that we act out of and that give meaning to our actions and our relationships inform these pre-understandings. As a younger English woman, I (Eleanor) brought to my conversation with Greta the pre-understanding that "thinness and youthfulness signify beauty". This pre-understanding was informed by several contexts. For example, in the cultures of my age and gender, there are rules about how people should look, which we learn about from sources like the media. These rules are "gendered": women are expected to be very thin, men not so much, as evidenced by the media's increasing attention to the American size zero. Rules about appearance are also age specific, as shown by the increase in cosmetic surgery to halt the ageing process. My pre-understanding that "thinness and youthfulness signify beauty" informed my choice not to comment on how Greta looked in the photograph lest I might imply that Greta no longer looked thin and beautiful. Therefore, we consider it important to reflect on how our contexts give meaning to and inform our actions and interactions with the older people with whom we work.

*   *   *

I (Josh) had been working with Gillian, a white British woman of seventy-two, who had just been diagnosed with dementia.

> Gillian and I were discussing what the diagnosis of dementia meant to her. She told me that it meant, "losing my marbles"; that she would gradually lose her memory, and eventually become reliant on others for simple day-to-day tasks, as had happened to her mother, who had also been told that she had dementia. I felt a kind of ineffable sadness at this point, and also a feeling of "what can I do for this person?", thinking of how awful this all sounded. I was unsure how to go on, when Gillian said, "It's funny, I know all this and I am really scared, but I will be able to cope . . . my mum and I, we often had laughs you know."

We can see how Gillian and I are connected in relationship as together we are trying to create a joint understanding of what it means for Gillian to be "losing her marbles". I am not only hearing information about Gillian's experience of dementia, but am also affected and moved by Gillian's words, and in my inner talks (Andersen, 1995) I reflect "how awful" this all sounded.

I was acting out of several contexts during my conversation with Gillian. I have direct experience of dementia in my family, from where I have taken the message that "dementia is always seen as a bad thing". This pre-understanding informed my actions and relationship with Gillian as I experienced "an ineffable sadness" and was unsure how to go on, which, in turn, would have affected Gillian. Later in the chapter, we explore further the contexts that gave meaning to my actions and provide some ideas on how we can begin to recognize which contexts we are acting out of and how to make use of our contexts in our work with older people.

Self-awareness

In our conversations with Greta and Gillian, we demonstrated self-awareness. By this, we are referring to the ability in the moment to recognize our thoughts and emotions. I (Eleanor) recognized that I felt uncomfortable and self-conscious about commenting on Greta's appearance in the photograph and unsure how to respond to her tears. Josh recognized that he felt an "ineffable sadness" and was thinking "how awful" Gillian's account of the deterioration associated with dementia sounded. The ability to recognize our thoughts and feelings, our pre-understandings, in this way is an important part of including our selves in our work, as it creates the opportunity to go on and use them as a resource. Self-awareness is a first step towards using our selves as a resource, but is limited. Just recognizing that "I feel uncomfortable", or "I see dementia as awful", does not give us a way to go on in our conversations. Isabelle Ekdawi, a co-author of this book, demonstrates through her work with William, an eighty-two-year-old man, how we can move from self-awareness to using our pre-understandings as a way to go on in our conversations.

Self-reflexivity

I (Isabelle) had been working with William, a thin, grey-haired man, who was overwhelmed by fears of illness. He walked seven miles a day, come rain or shine, to ward off ill health. William told me his mother died suddenly when he was three and he did not remember her. I wondered if the fear of illness and his lengthy walks were because he was afraid of dying suddenly like his mother. Also, I had heard other older people with whom I work say they fear dying. However, I did not want to assume this fear, so I asked William, "What is your worst fear?", to which he replied, "Not leaving a mark."

In Isabelle's conversation with William, she demonstrated an awareness of her pre-understanding that "William is afraid of dying". However, Isabelle did not assume that her idea was correct. Her self-awareness enabled her to use her pre-understanding to inform her question, "What is your worst fear?" In so doing, she was demonstrating self-reflexivity, which involves our becoming curious about our pre-understandings, what contexts inform them, and then changing how we act and how we respond to the other person accordingly (Burnham, 1993).

Isabelle demonstrated self-reflexivity in her conversation with William by using her pre-understanding as a resource (Cecchin, Lane, & Ray, 1994) to guide her interview. She did this by taking a number of steps.

- *Noticing her pre-understanding that "William is afraid of dying".*
  Here, Isabelle was demonstrating self-awareness.

- *Locating her pre-understanding in her personal and/or professional contexts by asking herself, "Where does that idea come from?"*
  Isabelle recognized that her pre-understanding that William must be afraid of dying came from her professional context, where she had heard other older people express fear of dying.

- *Using her pre-understanding as a "hypothesis" that was neither right nor wrong, but could be more or less useful in her conversation with William.*
  Isabelle approached a previously taken for granted assumption (pre-understanding) as a tentative hypothesis that she could explore in conversation with her client.

- *Drawing out themes from the hypothesis.*
  Using the hypothesis "he may be afraid of dying", she created a *"theme"* about "fear of dying".

- *Using the "theme" to inform a question she could ask of the client.*
  Isabelle asked William, "What is your worst fear?"

In this way, Isabelle used her contexts as a resource to create new information and different opportunities for developing her conversation with William. Recognizing that her professional context was informing her pre-understanding enabled her to ask questions informed by that context.

I (Eleanor), on the other hand, felt constrained and did not know how to respond to Greta's tears. If I had recognized that my culture, gender, and age were informing my pre-understanding about "thinness and youthfulness signifying beauty", I, too, may have created alternative ways to continue my conversation with Greta. For example, I could have been curious about Greta's ideas about beauty and asked questions such as: "Where have your ideas about beauty come from?"; "Who shares your views about thinness and beauty and who has different ideas?"; "Do men and women share similar or different ideas about what contributes to beauty?"; "What effect do my age and appearance have on our conversation?" To do this may have helped Greta and me to reflect on where her pre-understandings about age and beauty came from. It may have enabled Greta to consider whether there are different ways of thinking about ageing and beauty that we had not considered before that could be more useful to her than the dominant idea informing us. These questions could have created an opportunity for us to talk about the effects for Greta of talking with a younger woman and how we might manage this so as to make the conversations most useful to her.

Helping each other use our contexts as a resource

Isabelle was able to use her contexts as a resource to guide her questions with William in the moment. One way we have found to develop the sort of self-reflexivity Isabelle demonstrated is through the process of interviewing each other. We have found that supervision, peer supervision, or pre- or post-session conversations with colleagues (when working as a team) provide opportunities to interview in this way. The following is a summary of a conversation in which I (Eleanor) interviewed Josh about his talks with Gillian. We intended to use the interview (informed by Fredman, 1997) to develop Josh's self-reflexivity so that he might use his contexts as a resource in his work with Gillian.

I began by asking Josh, "Can we pick out the ideas or assumptions you are drawing on in your conversation with Gillian?" My intention was to explore Josh's pre-understandings about working with dementia and Gillian. I purposely used the words "ideas" and "assumptions", as these words seemed more familiar and therefore more meaningful to Josh. Josh highlighted his idea that "dementia is hopeless . . . a bad thing" and his belief that "Gillian must see it the same way as me . . . she thinks the same as me". I went on to enquire about what informed these ideas with questions such as "Where do these ideas come from?" I tentatively asked, "What might your family or your culture say about 'dementia being hopeless'? Do you think your age or stage of life has an influence on these ideas?" to further explore the ideas or pre-understandings Josh was drawing from each of those contexts. My intention here was to invite Josh to reflect upon the contexts that gave meaning to his pre-understandings.

> I (Josh) spoke of several of my family members who had had dementia, which had "brought with it depression and family problems . . . nothing had helped". I noted that, as a clinical psychologist, I have been "trained to cure people . . . but can't with dementia . . . that makes it seem hopeless to me." Eleanor's questions reminded me of "a storyline from a soap opera where dementia had been depicted in a very traumatic way . . . the person with dementia had almost been kept behind closed doors." I reflected on how, as a younger man, I felt constantly confronted with "messages about the perils of growing old . . . almost being taught to dread how I would look . . ."

Thus we highlighted Josh's family, his profession, his culture, and his age as important contexts that influenced or informed his pre-understanding that "dementia is hopeless". Having explored the pre-understandings Josh was drawing from these different contexts, I (Eleanor) asked, "How did these ideas affect how you acted with Gillian, what you did or did not do?", and "Which of these contexts has the greatest influence on your assumption that 'dementia is hopeless'?" My intention was to explore how our pre-understandings and the contexts that we act out of influence what we do. Furthermore, the contexts we act out of do not necessarily have equal impact on the meaning we ascribe and the actions that we take (Cronen & Pearce, 1980). In response to my questions, Josh was clear that his family experiences were the most significant influence. He followed this with the contexts of his clinical psychology training, then his age, and then he suggested that the wider cultural stories about dementia had some influence. He reflected that his pre-understanding that "dementia is hopeless" seemed to "make me lose my curiosity . . . I would usually ask lots of questions, check things out, but with Gillian I was not doing that, I was assuming I knew."

As a way of further clarifying, we went on to map the relationship between Josh's contexts of meaning and action, which is shown below in Figure 3.1 (*ibid.*). We did this by writing down Josh's pre-understanding "dementia is hopeless" and then including the different contexts that gave it meaning. Josh had said that the context of his family had the greatest influence over his pre-understanding so we viewed this as the "highest context" and, therefore, put this at the top of the map. We put the other contexts below, according to the strength of influence Josh saw them having over his pre-understanding (for example, "profession", then "age",

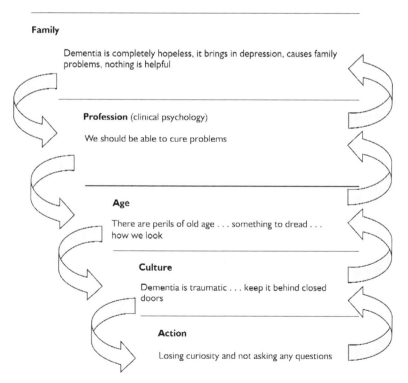

Pre-understanding: Dementia is hopeless

Family

Dementia is completely hopeless, it brings in depression, causes family problems, nothing is helpful

Profession (clinical psychology)

We should be able to cure problems

Age

There are perils of old age . . . something to dread . . . how we look

Culture

Dementia is traumatic . . . keep it behind closed doors

Action

Losing curiosity and not asking any questions

Figure 3.1. Josh's contexts of meaning and action.

and, at the bottom, "culture"). Drawing the contexts in this hierarchical way reminds us that one particular context (for example, "family") may exert a greater influence over our action than another and can give meaning to the contexts below or above. We can see later how mapping in this way enabled Josh to become an observer to his pre-understandings.

Having mapped his pre-understanding in this way, I asked Josh, "What has struck you about this mapping exercise?", and "What difference might it make to your conversations with Gillian?" My intention was to enable Josh to further develop his abilities in self-reflexivity by looking at what had already happened as well as hypothetically talking about what he might do differently in future conversations. Josh said he was struck by two things: first, how his "ideas about dementia are not the truth. . . they are influenced by all aspects of my life and experience", and second, "how much my assumption about dementia made me lose curiosity". Josh went on to explain how he thought that having this conversation meant he would be more likely to notice when he was making an assumption about "dementia being hopeless" or when he was losing his curiosity. He described them as "traps I can imagine looking out for."

By mapping the contexts of his meanings and actions, Josh was encouraged to become an observer to his own practice. Thus, he developed his self-reflexivity by identifying his pre-understandings, mapping the contexts that gave them meaning, and then reflecting on how they related to his actions. By recognizing his taken for granted ideas and noting where they came from, Josh was able to go on to recalibrate and reposition himself in his later work with Mr and Mrs Grant through the process of relational-reflexivity (Burnham, 2005), which we describe below. A few weeks after this interview, Josh described his work with Mr and Mrs Grant, a white, English, elderly couple. Mr Grant, eighty-five, had dementia. Josh engaged in a conversation with Mrs Grant quite differently from his conversation with Gillian.

> Mrs Grant talked about how awful it was for her to have to look after her husband. I (Josh) realized that I was becoming sad. I had a feeling of hopelessness and thought I ought to be able to do something. I was reminded of my conversation about Gillian and the understandings of dementia coming from both my professional and personal life, for

example, that "it is all hopeless". I wondered to myself about this, trying to be curious about it. In my inner talks, I asked myself, "Is it always hopeless when people have dementia?" Then I voiced this curiosity by saying to Mrs Grant, "Sometimes when we talk about dementia, we talk about times when hope is not around because things are often very difficult. I realize this is what we are doing now. Can I check, is this helpful to you?" She replied that it was "useful to get things off my chest", but that sometimes when we talked in this way she "felt down". I went on to ask, "When are the times that hope is around, when you don't feel so down?" She spoke of a time when she and her husband were dancing, "He still knows how to dance," she said, "and his face lights up." When I asked, "What is this time like?", she said it was "mixed", as she felt sad because they always used to dance but also, on reflection, he was clearly happy at this time. I asked, "What effect is talking about a time when hope is around having on you now?", and "Do you want to continue talking about times when you don't feel so down?" She quickly replied, "Yes I would rather talk like this, I need to focus on the positive. It helps me carry on."

Josh recognized his pre-understanding that "dementia is hopeless" and remembered that this is not the truth, but, rather, one of his perspectives. He recognized that his pre-understanding was informed by his personal and professional stories of dementia. He then used this pre-understanding as a hypothesis to generate a theme about "hope". He used this theme to inform his question "When are the times that hope is around, when you don't feel so down?" We can see how he is self-reflexive in the moment, as he uses his contexts as a resource and changes his behaviour accordingly. Mrs Grant seemed to value this way of talking over focusing on the "difficulties", as she described it as helping her "carry on".

Relational reflexivity

Josh not only recognized his pre-understandings and where they came from and changed his questioning accordingly, he also checked with Mrs Grant whether she found it helpful to talk about the difficulties she faced with dementia. This inclusion of Mrs Grant in how the conversation developed is an example of Josh being 'relationally reflexive' (Burnham, 2005). He does not assume that he must either talk about times of hope or about 'dementia as hopeless'; rather, he invites Mrs Grant to choose. In this way, he is not only examining his pre-understandings and the contexts that he acts out of, but is also considering the contexts he is acting into, that is, Mrs Grant's pre-understandings. Co-ordinating their resources in this way brought forth a very moving moment in their conversation, where Mrs Grant recalls her husband remembering how to dance as before. Josh's reflexivity within the relationship enabled Mrs Grant to remember this moment and acknowledge that she would rather talk about hope being around than not.

Working with our emotions

Daily, we hear older people's stories that move us in different and profound ways. We find ourselves experiencing a range of different emotions, depending on whom we are talking to, about what we are talking, and how we are talking. We believe that the emotions we experience offer us important information and can be used as a resource, but we have often struggled with knowing how best to make use of them as I (Eleanor) did in my work with Enid and Bill.

> Enid and Bill had very different views about Bill's "obsessions". He reported feeling more confident now at seventy-eight than he ever had in his life, and was able to resist the obsessions on occasions. He was proud to still visit art galleries and lectures at the University of the Third Age. Enid, on the other hand, stressed how she saw no change. She complained that Bill still checked the oven and wore a glove almost all the time to "stop contamination". She did not see going to galleries as any kind of achievement if it meant Bill washing his clothing several times afterwards. Bill said he found talking with us very useful and reassuring, yet Enid felt it made no difference but was happy to continue if Bill wanted to.

When working with couples, we can find ourselves confronted with opposing accounts and views. Working systemically, we actively invite these different perspectives. However, we have found we can be easily pulled towards one person's account or perspective (Jones & Asen, 2000). In my work with Enid and Bill, I found myself feeling thrilled with Bill's achievements, such as playing bowls, and frustrated that Enid did not see them in the same way. I recognized that my frustration could have affected the conversation with Bill and Enid. Although I had tried to conceal the frustration I was feeling, our emotions can show in our bodies, therefore affecting not only what questions we ask but also how we ask them (Griffith and Elliott Griffith, 1994). Therefore, I wanted to transform the emotion of frustration.

Emotional presupposing

In supervision we were introduced to the idea of "emotional pre-supposing" (Fredman, 2004, 2007), which can enable the practitioner to prepare for the "likely emotional flow" of a session. Emotional presupposing can help us reflect on and adapt our "emotional postures" that influence the type of relationship we create with the older people with whom we work. When referring to "emotional postures", Fredman (2007) draws on the work of Griffith and Elliott Griffith (1994), who suggest that our emotional postures involve our bodies' readiness to respond and focus our attention towards others and ourselves in different ways. Prior to the next session, Josh joined to help me prepare for the therapeutic conversation in a different way. He asked me a number of questions about my emotional posture and its possible effects on the way the conversation might evolve. These included: "How do you feel before meeting Enid and Bill?", to which I answered, "I feel 'despondent' as I know I will leave 'frustrated'." He went on to ask, "How do you think this posture of 'despondency' and 'frustration' might affect the conversation with Enid and Bill?", with the intention of encouraging my reflection upon how my emotional posture could affect our relationship. Josh checked, "Is this your preferred emotional posture?" I explained that it was not, and he then helped me consider other possible emotional postures I might adopt and their effect through questions such as, "If you adopted a different posture, what might that look like?" "How might that change what you are able to do in the session?" (Fredman, 2004).

I was able to reflect on how the emotional postures of despondency and frustration were not my preferred way of being with Enid and Bill. I recognized that they positioned Enid to continually defend her view and had an impact on how we all related together.

The questions Josh asked enabled me to see other possible positions I might adopt, such as a posture of "interest" towards Enid. In our next meeting, I gained Enid and Bill's permission to initially interview Enid while Bill listened. I revisited questions I had asked in our very first meeting, such as, "How are the obsessions affecting your life and relationship with Bill at the moment?" Enid gave lots of different examples about how the obsessions affected their lives from those we had heard about during our first session. I found myself genuinely curious to hear more of the detail. Just as we were about to end the session, Enid said, "Oh yes, and I meant to tell you, yesterday we left the house without Bill checking the oven and Tuesday last week he took his glove off when the neighbour popped in for a cup of tea."

Emotional presupposing gave me a way of transforming my emotions (Fredman, 2004). Considering my emotional posture, looking at what type of conversations and postures that would invite from Enid and Bill, and whether it was how I wanted to be with them, enabled me to experience different emotions and behave differently. Reconnecting with a position of curiosity (Cecchin, 1987) and interest in Enid's account, I invited her to talk differently and, for the first time, we heard from her about developments.

Sharing our selves

We find that sharing aspects of our selves with the older people we work with can be pivotal in enabling change. However, equally, we have had experiences where our sharing has not worked out as we hoped. Therefore, we are constantly faced with moment-to-moment dilemmas about when and how best to share. The times when our sharing has not seemed useful to the older person are, in the main, occasions where we have slipped into privileging our own stories above our client. An example of this is when I (Eleanor) was one of three professionals in a reflecting team (Andersen, 1987). (A reflecting team listens to the first part of an interview and then team members talk with each other tentatively about aspects of what they have heard to offer different perspectives to the clients and therapist. The clients and therapist listen to the conversation and later have an opportunity to reflect upon what the team said.)

The therapist had interviewed Jim, seventy-seven, about his partner having recently died and the effect this was having on him. During a reflecting conversation, I spoke about a recent loss I had experienced. I reflected how I had connected with Jim's story because "loss was something that was around for me". I was shocked by Jim's response to the reflections. He said, "I don't want that team next time. It's not really right for me." The therapist asked why this was the case, and Jim explained, '"The woman who said about losing someone, I appreciate her saying that but it felt hard hearing her saying that she's lost someone because she's only very young and has time on her side. She has been able to pull herself together and get on with her life, being able to be a therapist, and I can't even go to the corner shop. It's not for me, the team."

I decided to share with Jim about my recent loss, but I had not intended for him to make sense of it as he did. I had hoped he would feel listened to and validated and that my sharing would address the inherent power differential in the therapeutic relationship. With hindsight, my reflecting comments to Jim sit more closely with the practice of self disclosure, which runs the risk of sharing aspects of oneself for one's own cathartic benefit as opposed to for the benefit of the client (White, 2000). I had not considered the differences for a thirty-five-year-old woman and a seventy-seven-year-old man in the meaning and management of loss, and not thought about the effect on Jim. Following this unhelpful sharing with Jim, we were interested in moments in our practice where there had been a different outcome, where therapists or team members had shared something about themselves that had made a useful difference to the client.

Decentred sharing

I (Eleanor) got to know Grace while she was attending the day hospital. I wanted to review our work together before going on maternity leave. I thought Grace had made impressive changes in her life, which she did not always recognize. Our Camden and Islington systemic team offer consultations to practitioners and clients about their work together. Grace and I thought reviewing with the systemic team would offer us something different from just the two of us meeting to review. Therefore, a colleague interviewed both of us while Glenda Fredman and two trainee clinical psychologists were positioned as a reflecting team (Andersen, 1987).

Glenda reflected upon how she had been interested in Grace's struggles to keep depression out of her life. Glenda said she "had been particularly drawn to a comment Grace had made about her daughter saying to Grace, 'Don't end up like Granddad John after Nana died, don't just sit in that chair all day and fester like he did.'" Glenda had said she had been drawn to this comment as it had seemed to be important to Grace, since Grace had told us that it was this comment that "motivated her and got her going each day". Since Grace had said that she did not want to let her daughter down, or end up like her father, John, Glenda had wondered if Grace placed importance and value on being someone who got things done and was dependable. Glenda then went on to reflect upon how it had got her thinking about her own mother's struggles, as she had recently been discharged from hospital and was finding it difficult to "get going". Glenda had thought she might think with her mum if there were any conversations or things people had said to her, similar to Grace's daughter's comment, that "motivated her or got her going".

Grace still talks about the team's comments in that consultation. She reminds me frequently how "The doctor in the team was going to speak to her mother to see if she could try and do the same thing as I did. If the lady doctor thinks she is going to tell her mum what I did, I must have done something right." When she says this, she smiles and puffs her shoulders back.

When Josh and I reflected upon what we thought was happening in this episode that left the client boosted and had such a significant impact, we had an idea that it was something about the importance of her feeling someone had learnt or taken something from what she had to say. We started to theorize about what we thought Glenda had been doing and what was informing her actions. Looking back, I now recognize that I was encountering my first introduction to "outsider-witness practices" (Carey & Russell, 2003; White, 1997, 2000), an approach we have since started to use more regularly in our work in older people's services.

Glenda was working as part of a reflecting team, and saw the opportunity to practise as an outsider witness to Grace's story. This practice of reflecting is different from other types of reflecting conversations in a number of ways. First, White (2000) warns against the contemporary practice of praise. By this, he means offering positive reinforcement, congratulating, or pointing out positives. Although he recognizes that offering praise can seem to provide an antidote to the pathologizing stories of people's lives, he chose not to reflect in such a way, as to do so implies that someone has done well according to certain values and that the person offering the praise is in a position to make this judgement. So, we did not see Glenda saying how impressed she was about Grace making it to the session or reflecting back all the changes I had listed during my work with Grace; instead, we saw her do something different.

White has mapped four steps in the process of decentred sharing (Carey & Russell, 2003; White, 2002). First, *identifying the expression* refers to commenting upon which expressions caught one's attention or struck a chord. So, we heard Glenda say that she had been particularly drawn to Grace's comment that her daughter had told her, "Don't end up like Granddad John after Nana died . . . don't just sit in that chair all day and fester." The second stage is to *describe the image*, which requires the witness to describe what the expression suggested about the person's values, beliefs, purposes, hopes, dreams, and commitments. In other words, what image did the identified expression evoke about the person's life, identities or of the world more generally. Glenda had said how Grace's comment had seemed "important to Grace, because it motivated her—got her going". She also commented upon the possible value for Grace of "getting things done and being dependable". Third is *embodying responses*, which, as we see it, refers to locating what it is about you as a witness that meant you picked up on the particular expression and image. Or, to put it another way, what aspects of your experiences of life (either personal or professional) resonated with these expressions and the images evoked by the expressions. Glenda spoke of how this resonated with her mother's situation of having recently been discharged from hospital. The final part of what the outsider witness reflects upon is *acknowledging transport*. As the name suggests, this touches on where the above experience has taken you, where you have been transported to as a result of witnessing, or how the witnessing has changed you in some way. Glenda reflected that it had moved her to talk with her mother about what people may have said to her that might motivate and "get her going". In this way, Glenda had been transported to a different place with new ideas.

We have found that ensuring our sharing follows the four stages detailed above maximizes the chances of people like Jim and Grace's stories being privileged over our own. This is important in going some way to address the power imbalance inherent in our relationship as therapists working in public services with older people. White (2000) has suggested we should always strive towards "decentred practice". He sees decentring as a therapeutic posture, where one should be aiming to be both influential and decentred. The notion of "decentred" does not refer to the intensity of the therapist's engagement, but to how well they stay with the clients' stories, particular knowledges and skills, and keep the older person as the focus. In the example above, we saw Glenda using her personal story of her mother's experiences, but not losing sight of Grace's story and how the connection to her mother's story related back to the purpose of the consultation.

In the reflections I shared with Jim about a recent loss I had experienced, I had not spoken of the "expression" that caught my attention or described the "image". I had begun my reflecting from the third stage, "embodying the response". Furthermore, I did not speak of how I had been moved or transported through hearing Jim's story. In this sense, I was not connecting back to Jim's story but was allowing my story to become prominent, and so I was failing to "decentre". Our intention when working as outsider witnesses is to develop the older person's stories about themselves that they prefer, or to offer them more possibilities for how to be. During my reflections, I was not relating to Jim's preferred stories about himself.

We can help each other's sharing remain decentred by the interviewing therapist (or another team member) questioning the outsider witnesses. For example, to keep my sharing decentred with Jim, the interviewer could have asked me, "Was there a particular comment, expression or phrase Jim said that got you thinking about your loss?" Once I had identified the expression, she could have asked something like "So this phrase that struck you, what image of Jim's life, or who he is, did it evoke?" I could have spoken more of what I had gathered about aspects of Jim's life, his sense of himself as a person, or his values. Finally, the interviewer could have asked, "How has your thinking or experience of life been changed through hearing Jim's story?", followed by questions such as, "How is your life different for having been moved to this new place?"

Decentred practice has encouraged us to keep the older person in focus and ensure, where possible, that our sharing is not serving our personal agenda. Being open and transparent about where our hypotheses and questions come from is another way we attempt to ensure our sharing is decentred.

Transparency

I (Eleanor) walked into John and Graham's front room and sat by the open window. John talked about the impact of a recent fall on him. He could no longer do the cooking, he could no longer take daily walks in his local park, and he felt "continually miserable". I later asked Graham, "What effect did the fall have on your relationship?" He raised his eyebrows, frowned, and paused. I saw this pause as an opportunity to explain further. "I am asking these questions because I have an idea that when something happens, such as having a fall, it affects us in many different ways. It affects what we can and cannot do; it affects our relationships and how we view ourselves, and how others see us. I was wondering if it has brought you closer or changed the way you have to be with each other?" Graham thanked me, and said, "I'm glad you explained. I thought you might not be taking our relationship seriously because we are gay—you know, implying that a fall would split us up. Explaining made me realize you actually take our relationship seriously."

I (Eleanor) had noticed Graham's raised eyebrows and his change in bodily posture towards me when I asked about the effect of the fall on their relationship. I was not clear what exactly was informing this change in his emotional posture, but I hypothesized it may have had to do with their being in a gay relationship. This hypothesis was based on my experience of working with other older gay men and the prejudice they have received from health professionals. I decided to be transparent about the idea informing my question, as I had hoped it would show that my question came from a place of respect rather than a position of dismissing their relationship. Michael White and other narrative therapists (Roberts, 2005; White, 1992) have coined the term "transparency" (Rogers, 1980), which goes beyond self disclosure to include the sharing of information that comes from our own life experiences, conceptual models, or experiences of talking and working with families.

When we are transparent in this way we find it is important to monitor the verbal and non-verbal feedback from our clients. Thus, we can try to ensure that what we are doing seems useful to the older person. We have found that this can be particularly challenging when working with more than one person, as one person may find transparency helpful and another may experience it quite differently (Roberts, 2005). Therefore, we try not to make the assumption that being transparent is always a good thing or has the same effect for all people. With Graham and John, I could have checked this out and asked questions such as: "John, did you make sense of my explanation in the same way as Graham or did you see it differently?"; "What affect did my explanation have on what you felt able to talk about or not talk about?"; "If I had not explained my thinking, how might our conversation have been different?"

The degree to which we share our selves is dependent on our relationship with the client and on the position we take and are given in the work. As a reflecting team member, Glenda was able to talk to other team members about her experience and not directly to Grace; Grace was invited to listen, but not obliged to engage with Glenda or to respond to Glenda's words about her mother. Sharing a personal story, while continuing to centre the client, is more difficult when working on our own. Talking directly to a client about our personal experience risks their feeling obliged to respond, show interest, or comment on our story, thereby bringing us to the centre instead of the client.

Using different versions of our self

There are times when we are invited by our clients to share our personal opinions. It can be tricky knowing how best to respond so as to honour their request and acknowledge our positions of power and our knowledge, while recognizing the clients' expertise, abilities, knowledge, and resources (Freedman & Combs, 1996). Nuala was in her fifties and the main carer for her mother, Mary, who had dementia. Mary lived alone and chose not to have paid carers visit. She was known to frequently say, "The only way they will get me out of this flat is in a wooden box." Several professionals had advised Nuala that it would be best for her mother to be cared for in a home. Nuala had not found this advice useful, as she had understood it to mean she was not doing a very good job of caring for her mother.

> Nuala broke down in tears. She said, "I love my Mum but I can't go on like this, it's killing me. The constant phone calls during the night, the constant washing of bedclothes, and the daily battles of where she has misplaced things. Dave [husband] is at the end of his tether and is clear we should get Mum into a home before something terrible happens. I think he thinks if she doesn't go he might. What should I do? I know she has to go into a home but I just can't face it, I can't do it. Eleanor, please tell me what should I do?"

There are many ways we can respond to direct questions about our opinions. With Nuala, I (Eleanor) chose to talk from the different contexts or positions out of which I act. Therefore I replied, "As a daughter I can identify with your dilemma. I cannot imagine having to make that decision about my mum. Talking from the position of having been a granddaughter of someone with dementia, I would be likely to say, 'It is the best for everyone if she went to a care home', because I have seen what caring for someone with dementia can do to those family close by. Talking as a woman, I think there are ideas around that we are the 'caring ones' and should be the ones looking after the family. Yet, if I was to think from my position as a psychologist, I am tempted to ask you about what you would want me to say to you. Would you want me to tell you to 'hang in there', or do you want me to give you permission to move your mother to somewhere with twenty-four hour care?" Nuala listened intently to what I was saying and replied, "I see what you are saying. There is not a right or wrong answer here, is there? Everyone will have a different idea."

Nuala recognized that different people would have different views about her dilemma, but I was also suggesting that, as individuals, we would have different ideas dependent on the contexts we are acting out of. For example, I drew ideas from my professional context, my gender, and that of a daughter. Another way of thinking about this is that our identity is constructed of many different versions of our self (Pearce, 1989). Talking from the position of psychologist, I might offer a different perspective from what I might offer as a daughter or another woman. Explaining this to Nuala enabled us to go on to consider her different versions of self, what each might say she should or should not do about her current dilemma and towards helping her to decide about her mother's future. Furthermore, as the therapist, looking at what different aspects of my self might say about Nuala's dilemma enabled me to avoid replicating previously unhelpful interventions, such as giving advice that made Nuala feel a failure. In this way, I was able to co-ordinate with Nuala.

There are many other situations where older people have invited us to share our personal selves. Here are a few questions we have been asked by older people that you may find familiar. They require us to often make quick decisions as to whether or how to share our selves. "Where are you going on holiday?"; "Who are you going with?"; "Sorry to hear you were unwell, what was wrong?"; "Did you have far to come to see me today? Where do you live?"; "Are you married?" During my (Eleanor's) pregnancies I was asked many personal questions, such as "Can I touch the bump?"; "Do you know if it is a boy or girl?"; "Can you let me know when you have had it?"; "I love babies; can you send me a photograph?"

We each have different ideas about which questions feel appropriate to answer directly. We have found that, depending on our view of the relationship, we may feel all right sharing with one person, yet not with another. One way we have found useful to approach direct questions from our clients is to ask ourselves what is our therapeutic intent and the possible effect of our answering the question directly. For example, we have asked ourselves a number of questions, such as: "How come I am sharing this information?"; "What is my purpose in sharing this information?"; "What is my desired outcome or therapeutic hope?"; "In what ways do I think this might be useful to the client?"; "If I do / do not share this information what will be the meaning for the older person?" Once we have considered our possible responses, we can ask ourselves questions about the effect of our chosen response. For example, we might reflect on "What difference did my choice to share /

not share make to our conversation?", and "What opportunities did it create and what avenues did it close down?" "How might I do this differently next time?" We have found it amazing how quickly we can ask ourselves several of these questions before saying anything in response to the client's question. The answers to these sorts of questions have usually helpfully guided our decisions about what to say or not to say.

Reflections

We have found the use of our personal and professional selves in our work with older people essential to our practice. However, using our selves in this way is not without its challenges. In this chapter, we have shared some ideas of how and when we might make use of our selves. We have talked about how we attempt to move from self-awareness to becoming self-reflexive in our practice. Connected to self-reflexivity, we address how we can use both our pre-understandings and emotions as a resource and how we co-ordinate these relationally with our clients. We introduce the idea of practising as outsider witnesses to older people's stories as one way to encourage our sharing to be decentred, as well as using the practice of transparency. Finally, we show how we can make use of the many different versions of our selves to respond to clients' dilemmas from multiple perspectives.

References

Andersen, T. (1987). The reflecting team: dialogue and meta-dialogue in clinical work. *Family Process, 26*: 415–428.
Andersen, T. (1995). Reflecting processes; acts of informing and forming: You can borrow my eyes, but you must not take them away from me! In: S. Friedman (Ed.), *The Reflecting Team in Action. Collaborative Practice in Family Therapy.* (pp. 11–37). New York: Guilford.
Burnham, J. (1993). Systemic supervision: the evolution of reflexivity in the context of the supervisory relationship. *Human Systems: The Journal of Systemic Consultation and Management, 4* (Special Issue, 3 & 4): 349–381.

Burnham, J. (2005). Relational reflexivity: a tool for socially construct-
ing therapeutic relationships. In: C. Flaskas, B. Mason, & A. Perlesz
(Eds.), *The Space Between: Experience, Context, and Process in the
Therapeutic Relationship* (pp. 1–18). London: Karnac.

Carey, M., & Russell, S. (2003). Outsider-witness practices: some
answers to commonly asked questions. *International Journal of Narrative Therapy and Community Work, 1*: 3–16.

Cecchin, G. (1987). Hypothesising, circularity and neutrality revisited:
an invitation to curiosity. *Family Process, 26*: 404–413.

Cecchin, G., Lane, G., & Ray, W. A. (1994). *The Cybernetics of Prejudices
in the Practice of Psychotherapy*. London: Karnac.

Cronen, V. E., & Pearce, W. B. (1980). *Communication, Action and
Meaning*. New York: Praeger.

Cronen, V. E., & Pearce, W. B. (1985). Towards an explanation of how
the Milan method works: an invitation to a systemic epistemology
and the evolution of family. In: D. Campbell & R. Draper (Eds.),
Applications of Systemic Therapy: The Milan Approach (pp. 69–84).
London: Grune & Stratton.

Fredman, G. (2004). *Transforming Emotion: Conversations in Counselling
and Psychotherapy*. London: Whurr/Wiley.

Fredman, G. (2007). Preparing our selves for the therapeutic relationship. Revisiting "hypothesizing revisited". *Human Systems: The
Journal of Systemic Consultation & Management, 18*: 44–59.

Freedman, J., & Combs, G. (1996). *Narrative Therapy and the Social
Construction of Preferred Realities*: New York: Norton.

Griffith, J. L., & Elliott Griffith, M. (1994). *The Body Speaks. Therapeutic
Dialogues for Mind–Body Problems*. New York: Basic Books.

Jones, E., & Asen, E. (2000). *Systemic Couple Therapy and Depression*.
London: Karnac.

Pearce, W. B. (1989). *Communication and the Human Condition*.
Carbondale & Edwardsville, IL: Southern Illinois University Press.

Roberts, J. (2005). Transparency and self disclosure in family therapy:
dangers and possibilities. *Family Process, 44*: 45–63.

Rogers, C. (1980). *Way of Being*. Boston: Houghton Miffin.

White, M. (1992). Deconstruction and therapy. In: D. Epston &
M. White (Eds.), *Experience, Contradiction, Narrative and Imagination.
Selected papers of David Epston and Michael White 1989–1991* (pp. 109–
152). Adelaide: Dulwich Centre Publications.

White, M. (1997). *Narratives of Therapists Lives*. Adelaide: Dulwich
Centre Publications.

White, M. (2000). *Reflections on Narrative Practice: Essays and Interviews*. Adelaide: Dulwich Centre Publications.

White, M. (2002). Definitional ceremony and outsider-witness responses workshop. Notes. www.dulwichcentre.com.au (accessed 19 November).

CHAPTER FOUR

Creating contexts for talking and listening where older people feel comfortable and respected

Joshua Stott and Eleanor Martin

In this chapter, we explore creating contexts for talking and listening with older people where they can feel comfortable and respected by us. We will focus on initial meetings, outlining steps we take from our first contact with the older person and their significant others towards creating the sorts of therapeutic relationships where people feel heard and able to talk openly. We will follow the process of a session as it might happen. However, this chronology is somewhat artificial, since, in our experience, conversations usually involve weaving backwards and forwards between the processes we outline below.

Throughout the chapter, we will be introducing you to some of the people with whom we have worked. They have helped us to develop ways of "being with" older people that open space for conversations marked by mutual listening, appreciation, and respect. We have selected episodes of our practice that went well, and also examples that did not go well, since both have thrown light on important dilemmas and pointed us towards new possibilities for our practice.

Meeting and greeting

How we meet and greet people and the names and titles we use
to introduce ourselves and others set the context for how we go on,
as we learned from Josh's first meeting with Mary Charlesworth.

> I (Josh) had been sitting in the consulting room of a health centre
> preparing for a first meeting with an older client. Having just read the
> letter from her doctor who was "referring Mary Charlesworth . . . for
> psychological counselling", I got up to collect this client from the wait-
> ing area. On opening the door, I was taken aback to find an eighty-four-
> year-old woman apparently waiting to see me. I said, "Hello Mary?"
> and was met with a furrowed brow, which spoke to me of her imme-
> diate irritation. At the end of this first session, she told me she did not
> want further appointments and in her feedback form wrote, ". . .
> because my therapist called me the wrong name, I did not feel that he
> showed me respect. I like to be called Miss Charlesworth".

When I read Miss Charlesworth's comments I felt enormous
regret that my unintended clumsy beginning had left her feeling
disrespected by me. I was also disappointed that she had disengaged and did not access sessions that might have been useful for
her. One of the first things we consider in initial meetings with
clients is what they like to be called. In retrospect I reflected on how
come I had called this eighty-four-year old woman by her first
name, Mary, when many of our older clients have often told us that
they like to be called by their surnames, since they feel that this
"shows respect". I recognized that I had been taken by surprise to
find the client already waiting at my door when I had expected to
meet her in the waiting area. I also considered that I might have
been influenced by my team's practice of commonly referring to
older clients by their forename. My experience with Miss Charlesworth has left me careful in first meetings to ensure I ask clients,
"What name would you prefer me to call you?", mindful that I
cannot automatically assume that all older people would want to be
called by their surnames.

We go on in this chapter to discuss practices intended to create
therapeutic relationships where the older people with whom we
work do feel respected and comfortable. This reflexive process of recognizing our assumptions and where they come from, questioning

them and changing our actions accordingly, will be implicit through-out this chapter. In Chapter Three we offer a range of ways that prac-titioners can develop this sort of self and relational reflexivity. Here, we continue with Josh's encounter with Edith.

> Edith, a slim lady aged seventy-four, was dressed in a beige plaid skirt with a tucked in white blouse that appeared too big, as if filled with air where some of her weight used to be. As she leaned back in her chair, her vein-crossed lids falling over her eyes, I (Josh) thought to myself that she looked exhausted. She was talking about her "trouble with sleeping and eating". I asked what she meant by "trouble with sleeping and eating" as they could mean different things for different people. Her lids opened slightly, revealing blue eyes, as she told me that she thought it all went back to her "problems with partners". I asked her what she meant by "partners" as some people talk about partners in business and others about men or women with whom they are in a rela-tionship. She told me that she meant "relationships with men", and that she had always "gone for men who I knew were unavailable". I learnt that Edith's "real love" had been a married man. He had ended their relationship, moved country with his wife, and "now I have no one . . . I am dreadfully lonely . . . this has haunted my sleep and killed my appetite." At this point Edith stopped and said, "You know Josh, I could never talk about sexual relationships with my doctor; I just felt so dreadfully ashamed." I wondered aloud, "What is different here in our talking?", to which Edith replied, "I could not talk about that sort of thing with a doctor. I'm sure they would have judged me." I checked, "You thought your doctor might judge you if you talked about relation-ships?" Edith confirmed, "That's right. That means I have not been able to talk about a large part of my life with my GP."

One of the first things that clients get to know about us is our name and title. Edith was discussing the effect that the title of "doctor" had on her ability to talk. She appeared to have an under-standing that doctors were not people with whom one should discuss sexual relationships. Perhaps Edith's ideas about what she should and should not talk about with doctors were related to societal ideas about doctors as powerful professionals, who diag-nose disease rather than people with whom you share intimate personal aspects of your life. Or, perhaps, like many of the colleagues and clients we meet in our work, she had picked up the idea that older adults are asexual, or should not talk about sex. We wonder whether it was because of understandings like these that Edith did not share a large and important part of her life with her doctor. Understandings like Edith's that affect our actions, such as whether we talk about ourselves or not, are generated in the con- texts we live in and act out of (Cronen & Pearce, 1982). These contexts may include our society, our early history, our family life, and our peer group. We have found that these contexts determine what people do and do not share with us, as practitioners working with them. Edith and Miss Charlesworth show us how the context that we create together enables and inhibits different sorts of con- versations. It is the context that gives meaning to the communica- tion within those conversations (*ibid.*). For this reason, we pay close attention to the contexts we create with older people in our practice.

Contracting to create contexts of respect and comfort

Explaining how we work

June, aged seventy, told me (Eleanor) about her previous experience of family therapy. She recounted, "I went into this room with my husband and there were four people looking at us. It was like an interview, and then one of them started asking questions. After a while, the other three just started talking about me, as if I wasn't there. It was horrible, persecutory. I certainly won't be going back there."

We recognize the type of practice that June is describing as a reflecting team (Andersen, 1987) where a practitioner talks with clients while a team listens; the team then shares their reflections on what they have heard in front of the client. We often work in this way, and, like us, many of our clients say they find it helpful. However, June obviously did not. When I asked June how the format of the session was explained to her, June said she did not remember any clear explanation. June may have experienced the session as "horrible" and "persecutory" because she did not under- stand what was going to happen in the session or the practitioner's rationale for working like this with a team. This is not to say that it had not been explained, but rather a shared understanding had not been created.

We both work in contexts where there are legal and service policies and procedures that we are professionally obligated to follow. For example, we are required to discuss confidentiality with all our clients and there are clear guidelines for how we manage risk. We also have methods and techniques that are integral to the approach we take in our work with older people. For example, we consider and ask questions about relationships and the contexts that inform people's understandings. Therefore, we adopt certain practices because we have been taught to work in that way, or because we follow the procedures of the services in which we work. To create a meaningful context for working with a client, we endeavour to explain transparently those aspects of our work that are prescribed by the policies and procedures of our services and those that are an integral part of our therapeutic method. In a first meeting we usually begin by saying something like, "Can l begin by explaining how we will work here together so you can let me know if this fits for you and if it is OK to go on? Do let me know if you have any questions or what you want us to make clear . . ." In the example above, the practitioners could have explained to June what the session would involve, the roles and purpose of the team members in the room, and how long the meeting would take. They might also have checked with June and her husband whether they had explained themselves clearly and invited the couple to ask further questions for clarification if needed. We find that explaining and negotiating how we work in this way can make the difference between our engaging or disengaging the older people with whom we meet.

Each of us will find the way to explain how we work that fits best for us. When a team joins us, we usually explain something like, "My team members are here to help me think about your situation. We find that having more than one person in the room gives us more people to pay attention to you as we have more ears to listen and more heads to think about your situation. We find this helps us come up with lots of different ideas together for you. At some point the team will share their ideas with you and me here in the room. Is that all right? Do you have any questions about this?"

Starting to address power

Miss Charlesworth and June both had uncomfortable experiences with aspects of their sessions, but were unable to express their concerns directly to the practitioners working with them at that time. This illustrates how our positions as public service practitioners give us a lot of power in relation to our older clients and how it can be very easy for us to forget this. For example, as psychologists, we often have the power to end therapy and to make decisions regarding a person's care. If you are a doctor, you may have the power to diagnose or prescribe medication, or if you are a social worker, you may have the power to allocate or withdraw resources. Such power imbalances between practitioner and client may make it more difficult for the older person to feel able to express their concerns or dissatisfaction to us. Clarifying how we work, the contexts in which we work, and addressing the power differential, goes some way to addressing this imbalance. We have found that being clear about our respective duties, responsibilities, obligations, and rights makes it possible for clients to make informed choices about what they say and do. Therefore, we transparently set out the procedures we are obligated to follow and about which we have no choice. For example, the maximum number of sessions in our service is not negotiable, since the purchasers of our service set these. Also, we are obligated by our professional ethical guidelines and our services to disclose any concerns we have about risk. If June's therapists were obligated to work with a team, they could have given the couple the option to say that they did not want a team and the chance to discuss alternative options for therapy.

Implicit in the process of contracting how we will work is our commitment to creating a context of respect and comfort for the people participating in meetings with us. To redress the power imbalance we often address "respect" and "comfort" directly. For example, we might say something like, "We find that this sort of talking works best when people we meet with feel comfortable talking with us and when they feel that we are respecting them. What would you like us to agree so you can feel comfortable here and respected by me?" When Josh asked Edith this question she was able to tell him a little of what she wanted; that she wanted to be listened to, that she did not want to be judged, and that she would want to think about how their sessions would end well before they stopped meeting. Not everyone we have met is like Edith and can answer this question so readily. Even if it is difficult to answer, however, we have found it worth asking, since it sets the context that we wish to be respectful and make talking comfortable, and opens space for us to have a conversation about this. We wonder what difference this would have made to Miss Charlesworth's engagement with Josh if he had begun their session in this way.

Clarifying who shares what with whom

> Robert, seventy-three, and Harriet, sixty-five, had met with me (Josh) for help with the "little demon" of conflict that had "flared up" since Harriet had developed physical health problems. In our second session, Harriet noted that I was taking notes, and asked where they were kept. When she heard they were being stored in a locked filing cabinet, she asked who had the key. When she discovered that the filing cabinets were accessible to the entire multi-disciplinary team, she was "shocked and upset" to hear that "our personal information is being given to all those people". My stomach tightened and I thought, "Oh no, I obviously haven't made this clear!"

Harriet's expression of "shock" and "upset" led me to address whether I had been clear enough about confidentiality. At the beginning of our work together I had told Robert and Harriet, "What we talk about in these sessions will be confidential," explaining, "This means that what we talk about here is kept between us. We won't share information, unless we are concerned about your safety or that of others, in which case we may need to share information even if you don't want us to." Harriet and Robert had said they thought that "fair enough". I went on to say that I would also be taking notes that were kept in a locked cabinet, and that these were "also confidential, in the same way as our conversations".

Although I thought I had explained what I meant by confidentiality to Robert and Harriet, in retrospect I realized that I had not fully clarified what would be shared with whom, and in what circumstances. When I checked what they had understood by "confidentiality", I learnt that they believed it to mean, "Everything we say here is just between us three unless we are not safe." This prompted me to explain, "I work as part of a team of different professionals. All of us could contribute to your progress. For this reason I may talk with them about how you are doing to get their perspectives." I went on to clarify with the couple, "My team like

to know when you are doing well as well as when there are difficulties. How does this sound to you? . . . What would you like to be
shared about you? . . . If there are things you specifically do not
want me to share, can you let me know . . . how will you let me
know?"

Harriet was particularly keen that the team should know "when
we are doing well". Robert's request to "keep the detail of our troubles private" opened space for me to clarify again, "If I am concerned that either of you or someone else we talk about may be
harmed, I will need to discuss this with others. In that case, I will
let you know what I am going to say and who I talk to." As Robert
and Harriet were particularly concerned about the content of the
notes in the filing cabinet, I asked them, "What aspects of this meeting do you want us to record so we can remember it next time?" I
also asked them to comment on and contribute to the letters that I
was writing to referrers or other professionals working with them
(Fox, 2003). We often involve older people in co-writing records and
letters in this way.

Further on in our work, Robert told me that he had "slapped"
Harriet in the course of an argument and added, sighing, "I suppose you will have to tell someone about this . . . I suppose I need
help with this side of myself?" Clarifying the context for confidentiality at the start of our work gave Robert and Harriet an idea of
how I might view the "slapping" and how we might go on. Thus,
how we talk about confidentiality sets the context for the meaning
of subsequent disclosures and our consequent actions. In Chapter
Eight, Glenda Fredman, Sarah Johnson, and Goran Petronic address
confidentiality in the context of risk of self-harm.

Talking about talking

Before Miss Charlesworth sat down, she said, "I do not know why
I am here or who sent me. It's rather a mystery to me really."

Rarely do the older people we see refer themselves. Sometimes,
like Miss Charlesworth, they are not clear why they have been
referred or for what. Therefore, we do not assume that people meeting with us want or expect to talk about the referred problem or
that they want to talk with us at all. Hence, in first meetings, we
begin by asking ourselves whether the clients feel this is a suitable

time or place for talking. We also consider whether we are the person with whom the clients prefer to talk, or whether they have other members of their family, cultural, or religious community, or people of the same or different age, gender, race, or sexuality they might prefer or want to include. Furthermore, we take into account whether we have sufficiently created the sort of relationship to enable the kind of conversation they want in the way they want to have it. Miss Charlesworth questioned who had referred her and why. Usually, it is we who set the context for our conversation by "talking about talking" (Fredman, 1997) at the start of first meetings with questions like: 'Whose idea was it that we meet and talk together? What are your views on our talking here together? Is there anyone else you would prefer to talk with/like to include? Are there some things you do not want to talk about here/with me? How will I know if we are starting to talk in ways you do/do not want?' Having learnt earlier that Edith had never talked with her doctor about sexual relationships, I (Josh) wanted to be careful to create a context for talking about relationships that would be comfortable for her.

> Josh: Is this the first time you have talked about this?
>
> Edith: No, I talked to my neighbour about it and she got very competitive. She started telling me all about her woes and her own relationship failures.
>
> Josh: What effect did her response have on you?
>
> Edith: It made me clam up, not say any more, and feel very resentful of her.
>
> Josh: Is our talking about relationships similar or different to conversations with your neighbour?
>
> Edith: It is a very different thing.
>
> Josh: How is it different?
>
> Edith: Talking here makes me feel light in myself, and understood.

Edith and I were "talking about talking". I explored what she had talked about with whom; what she wanted others to know or not; when it might be good or not to talk; and the possible effects of her talking about her partners on other people and relationships in her life (Fredman, 1997). From this, I learnt that Edith could not talk with doctors about relationships for fear of being judged. As I am a doctor (albeit of clinical psychology), I was careful not to assume that Edith wanted to talk with me. I was also curious as to whether Edith wanted to talk about relationships at all, especially having heard her negative experience of talking about her relationship with her neighbour. So I asked, "Is our talking about relationships similar or different from conversations with your neighbour?", and learnt that Edith prefers to talk with me as "talking here makes me feel light in myself, and understood."

Checking with clients is an essential part of our talks as it helps us to get feedback about how useful and comfortable they are finding our conversations. Therefore, I was careful to check with Edith when I realized that we were moving away from talking about Edith's sleeping and eating, which she presented as issues she wanted to address in our first meeting, and we had started to talk about what she called her "deep and real fears".

> Josh: We started talking about sleeping and eating and now we are talking about what you call "deep and real fears". Are these the same things or different?
>
> Edith: Different.
>
> Josh: Which one would you like to talk about?
>
> Edith: Deep and real fears.

Aware of Edith's concerns about being "judged" by her doctors, I also checked to ensure that she was not feeling judged by me.

> Josh: I am aware that judgement entered your conversations with your doctor, and stopped you talking about these fears. Would it be OK to think about this?
>
> Edith: Yes.
>
> Josh: I just wondered . . . what could I do to stop "judgement" entering our conversations?
>
> Edith: You can talk like you have been. What I like is that you seem to want to know what this is like for me . . . not put pressure on me to be a certain way.

Josh: If our conversations stopped being like that, if it did feel like pressure, how could you let me know?

Edith: I don't think I would be able to tell you. You would have to notice.

Josh: What would I notice?

Edith: I think you would notice that I fell back in my chair and that I would start to . . . try and not answer you directly . . .

By "talking about talking", I learnt more from Edith. She taught me to notice if "judgement" was entering our conversation and how to keep clear of "pressure". In this way, we were able to create a comfortable and safe context for talking.

At the start of our work together, I had invited Edith to include other significant people in our meetings. For example, in my first appointment letter, I wrote, "You are welcome to invite anyone else whom you think might be helpful". When Edith came alone to her first meeting, I invited her to bring in the perspectives and voices of significant people in her network by asking, "Who knows you are meeting with me today?"; "Who will be interested in what comes out of our meeting?"; "What view might they take on your concerns?"; "Would you like them to join us?" These sorts of "who" questions can open space for people attending sessions on their own to include other people in later sessions. Initially, Edith had not wanted to bring anyone else to our meeting. After speaking about her "good friend", Madeline, at length during the first session, however, she asked if she could bring her next time, as she felt Madeline "understands me better than I do sometimes". Asking questions about significant people's views on an older person's situation can facilitate their seeing friends, relatives, or carers as potential resources to the work. Introducing people into the room in this way sets the context for relationships rather than individuals being the focus of the work (Hedges, 2005).

Madeline, whom Edith had described as "a straight talker", raised Edith's fear of dying right at the start of the session. She said, "I think that the problem is that Edith is frightened about dying, I think what we need to talk about is death." Madeline's idea that death must be talked about may have reflected a common belief in her culture that people need to talk about death, in order to resolve their fear of death. Thinking that this was just one view, and concerned that Edith may not want to talk about death, my first intention in the conversation was to find out if Edith shared this view, or wanted to talk about death at all. Therefore, Edith, Madeline, and I went on to "talk about talking" about death.

I asked Edith, "Madeline has an idea that it would be useful to talk about death. Do you have a similar view or a different view?" Edith said that she felt she had a similar view but was not sure. At this point she looked uncomfortable, falling back into her chair as she had told me she would when pressure entered our discussion. I became concerned about whether she was being compliant with Madeline's suggestion and did not really want to talk about death. Therefore I wondered aloud, "Is pressure around now? You mentioned that you would fall back into your chair if pressure entered our discussion and I noticed you doing that just now." Edith said that she did not feel pressure to talk about death; in fact she did "want to . . . I am just not sure how to go about it."

I was concerned that to step straight in and ask lots of questions about her fears of dying could feel unsafe, risky, or too frightening for Edith. Therefore, I wanted to further explore how Edith might want to talk about death. We have found "talking about talking" particularly useful in conversations about death, or sexual relationships with older people, which can be taboo topics to discuss in British society. "Talking about talking" allows us to explore the effects such a conversation might have on someone before actually talking about the issue itself. Therefore, I started to explore the effect of talking about death on Edith by asking, "What do you think talking about death might be like for you?" Edith responded that she would be "very scared". I went on to find out whether the effects that Edith had discussed were wanted or unwanted.

Josh: You'd be scared? Would that be a positive thing or a negative thing?

Edith: Well, what a strange question. I think it would be positive and negative—because I don't like feeling scared, but I do want to talk about it.

Josh: So I just want to check—you may want to talk about death, but it might frighten you?

Edith: Yes that's it. I do want to talk about it but I'm not sure . . . how will I be . . . I mean I might just get so scared I would not be able to cope.

Concerned to avoid creating a situation where Edith felt "not able to cope", I appealed to Madeline's "expert knowledge" of Edith.

Josh: Madeline, Edith said she does want to talk about death. She is also worried that she will be so scared she might not be able to cope. You have known her for a long time. How would you know if she were that scared?

Madeline: Well, Edith's not a great complainer. I think she would sit there, but she would . . . you know, she would sit there and not say anything.

Josh: Edith, is Madeline describing what you call "clam up"? Is that how you would describe what you do when you are too scared?

Edith: Yes . . . she is quite right.

Hoping to learn more from Edith and Madeline, I went on to explore what we might do should Edith start to be scared and to clam up.

Josh: If it gets like that, what would you like us to do about it?

Edith: Well, I'm not sure really.

Josh: Can I ask Madeline? To see if she has any ideas?

Edith: Yes . . . of course.

Josh: When Edith has been really scared in the past, what have you noticed has been helpful?

Madeline: Well, I have noticed that if you ask her how she is feeling, she will tell you and I have noticed that even just asking helps. Then we have done deep breaths before, haven't we Edie?

When older people have difficulty understanding

Some of our clients have difficulties taking part in conversations because of cognitive impairment. For example, they may find it hard to express themselves, understand what we are talking about, or follow conversation. Sometimes, we are unsure how well we are making ourselves understood. "Talking about talking" with the older person and their carers can help us co-ordinate in conversation, as Eleanor shows in her talks with Paul, sixty-eight, and his wife, Dora. Paul had a diagnosis of dementia. This conversation takes place at their first meeting. After introductions Eleanor, Paul, and Dora started to discuss how dementia might affect their talking together.

Eleanor: How can we make this conversation useful and comfortable for you both?

Dora: Well one thing we need to do is to help Paul understand.

Paul: Eh?

Eleanor: Sometimes when I have discussions with people with dementia, they find it hard to understand me. So can we talk about understanding? Would that be OK?

Paul: What?

Eleanor: Sometimes people with dementia find it hard to understand people. Is that so for you?

Paul: Might be.

Eleanor: If you don't understand me what will you do?

Paul: Eh?

Eleanor: Well, sometimes when people don't understand they leave the room. Other times they get angry and shout, other times they just don't speak. What would you do?

Paul: I will just not talk.

Eleanor: What should I do if this happens?

Paul: Eh?

Eleanor: Well, sometimes people would like me to repeat my questions, but shorter. Sometimes they want me to summarize what has happened.

Paul: Don't know.

Eleanor: Would it be OK to ask your wife how she has helped you to understand her?

Paul: OK.

Eleanor: Dora, I wondered what has helped you to make yourself understood with Paul?

Dora: First of all, he's a bit deaf, so you need to talk louder. You also need to use short sentences. I also think he can understand better when I say things because he knows me so well.

Eleanor: That sounds really good. If I'm not doing very well, can I ask you how you would ask that question?

Dora: OK.

This conversation illustrates how we might approach "talking about talking" with our older clients affected by cognitive impairments. I (Eleanor) began with the sorts of questions we typically would ask. These questions are open ended, such as, "If you don't understand me what will you do?" Paul's feedback suggested that it was not easy for him to respond to this sort of question. I felt uncomfortable with my style of questioning as I did not seem to be co-ordinating well with Paul, so I tried asking the question again in a different way, giving actual examples of what some people do if they do not understand. Paul found this easier to answer. White (2006) draws on Vygotsky's (1978) "scaffolding" to describe this process of responding to a person's feedback and adjusting the type of talk accordingly. White stressed that it is the responsibility of the practitioner to pay attention to clients' verbal and non-verbal feedback to gauge whether or not they are able to understand and communicate. He noted that practitioners need to adjust what they say and do so that clients can respond and make sense of the questions practitioners ask.

I (Eleanor) was in a dilemma as to whether or not to give examples in my own words, aware that Paul might feel an obligation to take on my suggestions or agree with me because of my position of power as a therapist. This could then place me in an expert, rather than curious, position (which we will discuss later) and close down avenues for further discussion and exploration. I did not want this to happen with Paul, yet I knew from feedback that Paul found it difficult to answer open-ended questions, which would normally allow a person to express their own view. I tried to resolve this dilemma by offering an open ended question first, for example,

"What would you do if you did not understand?" and then, if Paul struggled to answer this, I re-asked it offering several options ("leaving the room . . . not speaking . . . getting angry"). Giving options still gave Paul some choice. I also phrased these options in terms of actions rather than thoughts or beliefs.

The choice to ask what Paul might do is based on my experience that older people with cognitive impairment often find it easier to answer "doing" questions rather than the more abstract "thinking" or "belief" questions. I also consulted Dora about what she does to maximize understanding between her and Paul, approaching Dora as an expert on Paul and his communication abilities. These practices of scaffolding, inviting, and following feedback, and adjusting responses accordingly, as well as respecting a family's expertise on a client's abilities, are all practices we have found helpful in co-contracting with people with cognitive impairments. In Chapter Two, Glenda Fredman and Penny Rapaport address how we might include people who have hearing impairments in a conversation.

When people have different views on whether or how to talk

As the conversation with Dora and Paul continued, it emerged that Dora wanted to talk about the effects dementia was having on their lives and she felt it was important that Paul was there for this conversation. Paul, however, did not want to participate in the conversation. For me this raised the dilemma of how to go on with the couple when there were different views about whether or how the talk should happen.

In this example, Paul chose to leave the room. I believed that to insist that Paul stay would have been using the power I had as a practitioner in a way that was not respectful of his right to make a choice. This felt particularly salient in this setting because Paul, as an older man with dementia, was likely to have had many experiences where his choices were being taken away from him and I did not want to replicate this. Therefore, before he left the room, I clarified, "Paul, is it OK for Dora and me to continue talking about this?" I let Paul know he was welcome back in the room whenever he wanted to return and checked with him "How would you let me know if you want to come back?"

I also clarified whether Dora felt that the conversation could continue without Paul. Although Paul was satisfied for Dora and me to talk about dementia without him, Dora was unsure "if we can get anywhere without him here". Therefore, I asked, "How can we keep Paul involved in the conversation, while respecting his right not to be in the room?" We decided that I would keep Paul in mind by asking questions such as "If Paul were here what would he feel about that?" In addition, Dora and I discussed how Dora could talk to Paul later about our conversation. I asked questions such as: "What would you want to tell Paul about? What would Paul want to know? Who else would you both want to let know about the dementia? How will you decide this between yourselves?" Asking these sorts of questions had the effect of bringing the system into the room so Dora and I did not seem alone in our conversation (Hedges, 2005). Although I was working with only one person in the room at this point, I was still working with the system. Throughout my conversation with Dora and Paul and with Dora alone, I was addressing ways of talking about the effects of dementia. I was exploring what aspects of the news of dementia and its effects on Dora and Paul would be shared, with whom, and how. My intent in doing this was to co-create a respectful and comfortable "context for knowing and telling" about dementia with Dora and Paul (Dixon & Curtis, 2006; Fredman, 1997, p. 23).

Co-creating a focus for the work

There have been times when, having set the context for our work with older people and gleaned snippets of their stories, we have found ourselves thinking "I know what they need" or "I know what this is all about". Taking up this sort of "expert position" too quickly has tended to lead us into difficulties as I (Josh) found when I was a newly qualified clinical psychologist.

> I was sitting on a large orange sofa with the cushion bunched up around me because the springs had gone. On the wall to my right was a set of six shelves, each one lined with books and magazines in a higgledy-piggledy mess of colour. Cutting a head-shaped hole in this was a woman with a shock of white hair and bright blue eyes. Her name was Agnes. She was sitting in a white chair talking about her "collywobbles". They were strange things these collywobbles, "indescribable",

she said. A feeling "like a cold wave" would come over her and "things would start moving in [her] stomach". As we talked, I suggested that some of these collywobbles might be similar to what I called "anxiety", and could be an important focus for the session. I went on to explain to Agnes about how vicious circles of thoughts, feelings, and behaviour could form in response to threatening situations (Clark, 1986). Agnes seemed to like this idea. She nodded and smiled as I continued to expound my theory to her, and from this I guessed that she seemed to think it fitted for her. I went on to discuss how avoidance of feared situations could be contributing to the problem when she interrupted me. "You know Josh," she said, "It's not really that I'm frightened to go out. It is just there is nothing to go out for. All the people I love have moved away, and those that I do see, it's just not like before. I see all of these people walking around doing their business. I even know some of them. My daughter comes round a lot, but I just feel so different . . . alone . . . my whole community is disintegrated . . ."

I had first approached Agnes with my "expert clinical psychologist" ears. That is, I started to listen out for facts about her life that would confirm a model of what her problems were. In so doing, I was clear what should be the focus for the session and so was not checking this with Agnes. There are many reasons why my ears might be tuned to listen for "facts" in this way. I come from an educational system where answers are right or wrong. In my professional training I have been taught to listen for certain types of signs and symptoms and try to understand the underlying causes of a person's difficulties. In Agnes' situation, I started wondering how thoughts, feelings, and emotions might interlink in vicious circles and stopped listening to what Agnes was telling me. My understanding was more connected to my own ideas of what should be the focus than to what Agnes was saying. I connected "the collywobbles" to what I already knew from my cognitive behavioural theoretical framework as "anxiety". This "expertise" led me down the path of "talking to" and "educating" Agnes about anxiety. Thus, I did not connect with Agnes's understanding of the problem or check what focus she wanted. If Agnes had not let me know that my ideas did not fit for her, I might have imposed on her my own agenda, "anxiety", for the session.

We try to create the focus for our conversation jointly with clients rather than assume we know what needs to be talked about as I had started to do with Agnes. One client who I (Josh) felt this went better with was Mr Atayi, a seventy-six-year-old man, who described himself as black Ghanaian. He had come to see me due to the effects on his mental health of an ongoing dispute that he had with the justice system, which he said was "incredibly unfair". His GP had referred him because she thought he was "depressed as a result of these ongoing battles". Mr Atayi and I spent some time creating a context for our session together. We explored whose idea it was for him to see a psychologist, who else knew and what they thought about him coming for help. I heard how Mr Atayi had spoken only to his doctor about the referral and had not spoken to friends or family.

I then went on to create a focus with Mr Atayi by saying, "Imagine that it is now the end of our meeting and you are leaving here. You look back on our meeting and say to yourself, 'That was worthwhile, that was a good meeting'. What have we made sure we talked about here?" Mr Atayi responded, "We would have talked about my not being born in this country and whether my foreign looks and foreign land have made people prejudiced against me."

I could have gone on to ask further related questions, such as, "It is the end of our meeting . . ..what have we made clearer?" or "What have we worked out together?" An important component of these questions is that they require the person to project themselves to the end of the session (the future) and to look back on what the conversation would have involved. For this reason, we call them "future-oriented" questions (Penn, 1985). In order to further the sense of being projected forward into the future, these questions are worded in the present tense with the intention of quickly moving the client into a future where the "problem" is not around (Lang & McAdam, 1997). Thus, my initial question to Mr Atayi invited him to engage from the start in talking about his hopes and desires for the session and for his life. Mr Atayi did not say that he wanted to focus on "depression", as I initially anticipated, based on his GP's letter. Indeed, I did not hear the word depression mentioned; only that he wanted to talk about prejudice.

Listening for meaning

Although I had spoken with other people about their experiences of prejudice before, I was careful not to assume I understood what

Mr Atayi meant by "prejudice" in the same way I had too quickly assumed the meaning of Agnes's "collywobbles". Therefore, I went on to explore Mr Atayi's meanings of prejudice.

> Josh: So, for this meeting to be worthwhile, we would be talking about you not being born in this country . . . your different looks and the prejudice against you?
>
> Mr Atayi: Exactly.
>
> Josh: I have spoken with people about prejudice before, but I think everyone's experience is different. Would you help me understand what you are meaning by prejudice against you?
>
> Mr Atayi: I do not follow.
>
> Josh: Can you help me to understand how you are using this word prejudice?
>
> Mr Atayi: (Pause) Can I tell you a story to show you?
>
> Josh: Of course—please do.
>
> Mr Atayi: When I was young, Dr Stott, I was standing in a bank, when a masked man came in behind me. I saw his mask reflected on the glass in front of me. The man had a long object in one hand that I saw to be a knife. He went straight to the teller and ordered her to give him some money. I was young then, big, and I saw my chance. I grabbed him round the arms and shook, he dropped the knife and the police came. I was proud, and it was in the papers . . . that a black man—we were rare then—had stopped a robbery. I risked my life for the law in this country and all they give me is prejudice and unfair treatment.

In my conversation with Mr Atayi, I could have assumed that I understood what "prejudice" meant, as I had spoken with other people about their experiences of "prejudice" before. However, I was careful not to assume I understood exactly what Mr Atayi meant by this. Instead, I asked him, "Can you help me to understand how you are using this word prejudice?" This invited him to tell his moving story that tapped directly into his experiences of prejudice. In this way, my listening for his meanings, not for facts (Freedman & Combs, 1996), enabled Mr Atayi and me to begin creating a shared understanding of "prejudice". Conversely, when I responded to Agnes, I was listening for "facts" that fitted with a model that I had already assumed would explain her difficulties. I started to build up explanations about these "facts" that I believed to be true and started to become an expert on Agnes's life, her difficulties, and what I thought needed to happen to improve things. In so doing, I was losing sight of Agnes's hopes and meanings unique to her. One way I began *listening for meaning* with Mr Atayi was to tune into the key words or phrases that he was using. By attending to these key words I was able to join his language.

Tuning into key words

Mr Atayi talked about people being "prejudiced" against him. The word "prejudice" struck me as a key word in his talk. Key words, which carry important meanings for the person, are often associated with non-verbal expressions, such as pauses, change of voice tone or pitch, intonation, and change in body postures. I noticed Mr Atayi sigh and his voice seemed to catch as he uttered, "Prejudiced against me". Key words, such as Mr Atayi's "prejudice", tend to be those that hold significant meanings for the person. Such words will mean different things to different people. We find that we can only begin to understand the meaning of the word when we know how to use the word in the particular context of the person with whom we are talking (Wittgenstein, 1953). With Mr Atayi, this involved my understanding the word "prejudice" in the context of his having risked his life "for the law in this country" and receiving only "prejudice and unfair treatment".

> Josh: That is a remarkable story of bravery. I am getting some sense, but I wonder if you can help me further understand the unfair treatment and prejudice you have experienced subsequently?
>
> Mr Atayi: Despite my actions no one trusts me, no one thinks I am honourable. People question what I say, what I do, as if I am always after whatever I can get my hands on.
>
> Josh: So people have been prejudiced towards you through lack of trust and questioning your integrity, have I understood you?
>
> Mr Atayi: Yes, that is right—my integrity has constantly been brought into question.

Tuning into Mr Atayi's key words helped me join and use his language rather than impose my own. Using his language in this way ensured we stayed with the focus he identified as important for him in this conversation.

Summarizing, checking, and following feedback

To ensure that I was both understanding Mr Atayi and focusing on what was important for him, I summarized and checked with him throughout, relying on his verbal and non-verbal feedback to tell me whether I was on the right lines. I summarized tentatively to offer him the possibility of correcting or altering what I had said, ensuring that we were co-creating rather than my imposing meanings. If I introduced my own words, for example, "questioning your integrity", I tried to do this tentatively so as not to assume this phrase was fitting for Mr Atayi. Therefore I checked the fit of my words, asking, "Have I understood you?" and took Mr Atayi's adopting and using my word, "Yes, that is right my 'integrity' has constantly been brought into question", to suggest that we were co-ordinating our meanings. On reflection, I could have further checked with, "'Integrity' was my word; does that capture your experience or would another word fit better?"

Older people have told us that when they hear the words they have used fed back or summarized to them, they feel heard and understood. Hearing their own words coming from us also makes them reassess and sometimes change what they originally said. In this way, our summarizing does more than checking if we have understood; it also places the person in a position where they can step back and take a look at what they have said as it is repeated back to them. In this way, they are taking an observer perspective to themselves and are able to reflect on and evaluate their own perhaps previously taken for granted talk.

Having created shared meaning of "prejudice" together, Mr Atayi and I went on to develop the focus of our conversation in terms of his hopes and desires.

> Josh: So if we were to talk some more about your experiences of prejudice such as people not trusting you or your integrity being questioned, what could that make possible for you?
>
> Mr Atayi: I am not sure what you mean.
>
> Josh: If we were to discuss prejudice, what difference might that make to what you can or cannot do?

Mr Atayi: Well I think it would help me to understand what is behind people's behaviour towards me.

Josh: If you felt more able to understand what was behind people's behaviour, what difference would that make to you? What would you be able to do?

Mr Atayi: I think if I understood I might be less angry and if I was less angry I would get my point across better and everything would be easier.

Inviting Mr Atayi to connect his focus, "understanding prejudice against him", to future action, what he might be able to "do", opened space for him to describe his preferred future in terms of being "less angry" and "getting my point across better". This became the focus of our work over the next few months. Having articulated his desired developments in terms of actions, what he might do, also enabled Mr Atayi to notice more easily when he performed those actions. Hence, we were able to identify what made it possible for Mr Atayi to "be less angry" and to "get his point across", and, consequently, for him to do more of this. Older people have often told us that taking time to work out what they want to be different has contributed considerably towards their finding ways to go on. Mr Atayi's identifying his hopes for "understanding", his desire for "less anger", and his wish to "get my point across better" opened space for new possibilities such as "everything being easier".

In retrospect, I wonder whether the conversation may have evolved quite differently with Agnes, if I had used more of these practices in our talks. For example, if I had asked Agnes, "Let's say this session has been useful for you . . . what are you now able to do?", perhaps I might have learnt earlier that she had "nothing to go out for", that life was "just not like before" and heard about her sense of being "alone" since her community had "disintegrated". I may have tuned into Agnes's words, such as "collywobbles", and explored her unique meanings rather than assuming "collywobbles" to be the same as "anxiety". I may have summarized what I heard, checked and followed her feedback to ensure our joint understanding.

Learned not knowing

Talking with Agnes, I quickly slipped into an "expert position" on her life (Anderson & Goolishian, 1988). Thinking I knew all about her problems, I started educating Agnes about her experiences as if I had the authoritative knowledge. Assuming that I knew what she was talking about, I initially missed her meanings. With Mr Atayi, on the other hand, I was careful to adopt a "not knowing" stance (Anderson & Goolishian, 1988). Actively assuming I did not know more than he did about his life or his problems, I was genuinely curious to find out and understand more. Adopting this "not knowing" stance did not involve discarding all my "expertise". Rather, I recognized Mr Atayi's expertise in relation to his own life, explored his unique meanings with curiosity, and closely followed the feedback he was giving me, thus using my expertise to facilitate our conversation. By taking a "learned not knowing" approach to our conversation (Lang & McAdam, 1995) in this way, I endeavoured to see Mr Atayi as the expert on his life. This made me curious about his story.

When we approach our work from the perspective that our clients know their lives better than we do, we become curious and ask questions to facilitate our understanding. Throughout this chapter we have tried to adopt a stance of "curiosity" to develop conversations, holding the view that there is not one explanation for our clients' situations, but, rather, that there are a multiplicity of possible explanations and understandings (Cecchin, 1987). Adopting a stance of curiosity reminds us that we cannot assume we know what it is like for the older people we talk with; rather, we need to explore understandings and meanings together. When I thought I knew the "true meaning" of Agnes's "collywobbles", we began talking about different things: I about her "anxiety" and her about her being "alone". I was fortunate that Agnes pointed out to me that I had got the wrong end of the stick about her collywobbles, "You know Josh, it's not really that I'm frightened to go out . . ." This offered me the opportunity to explore Agnes's meanings of "collywobbles", which opened space for her to identify her wish to reconnect with her community.

Reflections

How we begin our conversations with older people can make the difference between our engaging with them or disconnecting from them. It is not always easy to "get it right", and many of the older people we have talked with have been generously forgiving of our blunders. However, we have found that our efforts to show respect through not making assumptions about whether people want to talk with us, what they want to talk about, and how we do that talking go some way to creating a context for useful and meaningful conversations.

References

Andersen, T. (1987). The reflecting team: dialogue and meta-dialogue in clinical work. *Family Process, 26*: 415–428.

Anderson, H., & Goolishian, H. (1988). Human systems as linguistic systems: preliminary and evolving ideas about the implications for clinical theory. *Family Process, 27*: 371–392.

Cecchin, G. (1987). Hypothesising, circularity and neutrality revisited: an invitation to curiosity. *Family Process, 26*: 404–413.

Clark, D. M. (1986). A cognitive approach to panic. *Behaviour Research and Therapy, 24*: 461–470.

Cronen, V. E., & Pearce, W. B. (1982). The coordinated management of meaning: a theory of communication. In: F. E. X. Dance (Ed.), *Human Communication Theory* (pp. 61–89). New York: Harper & Row.

Dixon, M., & Curtis, L. (2006). Contexts of knowing and telling. Reflections on dementia and the concepts of insight and awareness from a social constructionist perspective. *PSIGE Newsletter, 95*: 7–22.

Fox, H. (2003). Using therapeutic documents: a review. *The International Journal of Narrative Therapy and Community Work, 4*: 26–36.

Fredman, G. (1997). *Death Talk: Conversations with Children and Families*. London: Karnac.

Freedman, J., & Combs, G. (1996). *Narrative Therapy and the Social Construction of Preferred Realities*: New York: Norton.

Hedges, F. (2005). *An Introduction to Systemic Therapy with Individuals: A Social Constructionist Approach*. New York: Palgrave Macmillan.

Lang, P., & McAdam, E. (1995). Stories, giving accounts and systemic descriptions. Perspectives and positions in conversations. Feeding and fanning the winds of creative imagination. *Human Systems: the Journal of Systemic Consultation & Management, 6*: 71–103.

Lang, P., & McAdam, E. (1997). Narrative-ating: future dreams in present living: jottings on an honouring theme. *Human Systems: The Journal of Systemic Consultation & Management, 8*(1): 3–13.

Penn, P. (1985). Feed-forward: future questions, future maps. *Family Process, 24*: 299–310.

Vygotsky, L. S. (1978). *Mind in Society: The Development of Higher Psychological Processes.* Cambridge, MA: Harvard University Press.

White, M., (2006). Narrative practice with families with children: Externalising conversations revisited. In: M. White. & A. Morgan (Eds.), *Narrative Therapy with Children and their Families* (pp. –56). Adelaide: Dulwich Centre Publications.

Wittgenstein, L. (1953). *Philosophical Investigations.* Oxford: Blackwell.

CHAPTER FIVE

Older people and their significant systems: meeting with families and networks

Eleanor Anderson and Sarah Johnson

"There are so many people here." The interpreter was speaking for Ahmed, aged eighty. His wife, Fatima, seventy-two, sat next to him in a circle of eight mental health practitioners. Ahmed and Fatima bowed their heads and smiled in response as each person welcomed them, introducing their names and role in the team. Ahmed was to be discharged from the acute mental health ward the following week. The meeting had been called to plan support for them. Ahmed smiled and spoke again through the interpreter, "Thank you all for coming."

Like Ahmed, the older adults we work with are often connected in large networks of people, including their families, carers, and other helping practitioners, engaged to address their needs and offer resources. How we connect, listen, and respond to each other in these large systems affects the quality of the outcome for everyone. Adopting a "network-oriented" approach (Seikkula & Arnkil, 2006) means thinking of people in their networks of social relationships. We have found that systemic principles help us to clarify our intentions for a meeting, informing how we bring people together and the practices we use. This chapter addresses how we convene meetings using these principles to facilitate effective dialogue and to create respectful and collaborative communities for all in systems of care with older people.

Why we call the network together

In our services, we are asked to get involved when someone has a worry or concern. For example, a practitioner may be struggling to communicate with a family; or a family member might be worried about how the older person will manage when they are discharged because they seem so alone; or a team could be concerned that the older person or their family member is at risk and not be sure how to address it. Anyone, practitioners, the older client or family members can ask for help. For us, these sorts of requests for help often lead to our initiating a network meeting as I (Eleanor) did in response to the consultant psychiatrist's request for my help with the team's feeling "stuck".

> "Eleanor, as the family therapist here, we wonder if you can help us. It is a complex situation, and we are stuck," said the consultant psychiatrist as the ward round in the mental health day hospital was nearing its end. The team had been discussing Hussain, sixty-nine, who had Parkinson's disease, at times heard voices, and had terrifying dreams from his past. He had just left the acute mental health hospital. The discussion had at first focused on reviewing his numerous medications that were conflicting with each other. It had then moved on to his care at home.
>
> Hussain was married to Ruksana, who was fifty-five. They had emigrated from Bangladesh twenty-five years before. Ruksana spoke little English. I (Eleanor) heard the team's concerns that Ruksana was "very critical" of their care of Hussain. They complained that Ruksana was not always giving Hussain the prescribed medications, following instead her own ideas, and she sometimes locked him alone in their house. The Parkinson's disease was affecting Hussain's speech and his ability to talk to Ruksana. Their frequent arguments became "physical" when Ruksana tried to help Hussain. He had told one worker he wanted to leave Ruksana and another that he must be at home, and did not like respite care. Social Services, who had tried various ways to support the couple, had to change their plans frequently because they did not suit Ruksana, or she did not like the allocated workers. Team

members held strong views about different ways of managing the situation. I said, "It does sound complicated. I think it could be useful to meet all together to see if we can find a way forward."

Hussain's situation is not atypical in services for older people, where there are often large numbers of people or agencies involved with different opinions about how to get things right. Hussain, Ruksana, and the staff involved seemed to have many different views about Hussain's care. I hoped a meeting could facilitate communication and enhance relationships in the face of the strongly held differences: those in the family, those among the practitioners, and those between the family and the practitioners. I hoped to bring people together in a way that would create an "open dialogue" (Seikkula & Arnkil, 2006), a way of talking together that could help those involved find new ways of understanding, of seeing things, and, thus, of acting differently. I also intended to create a context to promote the safety of all: Hussain, Ruksana, and those working with them.

We find it helpful to suggest this sort of meeting when there are different views being expressed, when practitioners or clients feel "stuck" or are unsure how to go on, when there are concerns about safety, and when many people or several different agencies are involved. Network meetings can be a powerful turning point in effecting change if set up and facilitated in a thoughtful way, as Sarah's meeting with Rachel and her network shows.

> I (Sarah) was asked by Simon, a community psychiatric nurse working in the same mental health team as me, to help with Rachel, sixty-seven, who lived alone. She had made several previous suicide attempts, and was now saying that ideas of trying to take her own life were again coming into her mind. Simon initiated the meeting with all the professionals involved and with Rachel's son, who lived some distance away. Everyone present at the meeting addressed Rachel's concerns about the suicidal thoughts, what support she would like, and what resources team members could offer to keep her safe. I drew attention to Rachel's personal resources and abilities: for example, her ability to provide us all with tea and biscuits at the start of the meeting. By the end of the meeting, Rachel said that, to her surprise, she had started to "feel better already" and her son said he "liked being part of a team with mother . . . it feels good working together."

This meeting created a "collaborative community" with and for Rachel, her son, and the professionals involved by pooling the resources of those attending. Rachel was involved at each stage: setting up the meeting, deciding who should attend, actively participating in the talking, and generating a plan. We find meetings like this can help keep family members informed and involved, honour their contributions to the work, facilitate working together, and enhance working relationships. They are an antidote to isolation, not only for older people, but also for practitioners who work alone. These sorts of network meetings can offer a space to witness difficulties and create an opportunity to talk about what is not working so that everyone concerned begins to be aware of dilemmas and difficulties. They also enable progress and achievements to be witnessed and celebrated by everyone. Thus, Rachel was able to describe and show all people present what she had already been doing to keep away depression and suicidal thoughts. In this chapter, we go on to discuss how we might enable planning and co-ordinating with all those involved and concerned to make possible the sorts of outcome achieved by the network meeting with Rachel and her family.

Planning for network meetings

We plan for large network meetings with the intention of creating a respectful context where everyone can have a chance to talk and be listened to. We have found that careful attention to the planning process itself can give those involved hope and energy well before the meeting begins.

Who conducts the meeting

It is difficult for the person who is most concerned about the situation to conduct a large network meeting. This is particularly so if he or she is intent on changing things or has strong ideas about what should happen. When we have been in this position, we have found it challenging to create a neutral space to allow all voices, particularly those with different perspectives from our own, to be heard in an open and non-judgemental way. In this sort of situation, we have found it more necessary to have a conductor who can take the "outsider position" (Seikkula & Arnkil, 2006). Thus, the consultant physician chairing the meeting with Mary and her children, below, found it difficult to create a neutral space for all voices in the meeting, since she was intent on reassuring Mary and convincing her son, Brian, that moving to residential care was the best option.

I (Sarah) sat in the day room of the physical health ward watching Mary, an Irish widow, aged seventy-nine, who was sitting in a wheelchair, half-listening. It was very hot and Mary looked tired. She was seated between her daughter, Lisa, and her son, Brian, while eight members of the multi-disciplinary team were seated around the other sides of the room. The team had called the network meeting to discuss arrangements for Mary's discharge from the ward. She was in the early stages of dementia and had experienced many falls.

The consultant physician began by introducing herself to Mary and her family, asking the rest of the team to introduce themselves. She told the family that the meeting was to discuss the support Mary needed when she left hospital. Looking at Mary, Lisa tentatively said that she had discussed with her mother that she did not think she would be able to look after her at home as much as she needed. The physician turned to Mary and gently said, "I know this is hard for you, we want you to be as independent as possible but we are worried that you will fall and have to come into hospital again if you go home. Sometimes people are safer in a residential home." Raising his voice, Brian said, "No one from our family has ever gone into a home before . . . I can't bear to think of Mum sitting in a room full of old people." Mary became very distressed hearing this, and screamed, "There is nothing wrong with me. I want to go home." Brian shouted at the physician, "Can't you see she is upset." Lisa started crying. I felt upset at seeing their distress and thought, "What can I say to help?" The physician then turned to me and said, "Sarah, would you like to say something?" I said, "I can see this is upsetting for everyone. I am wondering if I have correctly understood everyone's position." I went on to summarize my understanding of each person's point of view and invited further perspectives from everyone present. In this way, we were able to hear and discuss the differences between Lisa and Brian.

The different positions we take in a meeting afford us different rights and responsibilities (Davies & Harré, 1990). For example, in the meeting with Mary, Lisa, and Brian, the consultant physician took up the position of conductor of the meeting. She was also positioned as the leader of the team and the "expert" in medical matters. When she asked me to "say something", as the psychologist on the team, the physician positioned me as "the person who helps people talk about emotional matters". Perhaps she was also inviting me to take an "outsider" position as she struggled to invite all perspectives in a non-judgemental way. It is difficult to conduct a meeting, help people talk about feelings, and offer expert medical opinions at the same time. The conductor is not there to advise or interpret, but to facilitate all voices. Therefore, it was difficult for the physician to hold her position of conductor, when, as the "medical expert" she had advice and opinions she wanted and needed to give.

When planning a network meeting we talk about who "conducts" the meeting, rather than who "chairs" it. A conductor is not a decision maker, or an "expert" who knows the "right way". Rather, conductors position themselves as peers who are separate enough from the situation to facilitate. Therefore, the team decided that I (Eleanor) was the best person to conduct Hussain's network meeting, since I was sufficiently "outside" the situation.

Clients need to feel comfortable with the choice of conductor. Therefore, we discuss the conductor's presence when we are inviting people. When we are conducting the meeting, we have found it useful to see the older client beforehand if possible, even if only briefly just before the meeting begins. Thus, I joined Belinda, Hussain's community psychiatric nurse, when she talked to Hussain about joining us. When Belinda later met with Ruksana, she explained that I would be conducting the meeting.

In our organizations, it is not always possible to have an outside conductor in a meeting. However, if we are clear about the responsibilities of the conductor, then we can consider who might be best placed in the team to act in as neutral a way as possible. When we have had to hold both a therapeutic position with a client and were also required to conduct a network meeting, we have found it helpful to think about ourselves as wearing different "hats". We make this explicit in the meeting, as I (Sarah) did at our next meeting with Rachel and her network when I said, "Today I am wearing two hats—the hat of the conductor of this meeting and the hat of Rachel's clinical psychologist. With my 'conductor of the meeting hat' on, I am inviting each of you to let us know what progress you have noticed since we last met with Rachel and her family. It would be good to hear from all of you." After we had heard the views of the family and all practitioners present, I went on to speak from my position of Rachel's therapist by saying, "Now, speaking with my 'clinical psychologist for Rachel' hat on, I would like to add that Rachel has agreed for me to let you know that she sees more light at the end of the tunnel these days—have I got that right Rachel?"

Deciding whom to invite to a meeting

To help us decide whom to invite to a meeting, we consider "Who wants to have a conversation with whom about what?"; "Who is concerned, involved, and offers resources to the problem?"; "What is the relationship in focus?" (see Chapter Two). We also invite colleagues to consider "Who else could be of help and is able to participate in the meeting?" (Seikkula & Arnkil, 2006) to help us identify who has resources to offer. Thus, these questions help us to identify those "key contributors" whose presence is essential to the meeting's progress.

> When I (Eleanor) asked these questions at the ward round, I learned that Ruksana and Hussain might want help in talking together. All thought that Ruksana would welcome an opportunity to talk about her dissatisfaction with the care her husband was receiving through an interpreter. Communication within such a large system was felt to be the main difficulty. With the intention of exploring resources, I asked, "Who would be of help and is able to participate in the meeting?" All felt that it was important for the consultant psychiatrist to attend, as her concerns had initiated the meeting. The social worker, Joan, was important, as she would need to implement any plans. Because Belinda, Hussain's community psychiatric nurse, seemed to get on with both Ruksana and Hussain, people suggested she could help, as could Peter, the day hospital manager who was particularly close to Hussain. Clearly, an interpreter would be essential

When conflict is anticipated

In our teams, there have been times when some practitioners who know about relationship difficulties between family members and staff have raised concerns about inviting people to a meeting for fear that "things will get out of hand" or "there may be fights in the meeting". When conflict is anticipated, it can seem easier not to invite people who are not getting along.

> The professionals wondered if Hussain's and Ruksana's relationship was too volatile for them to meet together. They worried that Ruksana might get angry and walk out in the middle of the meeting. Peter, the day hospital manager, was worried that he might "lose it" with Ruksana, because of his angry feelings towards her. We wondered if Ruksana would even agree to attend, because of her negative feelings about Peter. Peter was also concerned that if Ruksana did come, her needs rather than Hussain's might dominate the meeting.

Thinking about our hopes, intentions, and preferred outcomes for meetings can help us consider whether a person's attendance will enable or constrain the purpose of the meeting and can open space to address how best to include them. Therefore, I asked, "What are our intentions for the meeting if everyone does come?" One of the nurses said, "If we could manage to talk together, maybe Ruksana would come to understand things from our team's point of view." The social worker said, "Perhaps we might begin to see things from Ruksana's point of view as well." We also wondered if it would be helpful for Hussain and Ruksana to have an opportunity for each to witness the other's difficulties and progress in a more neutral place.

There are times when an older person or a practitioner whom we think would be a helpful resource at the meeting feels reluctant to attend. Sometimes, someone may say "yes", but their body language or tone of voice clearly signals their lack of enthusiasm. Our sensitivity to a reluctance to meet, and the questions we then ask, can make a difference to engaging people, to enabling them to feel heard, and to helping them to begin to think differently about the difficulties of talking together (Public Conversations Project, 1995). The following is a conversation I had with Peter, the day hospital manager working with Hussain, who had worried about attending the meeting with Ruksana in case he, Peter, "lost it".

> Eleanor: Peter, what are your hopes for the meeting, for talking to Hussain and Ruksana with the other professionals?

Peter: Well, of course I hope we can resolve things so Ruksana and I can at least be civil when we meet. But I'm not very hopeful. Ruksana makes it so hard for us all. She scowls every time I see her—shoots daggers at me with her eyes. Sitting in a meeting with her won't be easy. I know her life has been difficult, but I get so angry with her. A difficult life is no excuse for bad behaviour.

Eleanor: How do you think we could manage the meeting so that the anger doesn't get in the way?

Peter: I don't know. Pretty impossible, I think, with Ruksana. Having an interpreter will help, maybe . . . and you conducting the meeting. Except just seeing me makes Ruksana angry. I think it is best if I am not there. I won't put up with her almost certainly being rude to everyone in the meeting. She doesn't like me. But Hussain wants me to be there.

Eleanor: If I understand correctly, you don't want to be in the meeting because of the anger *and* you do want to be there for Hussain?

Peter: Yes, that's it.

Eleanor: What do you think you could do personally to prevent this anger coming between you?

Peter: I can't think of anything . . . [a long pause] . . . if I try not to make too much eye contact with her it might be better? I'll be there for Hussain, and help him to say what he wants to say. I worry that his point of view gets lost when everyone is so focused on Ruksana, and he finds speaking so difficult.

Eleanor: So if I see you looking away from Ruksana that will mean anger is around? Anything else?

Peter: (laughing) Maybe you'll see me clenching my teeth, biting my tongue . . .

Eleanor: So when that happens, what would it be helpful for me to do?

Peter: I don't know. I think just knowing you know I'm near to the end of my tether will help. What do you suggest?

Eleanor: Well, I often ask a question at that point, to help us understand the difficulties for each of you. Much like we are doing now. Hopefully, from there we can begin to find a way through. How would that fit for you?

Peter: Well, we'll see. At least I'll know what you are trying to do.

I (Eleanor) went on to talk with Peter about what in the past had worked well in communicating with Ruksana, and how else, as conductor of the meeting, I could help everyone's voice to be heard. In this conversation with Peter, I used the Public Conversations Project (1995) schema to help me understand both Peter's concerns and his hopes for the meeting; to help Peter and myself to become aware of these concerns; to build a collaborative relationship, and to enable me to become an informed facilitator in the meeting. I talked about "the" anger, not locating the anger "in" Peter or Ruksana, but rather as an entity external to them both that gets in the way of their communication (White, 1988). I then named the dilemma, "If I understand, you don't want to be in the meeting because of the anger *and* you do want to be there for Hussain?", using the word "and" rather than "but" to clarify that both positions hold equal weight. I asked about Peter's hopes for the meeting. Thus, in the context of Peter knowing what he would like to achieve, I was able to go on to explore how the meeting could be managed "so that the anger does not get in the way." I based my question, "What do you think you could do personally to prevent this anger coming between you?" on The Public Conversations Project (1995) guideline, which points us toward asking what people would "want to personally restrain or practise in order to participate as their 'best' selves in such a meeting".

Including the older person affected by dementia or mental health difficulties

When practitioners are concerned about the effect of mental health problems or dementia on the older person's ability to participate or understand, we discuss whether or not to include the older person in a large meeting. For example, the practitioners working with Hussain expressed concerns about whether to invite him to such a large meeting since his speech was so poor, and people wondered whether he was beginning to develop cognitive problems, making it difficult for him to understand.

> The practitioners wondered if it would be better to have the large meeting without Hussain and a smaller one for him with Ruksana and only one or two practitioners. I (Eleanor) invited the team to weigh up the opportunities and constraints of Hussain attending by asking, "What

effect would it have if we were to include Hussain?" Peter said he thought that Hussain might find being part of a big meeting "support-ive", that he was a "proud man" and might "be deeply offended, feel not respected, if he were excluded." I then invited Peter to reflect on what could help Hussain's participation by asking, "If Hussain comes to the meeting, what will help him to participate?" Peter felt that Hussain could manage the meeting if we talked with him beforehand to find out what could help him during the meeting. Peter proposed that he sit next to Hussain, since "we understand each other fairly well . . . and I can check his understanding . . . and repeat what people say directly to Hussain if necessary." He suggested that it might help to have someone available to go out of the room with Hussain if he felt it was getting too much for him.

If we anticipate the older person having difficulties following everything said in a large meeting, perhaps due to cognitive or hearing difficulties, we need to be even more careful to make sure we are helping them to participate in the meeting.

Mary, who could not concentrate for long, had wanted to come to the meeting with her children, Lisa and Brian, to discuss the plans for her future. However, sometimes she found it hard to understand what was being said, particularly when several people were speaking at once. I (Sarah) was careful to make eye contact when I spoke to her and to speak slowly enough and in short sentences to help her follow. I regu-larly checked whether she wanted others to slow down, and offered a summary of the main points discussed when someone else had been speaking.

It can be too easy to assume an older person's inability to partic-ipate. My team and I (Eleanor) learned this when we did not invite Doris, seventy-four, to a meeting, assuming that because she suffered from almost constant agonizing delusions, she was "too ill to attend". Doris's niece misunderstood our invitation and brought Doris to the large meeting. To our amazement, Doris was able to respond and participate in the meeting, so much so that it was a turning point in her recovery.

If someone is unable to attend a meeting

Sometimes an important member of the network is unable to attend a meeting. This may be because of physical reasons such as illness or dementia, or it might be difficult to find a time that is convenient for everyone. A close family member might want to be involved, but lives too far away to attend. If someone is unable to attend, there are alternative ways we can enable a person's voice to be heard and for them to receive feedback about the meeting. For example, we may ask what they would like said at the meeting on their behalf, or we may offer them the opportunity to have someone represent them in their absence.

Some older people have opted to have a representative or advocate sit alongside them in the meeting and to talk for them (Iveson, 1990). We have also given them the opportunity to elect a person to sit in the meeting instead of them to listen from their position, and to participate in the meeting from their perspective. In this situation, we try to hold a separate meeting with the older person and their representative so the older person can brief the representative before the meeting. Alternatively, the older person may prefer us to help them prepare a written message, audiotape, or videotape to be presented at the meeting in their absence. We can also keep the absent member's views in mind throughout the meeting by asking questions such as "I wonder what John would say about this, if he were here today?" Or "Before the dementia, I wonder what advice Loretta would have given us?" Finally, we talk about how and when the absent person would like to find out what happened in the meeting. They may prefer a copy of the minutes of the meeting, or something less formal in writing, or they may prefer to meet to talk about it, or both.

Engaging the network

How we invite people

How we invite all those involved makes a difference to a meeting's progress, or even whether or not it happens. We have found that standard letters are least likely to engage busy people working in time-pressured services. Therefore, we try to make time to call or talk with people to explain the purpose of the meeting and why we would value their contribution (McNamee, 2002; Public Conversations Project, 1995). We intend to give the message that we are "not going to tell people what to do". Instead we try to let them know that "we want to connect"; "need your help"; "are interested in hearing what you want to say"; and "would like to share what we know". Therefore, we highlight the unique contribution that each person can offer to the situation. For example, when we invited Hussain's network we said, "We would value your contribution since you have known Hussain before the Parkinson's disease began to interfere with his life", or "Since you have been working with Hussain and Ruksana, you can offer us a useful perspective on . . .", or "The family will probably want to ask questions about (medication/housing) so your presence will be helpful to all of us."

Who invites whom

We spend some time thinking about who is going to invite whom to the meeting. If a practitioner has asked for the meeting we suggest that they invite whoever could make a useful contribution to the issue they want to address. We also suggest that the practitioner best able to engage the older person meets with him or her to invite them to the meeting, asks whom the older person would like to invite, and discusses what needs to be taken into consideration to plan a co-operative meeting. We offer the older person the opportunity to invite other members of the family. However, they may prefer a practitioner to invite their family, like Olive in Chapter Two, who asked Philippa to invite her younger daughter, Margaret because "I don't want her to think I am putting pressure on her." We decided that Belinda, the community psychiatric nurse, and I (Eleanor) would meet with Hussain to invite him to the meeting. Hussain had a good relationship with Belinda and we also thought it would be helpful for him to be introduced to me as I would be conducting the meeting.

> Belinda said, "Hussain, we are planning a meeting of everyone involved in your care because we are concerned that we are not co-ordinating everything as well as we can for you. We wondered whether you would like to help us prepare for this meeting and whether you want to come to give us your point of view?" We then told Hussain who wanted to attend this meeting and asked whom else he felt was important to include. With halting speech, Hussain slowly told

us he wanted to be at the meeting. He particularly wanted Peter there, and hoped Ruksana would come. He thought Belinda should be the one to invite Ruksana because she might not come if he asked. He thought Ruksana might want to bring her friend, who often helped interpret for her and gave her support. Until this conversation, we had not been aware of Ruksana's friend.

When Belinda asked Ruksana to attend, through an interpreter, she said "Ruksana, we are concerned because we are not sure we are helping Hussain and you in the best way. It would help us if you could come to a meeting with Hussain and the other members of our team, so we can see if, together, we can all find a better way. Hussain says he is able to come. Would you be able to come? Hussain wondered if you want your friend, Najwa, to come as well?" Ruksana was pleased with everyone who was attending, but was concerned about Peter, the day hospital manager, whom she said she did not like. Belinda asked her, "What could we do to make the talking with all of us and Peter helpful to you in this meeting?", which opened space for Ruksana to say that she would feel all right if the rest of the team were there, if they listened to her point of view, and if she could sit next to her friend, Najwa.

Belinda positioned "the team" as asking for the help of both Hussain and Ruksana. By talking about the concerns the team had with their own ability to co-ordinate everything, therefore, Belinda was careful not to locate the concerns in either Hussain or Ruksana's behaviour, which could be perceived as blaming, potentially making it more likely that the invitation to attend was rejected. Clarifying who will conduct the meeting, who will be attending, and what will be happening helps everyone involved to know what to expect.

When and where to have the meeting

Finding a time that is convenient for everyone to attend a large meeting can be daunting. When there are large numbers of people involved, we consider who are the key contributors, and try to arrange the meeting around their preferred times. For example, we say, "It is most important to have your voice at this meeting because . . . When are the best times for you, and we will try to work around that?" When Belinda and I met with Hussain, I said, "I will be inviting everyone to the meeting and I will conduct the meeting. Would it be easier for you to have the meeting at your home? We could arrange for people to join us there. Or you may prefer the hospital?" Belinda also asked this of Ruksana, and both preferred their home.

If it helps a key contributor to attend a meeting, we may offer to hold the meeting at their venue. In this case we are clear to clarify, "If it is more convenient for you to host the meeting, I would be pleased to conduct it at your base." Distinguishing who "hosts" the meeting from who "conducts" it well before we meet helps to clarify who takes responsibility for leading the meeting.

Flexibility and attention to details like this can make a major difference to people being present at a meeting or not. Thus, Hussain's meeting was planned to begin about fifteen minutes after the ambulance had brought him home from the day hospital, giving him time to have a drink and settle before beginning.

In summary, then, we find it useful to ask ourselves the following questions when we talk to someone about a meeting:

- Have we clarified the purpose of the meeting?
- Have we asked their views about having the meeting?
- Have we discussed who will attend?
- Have we discussed the format, structure and process of the meeting?
- Have we discussed the preferred venue?

Facilitating collaborative dialogue

Engaging everyone involved begins at the planning stage and continues throughout the meeting. If possible, we try to plan a meeting along the lines we have already outlined above. Whether or not we have been able to do this, we find it invaluable to start with a pre-meeting.

Starting with a pre-meeting

When we schedule the time for the meeting, we ask the practitioners working with the older person to arrive fifteen minutes before the older person and their family join us to allow time to clarify our positions and responsibilities in the meeting and to prepare our "emotional postures" (Fredman, 2007; see also Chapter Two). We also use this time to address practicalities that will further help communication, like audibility, seating, language and how we will use an interpreter if appropriate. People rarely arrive all at once for large network meetings. How we greet both clients and practitioners as they arrive sets the tone for the meeting. If people are sitting waiting for others to arrive, we introduce people informally if they do not know each other.

Fredman (2007) describes how she uses pre-meeting discussions about seating arrangements to "position ourselves in order to create spaces and opportunities for people to connect and collaborate with each other, so that they can feel comfortable and respected by us all" (p. 56). So, for example, before Mary's network meeting we might have asked, "How might we arrange our seating so that Mary, her daughter, and son can feel comfortable and respected by us here today? For example—does anyone have some ideas about where Mary would prefer to sit? Who knows her best? Is there anyone with whom you think she would feel more comfortable sitting? Whom would she like to keep an eye on? What about the other family members?" We might also have conversations with the family beforehand to clarify what would help them feel most comfortable and able to participate.

Introductions

Our intention is to help everyone feel at ease and comfortable at the beginning of the meeting. Therefore the conductor starts by giving the older person and their family time to look around the room and take in who is present. We might start by asking the older person and family members, "Is there anyone here you recognize . . . who looks familiar . . . who do you already know in the room?" When the client identifies familiar faces, we ask, "Could you introduce us?" and then continue, "Who is unfamiliar to you . . . any faces you do not recognise? Whom would you like to be introduced to first?"

Hussain noted his connection with Peter, Belinda, and me (Eleanor). He asked to be introduced to the new occupational therapist, whom he had not met. Ruksana seemed pleased to introduce us to Najwa, "We are cousins and also good friends for a long time."

In this way, we are able to "map the system" by noting connections and exploring relationships. The conductor asks, "Who called this meeting?", "Why did they think it might be helpful?", and "Who else knows about the meeting, is interested, or wanted to come?"

Contracting

Making a contract at the start of the meeting enables us to "generate safety and minimize anxiety" (Seikkula & Arnkil, 2006). The conductor explains how we will work in the meeting. He or she clarifies when the meeting will finish and lets everyone know that there will be enough time to talk about plans at the end of the meeting.

Near the start of the meeting the conductor usually says something like, "We find it useful to begin by thinking about what we need to do to create a respectful environment here so everyone feels able to express their views. We expect to hear lots of different ideas. And it is important that everyone has their say . . . that we all get to hear everyone's voice. Everyone will have a turn both to talk and to listen. So, what is important for us to agree so we can be sure that everyone can speak, can listen, and can be heard? Who wants to begin? We will ask everyone."

Creating a focus together

At the start, the conductor invites everyone to think forward to the end of the meeting to create a focus for the meeting together. Thus, we use questions that invite people to look to the future (Penn, 1985) and to start anticipating solutions (de Shazer, 1985, 1990) right from the beginning. For example, we might ask, "Imagine we are now at the end of this meeting and you say to yourself, 'That was very good, very useful. Now I know how to go on . . .' What have we discussed here today? . . . What have we sorted out? . . . What are you able to do?"

> When I began like this at Hussain's meeting, through the interpreter, Ruksana said, "I am so worried about Hussain. He is getting worse . . . not eating right. No one listens to me when I say so." I asked,

"So Ruksana, let us say it is next month and we listened very well here today . . . so that everything you wanted is sorted out . . . so what can you and Hussain do now . . . since everything is sorted?" Ruksana told us that Hussain's health would be better if he ate and that she would be less worried if his health problems "got sorted". I wrote each issue down. She nodded when I said we would make sure we talked about them in the meeting.

Ruksana began by answering in a way that did not look to the future, and instead complained about the present. When I gently persisted in inviting her to imagine and explore her preferred future, "let us say it is next month and we listened well today . . . so that everything you wanted is sorted . . ." she was able to answer. Hence, we were able to go on to invite the perspectives of Hussain and the practitioners in the meeting towards creating a focus for the meeting together. This jointly created focus included helping Hussain to enjoy his food and Ruksana to feel he was eating well. Everyone present also wanted to ensure that Hussain was receiving his medication regularly.

Involving everyone in a large meeting can be difficult. A common occurrence is that a question is asked, one person answers it, and discussion begins on the basis of that one person's answer. This leaves some people's perspectives unspoken and unheard and can interfere with our jointly generating a focus for the meeting. If this happens, we have found it useful to say something like, "Before we talk in such detail, I would find it helpful to hear first what each of you would like to address here today so we can try to make space for all your agendas in the time we have together." When there are different ideas for the focus we have found it helpful to summarize these, and ask people to prioritize, "As we only have limited time to cover all issues today, what do you want to prioritize?"

We try to ask everyone for their views and invite their different perspectives with questions such as, "Do you *see* it the same way, or differently?", or, if there are large numbers of people, we might ask, "Does anyone see it differently?" We take care how we use language. How we each *see* something is more neutral than asking if people *agree* or *disagree*. Asking about the views of people who are unable to attend helps to keep these people in the picture even if they are not present.

*Creating a respectful listening and talking context
with many people*

When we conduct network meetings, we move the conversation around the room, inviting people to take turns in speaking and listening, so that all people present can talk and be heard, can listen, and have their own thoughts. It can be difficult for people to speak out in a large meeting, and even professionals may find it daunting to "think aloud" in the presence of others. Therefore, when we invite someone to talk with us we give that person our full attention. We make eye contact and use our body as well as our words to let them know that we are interested in what they have to say. We make sure that the speaker is not interrupted and help bring forth the speaker's ideas by asking open questions.

By purposively separating listening and speaking in meetings, we also intend to create space for "reflecting processes" (Andersen, 1995), whereby those listening can have their own thoughts and be touched and moved by the words of the speaker. If someone is talking to a person directly, they usually feel obliged to respond so that any "inner talks" or thinking to themselves are silenced or constrained. When a person listens to someone talking about them, on the other hand, they can tune in and out of the talks and thus be freer to have an inner dialogue, thinking to themselves about what they are hearing (*ibid.*). By talking with only one person at a time and by talking in the third person ("he", "she" or "they") about the others in the room, rather than in the second person ("you") to the other person directly, therefore, the conductor of the meeting can intentionally create space for this sort of reflecting process.

We make our intentions for this sort of talking transparent so as to avoid clients feeling we are disrespecting them in our talking about them rather than talking to them. Therefore, in Hussain's meeting, I (Eleanor) said, "Hussain, I am going to ask everyone to talk with me about how they think you are getting on with eating. They will talk to me about you, not directly to you, so you can have a chance to listen and have your own thoughts about what they say. And then I will come back and ask you how you see things. Is this all right for you?" Hussain nodded. I then said, "Peter, could you tell me how the staff at the day hospital sees Hussain's eating?" I continued to ask each member of the network present, with everyone speaking about Hussain in the third person as he listened.

In network meetings, we try to enable a conversation that first invites understanding and witnessing rather than looks immediately for agreements or solutions. This is particularly important when we are working with people holding strongly opposing views.

> Ruksana had been particularly worried about Hussain's food, saying he was "barely eating". Peter talked about how well Hussain ate at the day hospital, and Lucy, one of Hussain's carers, said she thought Hussain ate well when she looked after him. Ruksana glared as they talked. Positioning the practitioners to listen, I explored with Ruksana what she meant by "barely eating", asking for "examples to help us understand". Thus, we learnt about Ruksana's views on "good food". Lucy followed on to share her experience of what Hussain could swallow and other practitioners gave examples of food that other older people with Parkinson's disease could enjoy. As the conversation about food continued, the practitioners and Ruksana seemed to move towards more common ground in their approach to Hussain's eating.

To create a context that encourages all voices in a meeting, we try to show that we are listening in a way that is open and accepting. Even if we are not in the position of conductor, it is still possible to do this throughout the meeting. We try to

- summarize and clarify what we have heard
- use the language of the person
- check our understanding and explore the meaning of words people use
- avoid knowing too quickly.

To prevent the focus that all have agreed at the beginning of a meeting getting lost during discussion, we might stop and summarize partway through the meeting. Sometimes, we go on to refocus the meeting. In Hussain's meeting, I said, "It is halfway through our time, and we wanted to talk about ensuring that Hussain enjoys his food and that Ruksana feels he is eating well. You also wanted to address how Hussain can receive his medication regularly. We have been focusing on the eating. Do we all want to continue with this or go on to sorting out the medication, or something else? What is most important for us to sort out today?"

When there are strong emotions

Meetings in older adult services often deal with distressing topics such as leaving one's home forever, serious illness where little can be done to change a slow, worsening progression, or frightening symptoms associated with mental illness. Therefore, it is not unusual for people to become upset in meetings. Talking about such difficult issues affects us as practitioners as well. Although we have more chance to control the process, it is common for practitioners to feel uncomfortable with the open expression of feelings and the display of strong emotion in network meetings. Often we have heard practitioners say they were uncertain whether to respond, how to respond, or who should respond when people express their feelings in large meetings.

We are careful not to draw attention to people's non-verbal expressions of feeling that we may notice but that are not obviously intended as a public communication. However, when an older person, like Mary, weeps openly in a meeting, or a family member, like her son Brian, shouts loudly, we take this as a communication and an "invitation to respond" (Fredman, 2004). If an expression of feeling is intended for our witnessing, we believe that it does not matter who takes the lead. What is important is that there is a response to what has been said or expressed. We believe that "for a human being nothing is as terrible as remaining without a response" (Bakhtin, 1986, p. 127), whereas hearing and acknowledging emotions that affect everyone, clients and professionals, can create a feeling of togetherness in the face of difficult situations (Seikkula & Arnkill, 2006).

There are several ways we can respond to the display of emotion. These include repeating what has been said or asking more about it. We try not to respond too quickly, making assumptions about or interpreting how someone is feeling. For example, we are careful not to say, "We hear how angry you are feeling", as we may be misnaming an expression of frustration, outrage, or powerlessness. Instead, we might ask, "How would you name what you feel is happening for you?", or "I can see that you feel strongly about this. What is it about this that is important to you?" Having had emotion acknowledged and concerns identified, it may not be appropriate for people to continue to talk about their feelings in a large network meeting, and, indeed, they may not want to. We may ask if people would like to talk at more length about these issues at another time with someone else.

When there is criticism and blame

There are times when we have found ourselves pulled between wanting to protect the older person from criticism or humiliation and also wanting to acknowledge the distress of their critical or undermining carer.

> Lisa said, "Mum is really impossible. She urinates in waste paper bins . . . and I found poo . . . she just doesn't seem to care." Lisa's voice became shriller and louder as she talked. "It reminds me of when I was thirteen . . . It's as if she has all the rights here and I have none . . . I have to wash clothes all the time . . ." As Lisa talked, her mother, Mary, rocked back and forth, half-crying and repeating, "Oh my dear, oh my dear" over and over again. Brian looked dumbstruck.

My (Sarah's) inner thoughts were that it was important not to interrupt Lisa. I assumed she had shown her mother her frustration before in much this way. However, I was concerned that if I sounded sympathetic to Lisa, Brian might see me as allying with her and away from him. Trying to engage with Lisa's complaint, witness and appreciate her experience, as well as shift the focus of criticism away from Mary, I enquired about the effect of the problem on Lisa.

> Sarah: Lisa, what effect is this having on you?
>
> Lisa: (bursting into tears) You have no idea. I have lost my mum. It's like she is a child. I don't know what to do.
>
> Sarah: What is it like for you Lisa, having to take care of your mum in this way?
>
> Lisa: (crying) It's the wrong order. Mum used to care for me.
>
> Sarah: Do you think your Mum recognizes what you are going through?
>
> (At this point Mary's whimpering becomes a cry.)
>
> Lisa: I don't know. I don't think so.

Brian: I think she does.

Sarah: What do you think your mum understands, Brian?

Brian: It must be so humiliating.

Lisa: (turning to her mother) Come to think of it Mum, six months ago you said you were good for nothing. I feel so bad being so critical. I'm sorry Mum.

Sarah: (turning to Mary) I'm finding it difficult to look after everyone here, Mary. Maybe I should have stopped Lisa talking earlier? I left you all to talk like this, which has been very upsetting for you all.

Mary: (through her tears) No, no, it's good. She can say what she needs to and so can I.

Shifting the focus from Mary's behaviour to *the effect* of Mary's behaviour on Lisa acknowledged and witnessed what the situation was doing to them both and to their relationship with each other. When Lisa felt she had been heard and acknowledged, this opened space for a different kind of talking. It allowed Lisa to express how she was feeling, and Brian and Mary to witness and respond to Lisa's expression. When I was transparent about the process, by noting, "Maybe I should have stopped Lisa talking earlier, Mary? I left you all to talk like this which has been very upsetting for you all", my intention was to involve Mary in setting the pace of the conversation, and to allow her a space to be heard.

If someone finds it too difficult to continue in a meeting

Occasionally, no matter how carefully we plan, someone may find it too difficult to continue in a meeting. When a person suddenly walks out of a meeting, it can be difficult to know how best to respond. If a person is intent on going, we never insist they remain. If possible, another member of the team sees if the person is still in the building, ensures they are safe, and offers the opportunity to talk, or contacts them later to see how they are. If the person does not return, we tend to focus the conversation on "what can we still discuss without John's presence here?" "How can we be sure he is informed about our discussion?" "Who will talk with him about what we have said?"

We always end a meeting like this with a plan for who might contact the person who left, since walking out is a communication that needs a response. If we set another meeting date, we discuss with the person who left what needs to happen so that they can stay in the next meeting if they still want to attend. They might, for example, prefer to talk to someone on their own.

Ending a meeting: joint action planning

The conductor takes responsibility for drawing the meeting to a close. When we conduct meetings, we prepare people for the end of the meeting by clarifying at the beginning how long the meeting will last and agreeing the focus for what people want by the end. We also keep the ending in mind throughout by offering reminders of the time left and by summarizing and re-checking the focus of the meeting.

An important part of the conductor's task is to structure the meeting in such a way that all present can contribute and agree an action plan by the end of the meeting. Therefore, we usually check how people want to take what has been discussed forward, rather than make assumptions about, or prescribe, what should happen. For example, we might say, "Shall we decide who will take responsibility for taking each idea forward?", and "Who will discuss what, with whom and when?"

To avoid coming to rapid conclusions and decisions that might cut off other options too soon, we ask questions such as, "Do we need a follow-up meeting to review developments, or to continue a discussion?"; "Who else needs to know what has been agreed and how and when do we let them know—verbally, or in minutes of the meeting, or in staff handover?"; "What other decisions have to be made and where will this happen?" Finally, we try to finish by thanking everyone for their contributions.

Documenting a meeting

Leaving the meeting is never the end, particularly for the person who has to document it. We use written minutes to provide a record of the meeting for those present and those unable to be there. We record positive developments reported in the meeting in detail, since witnessing achievements and acknowledging how these were attained make an important contribution to consolidating progress (White & Epston, 1990). The minutes reflect the future focus of the meeting by documenting who has agreed to do what and when. Finally, we give the date and place of the next meeting.

We attend carefully to the language we use in our written record, wherever possible using the actual words of the participants in the meeting, avoiding jargon and medical terms, unless they are explained. For older adults, who often have trouble reading small print, we use large, easily readable type, and leave spaces between paragraphs, making the whole as easy to read as possible.

Having agreed towards the end of the meeting who will receive the minutes, we circulate them with a covering letter or acknowledgment slip that lets everyone know they can correct them if what happened has not been recorded accurately.

In conclusion

The process of writing this chapter involved many conversations with each other, with colleagues, and with clients about why we were doing what we did, the feelings this engendered, analyses of what we could have done differently at times of impasse, as well as our wide reading of how others are working with wider systems in different contexts. We were delighted to discover that, as we wrote, our practices developed. In the same way, we hope that your reading of this chapter might enable you to develop your practices with the meetings in which you will inevitably take part in your work with older adults and their wider systems.

References

Andersen, T. (1995). Reflecting processes; acts of informing and forming: You can borrow my eyes, but you must not take them away from me! In: S. Friedman (Ed.), *The Reflecting Team in Action. Collaborative Practice in Family Therapy.* (pp. 11–37). New York: Guilford.

Bakhtin, M. (1986). *Speech Genres and Other Late Essays.* Austin, TX: University of Texas Press.

Davies, B., & Harré, R. (1990). Positioning: the social construction of selves. *Journal for the Theory of Social Behaviour, 20:* 43–63.

de Shazer, S. (1985). *Keys to Solution in Brief Therapy.* London: Norton.

de Shazer, S. (1990). What is it about brief therapy that works? In: J. Zeig & S. Gillian (Eds.), *Brief Therapy, Myths, Methods, and Metaphors* (pp. 90–99). New York: Brunner/Mazel.

Fredman, G. (2004). *Transforming Emotion: Conversations in Counselling and Psychotherapy.* London: Whurr/Wiley.

Fredman, G. (2007). Preparing our selves for the therapeutic relationship. Revisiting "hypothesizing revisited". *Human Systems: The Journal of Systemic Consultation & Management, 18:* 44–59.

McNamee, S. (2002). Hearing marginalised voices in therapy. Paper presented to Kensington Consultation Centre Conference, London.

Penn, P. (1985). Feed-forward: future questions, future maps. *Family Process, 24:* 299–310.

Public Conversations Project (1995). *Public Conversations Project* www.publicconversations.org/pcp/pcp.html (accessed 19 November).

Seikkula, J., & Arnkil, T. E. (2006). *Dialogical Meetings in Social Networks.* London: Karnac.

White, M. (1988). The externalising of the problem and the re-authoring of lives and relationships. *Dulwich Centre Newsletter,* Summer: 5–28.

White, M., & Epston, D. (1990). *Narrative Means to Therapeutic Ends.* Adelaide: Dulwich Centre Publications.

CHAPTER SIX

Working with older people in contexts of difference and discrimination

Isabelle Ekdawi and Esther Hansen

I (Esther) was sitting opposite Bob, a ninety-two-year-old former university professor who had been referred to see a psychologist by the team psychiatrist. Bob was dressed in a smart shirt and trousers and had white, neatly combed hair. I asked him what he hoped to get out of our first meeting. Bob paused and said he had "no hopes" for our work together "because you have probably already read my notes—they say I have a paranoid personality disorder." Bob added, "You could not possibly understand my life or experiences due to your young age, but I am willing to give it a try, as I am feeling so depressed and hopeless." I asked him what difference he thought my age would make to what he felt able or unable to talk about with me. He paused for a few seconds and then said, "When you are young you have numerous opportunities to show the many different parts of who you are through your work, friendships, relationships, family, interests, and hopes for the future. But when you are my age . . . what opportunities do I have to show any other part of who I am . . . how can you understand that?"

Bob identifies work, friendships, relationships, family, as well as interests and hopes for the future as some of the many contexts that enable him to "show the many different parts" of his self. Within his working context, he had experienced himself as a competent, organized, highly regarded, professional man, and within his family context as a strong, loving, fun father. However, it has been more difficult for him to connect with or show these versions of himself within the context of a psychiatric day hospital, where he is ascribed the identity of "patient", and given the label of "paranoid personality disorder". Thus, Bob talks of the diminished identity older people can experience if contexts for performing and expressing the different versions of themselves are not available.

Bob also specifically points to age as a difference between himself and me (Esther), the psychologist. For older clients like Bob, this age difference can feel like a huge disparity between themselves and the younger practitioner. When the older people with whom we work also differ from us in terms of gender, ethnicity, culture, spirituality, sexuality, class, or ability, it might sometimes seem as if we have an enormous gulf to cross to create understanding. In this chapter, we explore how to help the older people with whom we work move from a position of what we might call "diminished identity", where they are able to access or show only a limited range, or less valued versions, of themselves to an "enhanced" identity, where they can speak of and live a range of preferred versions of self. We address the therapeutic dilemmas involved in this challenge, particularly in contexts of difference and discrimination. We also address how, as younger practitioners, we might begin to bridge differences between ourselves and the older people with whom we work, so that we can understand each other and develop a trusting working relationship. We approach difference not merely as an obstacle to be overcome, but as potentially enriching of us and both forming and informing our relationships with clients. Our challenge in a conversation such as the one featured above with Bob is to communicate in a way in which the older person feels understood and respected, despite the gap perceived due to the age difference.

We, the authors, are white, middle-class, and female clinical psychologists of working age. Our own personal contexts inform how we join and what we bring to our conversations with older adults, their carers, and families. For example, I (Isabelle) am in my early forties, I come from a mixed ethnic and cultural background consisting of a white British mother from working-class origins and an Egyptian father of middle-class origins, who belonged to a marginalized, minority religion in Egypt. Although I largely identify as heterosexual, I have also had a relationship with a woman. I (Esther) am thirty-one and identify myself as heterosexual, from a white European (Luxembourg), non-English-speaking background. My mother lived as a Luxembourgish child in post-war Canada until she was sixteen, and returned to marry my father. Both came from working-class origins. These contexts inform what we might attend to, note down, or ask further questions about.

Supporting preferred identities

We believe that people are more vulnerable to experiencing "diminished identity" in contexts where they feel different from others and where this difference either is not valued or is seen as negative. We have both had the experience of feeling less able to show the selves that we would usually value and enjoy when we have felt different from those around us and when we have a sense that the way we are different is not valued or appreciated.

Bob pointed to the difference in age between himself and Esther and questioned whether she could appreciate his "life or experiences". He also doubted her ability to help him, perhaps assuming that his diagnosis of "paranoid personality disorder" had prejudiced her ability to see beyond this negative self-description. We want to enable the older people we work with to show the versions of their selves that they value most highly. Therefore, I (Esther) wanted to enable Bob to be seen by others as a complex, intelligent human being with vast life experiences, rather than only as an "old man" with a "paranoid personality disorder". These "thin descriptions" (Geertz, 1973) tell us very little about people like Bob's resources, abilities, values, and beliefs, and, therefore, limit the ways in which they can show and experience their preferred identities.

Discourses that inform older people and services

When Bob went on to ask Esther, "Haven't you got somebody younger you should see? It would be more worthwhile seeing

them, they have more life left to live", he was touching on a common shared viewpoint that older people are less deserving of help
than younger people, or that they are "a drain on society". This
commonly shared viewpoint is a powerful discourse held within
white British culture and connects to other stories embedded in this
culture, such as "you cannot teach an old dog new tricks". These
discourses are often taken as the "truth", rather than as stories
coming from particular cultural contexts. Therefore, they remain
unchallenged. It is unlikely that Bob was aware that his words were
reflecting this dominant discourse and more likely that he believed
his opinion to be a "fact".

> Later in therapy, Bob told me (Esther), "I don't want to go to a day
> centre . . . it is full of old people . . . I have nothing to say to them."
> Unsure if Bob was referring to the educational difference between
> himself and the other older people attending the day centre, I (Esther)
> checked, "Is this about the difference between you and them . . . I mean,
> there are no other professors here?", to which Bob replied, "No, it's not
> that . . . I just don't like old people—they bore me."

Bob seemed to be drawing on the discourse that older people
have nothing to contribute, and that younger people are more interesting. The phrase "young at heart", meant as a compliment about
an older person, is an expression embedded in this discourse, since
it implies that youth is what is valued and aspired to, while attrib-
utes acquired in old age are less valuable. If these discourses go
unnoticed, an older person could come to accept these expressions
of ageism as realities, and internalize them. It is not unusual for
older persons to see ageing through the lens of this sort of discourse, hence placing negative value judgements both on themselves and on other older people, so that the meanings they give to
their lives, and the actions they take in their lives are guided by
them.

> I (Isabelle) recently spoke with Rose, a seventy-six-year-old Greek
> woman who had been suffering for some time with hip pain. She had
> not complained about the pain and tried to ignore it, saying to herself,
> "Well, what do you expect when you are old", until one day she
> collapsed in the street. In hospital, she was told that she had
> osteoarthritis and needed a hip replacement. Rose said, "I could not
> believe it. I thought I would just have to put up with this, that pain is

part of life now at my age. But they tell me I should not be having pain
. . . that it is treatable."

Rose's attitude to her pain had been influenced by what we
would describe as the "loss" discourse of ageing. This discourse
holds that as we age, we will inevitably lose physical and cognitive
abilities, and that pain, poor mobility, cognitive decline, and low
mood are all part of the normal process of getting old. Such discourses can become embedded into the fabric of organizations too,
contributing to institutional ageism. We noticed that referrals of
older people to our service for help with low mood were infre-
quent. When we discussed this with primary care staff, many told
us, "It is normal to feel low in old age", or "Yes, I see a lot of un-
happy old people—that's part and parcel of growing old". Since
then we have set up training to primary care staff aimed at challenging the discourse of loss, thereby helping practitioners recognize low mood as something for which an older person could
receive help, rather than just as an accepted part of getting older.
Initially, we offered a day of workshops for primary care staff to
launch our training pack aimed at recognizing low mood in older
age. This pack contained examples of questions to ask the older
person, as well as possible referral routes once low mood had been
identified. Since then, we have found that ongoing support in the
form of training sessions to district nurses, whose caseloads are
largely made up of older people, and supervision for community
matrons, who supervise district nurses, has been more successful in
increasing appropriate referral rates to our psychology service for
older people struggling with low mood.

Discourses about sexuality

I (Isabelle) was in a multi-disciplinary meeting. A colleague was
discussing his assessment of a male client, whom he described as
"never been married". I wondered if this colleague was equating
"never been married" to "never had a significant relationship", and
was, therefore, not allowing for the possibility that the client may have
been gay. I was struck by how much more sexuality was talked about
in my previous adult mental health work setting, compared to the older
adults setting. Therefore, I asked about "other significant relationships

that this man may have had, with either men or women". My colleague then recalled that the client had mentioned a "male friend", and was clearly curious to find out more about this relationship.

We are all likely to get lured into dominant discourses about old age. The example above reflects the dominant view of older people as asexual or heterosexual. This widely held view, which generates many assumptions informing how we talk and act with older people, can inhibit our curiosity about important aspects of their lives, such as sexuality. In this example, I (Isabelle) was able to ask a question that challenged assumptions and opened space for other descriptions of that older man to emerge. The client subsequently had different conversations with my colleague, since a curiosity about this older person's relationships had been kindled. It turned out this older man had had many sexual relationships in his life, and had been living with his male partner until that partner's recent death. The subsequent conversations invited different descriptions of this man that reflected more of the complexities of his life.

Older people might face a double stigma, arising, for example, from ageist and heterosexist/homophobic attitudes within society, or even triple discrimination for those older people who may come from an ethnic minority background (Berger, 1984; Kehoe, 1986). As practitioners, we try to remain mindful of replicating discourses that offer "thin" descriptions of older people's lives in order to honour the many different facets of the person. Thus, we hope to help people to live and tell their preferred versions of their selves.

Challenging discourses that diminish identities

I (Isabelle) was meeting Priscilla, a seventy-seven-year-old white British woman, in a large, cluttered room off a hospital medical ward. I struggled to make a space for her hospital wheelchair, and turned my chair to face her. Priscilla told me that she wanted to write to Julian, her boyfriend, thirty-two years her junior, to "know once and for all where I stand." The hospital staff working with Priscilla and Julian had giggled when talking about Priscilla's relationship with her "toy-boy", who was widowed and had two young children to support. They believed he was financially abusing her. He had apparently taken her pension book and broken off all contact with Priscilla when this was discovered by her social worker. In conversation with Priscilla, I found myself thinking that her relationship with Julian had ended because Julian no longer had access to her finances, and that there was therefore no point in Priscilla trying to contact Julian as he would not be interested in her any more. The conversation that followed included my asking, "What ideas do you have about why Julian has not written to you? . . . What would your social worker say about why he hasn't written? . . . What do you think might have given the social worker this idea?"

In this conversation I got drawn into the story of the hospital staff and society in general that younger men who go out with much older women are "gold diggers" and only interested in them for their money. It connects to common beliefs that older people are not sexually active, and that older women cannot be sexually attractive (Gergen, 1990), thus there must be another (for example, financially exploitative) motive for a younger man to be interested in an older woman. These discourses are so strong that they drew me into asking questions that had no useful therapeutic effect. In response, Priscilla adopted a defensive position, justifying her relationship with Julian. For example, she told me that she thought the social worker did not like Julian, and had "no business looking into my financial affairs".

The conversation was going nowhere, I was not sure what to do next and Priscilla seemed to be growing irritable. I took these cues as an alarm bell, an indication that I needed to do something different. Therefore I started to reflect on the position I was taking and the discourses informing my questions by asking myself, "What ideas or whose voice do I privilege when asking these questions?" This helped me notice how I, too, had become attached to the "gold diggers" discourse so that I could not understand why Julian was interested in Priscilla. Once I was aware that I had become drawn into these discourses, I was able to reflect on the effect of my questions and to notice that they had positioned Priscilla to have to justify her relationship with Julian, thereby closing opportunities for Priscilla to tell more life-enhancing stories that could offer ways forward. We have found Cecchin and colleagues' ideas about prejudices to be particularly useful in helping us in these sorts of situations (Cecchin, Lane, & Ray, 1994). They suggest that we all have prejudices, some of which might be useful to the client, but that we are not able to use these as potential resources unless we become aware of them. Once we are able to look at where our ideas have come from, either as I did above, or through challenges from our colleagues, we can then become more distant and less "loyal" to these ideas. Only then are we able to make useful judgements about how helpful they may be to our clients in a particular situation.

> Having noted the constraining effect of my prejudices on our conversation, I took a more curious (Cecchin, 1987) position, asking Priscilla, "What were you hoping for by writing to Julian again?" Priscilla said that she wanted to "have a relationship with Julian". I went on to ask, "What does this say about what is important to you in your life—what you value?" Priscilla told me that she was a Quaker, explaining that a Quaker "sees God in everyone and so I also see God in Julian." Priscilla did "not want to be the sort of person who is cynical about everyone . . . sees the worst in everyone. It is easy to see bad in people, but I don't want to do that all the time. If you do that, you end up being bitter, and not trusting anyone. How can that make you happy?"

Thus, I came to understand the nature of Priscilla's relationship with Julian from her perspective. Becoming aware of my prejudices about intergenerational intimate relationships, I regained my curiosity to explore the meanings for Priscilla of her relationship with Julian as well as her hopes and plans. As I challenged my prejudices, I also noticed my body language and tone of voice changing towards Priscilla. As I relaxed in my body, I leaned towards Priscilla more and the tone of my voice softened.

My earlier ideas about Priscilla's relationship with Julian had been strongly affected by dominant cultural assumptions about the meaning of older women having relationships with younger men. These assumptions had begun to get in the way of my understanding of Priscilla's experiences and of their relationship. If we privilege our own view or a negative perspective from the dominant culture, we may act to diminish or undermine the identity of the other. By this, we mean that we do not enable the person's preferred versions of himself or herself to emerge, but, rather, we impose a narrow definition of identity on them, which can be dehumanizing. Here, Priscilla was seen by the professional system as an older woman not smart enough to see that Julian was conning her into a relationship with him simply to gain access to her money. She was not seen as a spiritual woman for whom generosity and close relationships were more important than material wealth. In Chapter Three, Eleanor Martin and Joshua Stott offer us a repertoire of practices to help us to stay mindful of our assumptions and to use our self-reflexivity as a resource in our work with older people.

Using language that does not diminish identities

I (Esther) was discussing the assessment report I was due to write with Raymond, a retired civil servant in his early seventies. John, who lived with Raymond, had joined the session since they were both committed to eradicating worries from Raymond's life. Raymond said that he did not want me to mention in the letter that he was gay. He said that it was important to him that he was gay, but that he did not want others, in health settings, to know as it might, although it should not, make a difference to the care he would receive. Tentatively, I asked what Raymond thought of my noting that he was living at home with his "partner". Raymond seemed pleased with this, and pointed out to John, "We've never used the word 'partner' before." John explained to me that they had only used the word "boyfriend". I asked what difference "partner" would make for Raymond. He answered, "It is great— I now have a word for John—it is better at describing our relationship." I turned to John and asked whether he had a similar or different view. John said he was "excited" with this word. He explained that it gave a new meaning to their relationship, since it said something about commitment to each other. The word "partner" opened space for a lively conversation between these two men about the quality and nature of their relationship. At the end, Raymond said, "Thank you for offering me a way to talk about John and me."

Raymond and John belong to a cohort of men who were surrounded by social pressures to be reformed into heterosexual men, where "gay" was seen as deviant, a sign of defectiveness, and was also illegal. They now find themselves surrounded by more liberal, although still largely heterosexist, views. These contexts might have precluded them from developing words other than "boyfriend" to describe their relationship, which is a term that often implies a temporary, less important relationship than the term "partner". The language of "partner" offered them another description, which opened up different ways of making meaning of their relationship and pointed to their commitment to each other.

Heterosexist discourses can shape our language, the meanings we co-create with our clients, and, therefore, also our relationship with our clients. Resisting these dominant discourses, engaging our curiosity, and paying attention to the language we use can open space for conversations that invite life-enhancing stories. There are many different words we can use to tell one story and, depending on the language we use, new meanings and possibilities can arise. John and Raymond experienced the offer of a new language as enriching of their identities and relationship.

Our conversation with Mr and Mrs Jackson also illustrates how important it is for us to be mindful of generational influences on language in relation to race.

> Mr and Mrs Jackson had come to Britain from the West Indies in the 1950s. They had both worked extremely hard and raised three sons, who were all successfully employed. They came to see us because there were "bad problems in the marriage" ever since Mr Jackson had started urging his wife to return home, whereas she wanted to "stay where the family is . . . close to good friends . . . watch the grandchildren grow up one day". In our second meeting, the couple began to argue noisily in response to Mr Jackson's question to his wife, "What has this country ever offered us?" Every time Mrs Jackson said, "It has been good to us and our children", Mr Jackson responded by clicking his tongue and sucking his teeth. I (Esther) asked, "In the fifties, did this country treat black men differently from black women—or was it the same?" Mrs Jackson seemed to flinch at my question and Mr Jackson explained, "She doesn't like it when people call us black. She finds it insulting."

In both our generations, the word "black" is viewed as empowering. Our contemporaries educated in Britain usually hold the view that ethnicity is an important context for all of us and failure to pay attention to and name racial difference reflects a denial of our different privileges, or "colour blindness". We are also aware that in Mr and Mrs Jackson's generation, and in the generations of our grandparents, there was an idea that it was polite to avoid using the term "black" in relation to people of colour, and that drawing attention to differences in ethnicity was seen as racism. Many of the older people we meet still use terms such as "coloured people" to describe "black people", with the intention of being polite, whereas this term is nowadays often viewed as patronizing or diminishing the importance of the person's ethnicity. Mindful that a word or phrase can work to enhance the identity of a member of one generation while diminishing the identity of a member from a different generation, we try to take care to check with our older clients what words they prefer to use and what meanings they give to words we use. Sometimes, we reflect with our older clients on the changes in language over time and then ask them, "What words would you prefer that I use to describe your culture / your background / where you come from? Would you include your ethnicity / race / culture in a description of yourself, in the way younger people do in London these days?"

Working with older people has helped us become more sensitized to the effect on them of particular words. For example, "old codger" is not always seen as an affectionate term, but often experienced as patronizing and belittling. Our witnessing the effect of age and racial discrimination through our contact with older people has helped us to become aware of the discourses that inform our own conversations.

Assuming difference or similarity

Beth, a white, working-class woman in her eighties, opened the door to her flat and let me (Isabelle) in. She slowly made her way back to her armchair using two walking sticks. She sat down and made herself comfortable. I sat in the armchair nearby. This was our fifth meeting. Beth told me that since we last met she had been reflecting on what might be contributing to the "depression" she had experienced over many years. She said, "There have been many aspects of my past that I feel ashamed of, particularly how I behaved while married to my husband. I am not sure whether I want to go into detail, but I had sexual encounters with women. My husband never knew and I am not sure whether I can talk more to you about this as you are a middle-class woman who would, quite understandably, feel that what I did was wrong."

My (Isabelle's) accent, posture, and appearance may have told Beth that I am a white middle-class woman. Beth may also have assumed that I am heterosexual, and possibly married. However, I must also have communicated something else for Beth to risk talking to me about the differences she perceived between us. In our previous conversations, we seem to have created together a safe enough context, along the lines Josh Stott and Eleanor Martin describe in Chapter Four, for Beth to begin to discuss her "sexual encounters with women". It is probable that, like Beth, the older people with whom we work will make assumptions about our beliefs and values based on their perceptions of our class, age, culture, ethnicity, gender, sexuality, and religion. Therefore, we are mindful of what and how we might communicate about ourselves, both directly and indirectly. We reflect on the possible effect we have on others, how they might perceive us, and how this might affect our therapeutic relationship.

As well as communicating with words, we communicate a great deal with our bodies, our postures, our accents, and our clothes. So we "cannot not communicate" (Watzlawick, Beavin Bavelas, & Jackson, 1967, p. 51) something about who we are to clients. Some professions or services have dress codes or a uniform, with the intention of presenting a neutral style that can reflect a white, middle-class, professional culture, which may or may not fit for all our clients. Boyd-Franklin (1989) talks about the non-verbal cues, or "vibes", that we give off through our appearance, colour, class, clothing, language, and accent, as well as what we communicate about ourselves in terms of our genuine respect for, and warmth towards, our clients. Some older clients from minority ethnic groups have specifically told us that they have learnt to become very attuned to these "vibes" that tell them whether or not they can trust a white person. People who have experienced prejudice or critical judgements learn to rely not just on the verbal content of an exchange, but also on non-verbal cues. Therefore, how we listen and our willingness and interest to hear the clients' viewpoints tell them whether or not our words are spoken with genuine warmth and respect, by someone who truly wants to connect with them.

O'Brian (1990) and Boyd-Franklin (1989) point to the risks of assuming that we share common beliefs, ideas, or meanings with clients who may appear similar to us, for example in terms of race, class, culture or gender. Assuming similarity without checking has often stifled our curiosity so that we have found ourselves believing we already know what the clients believe, or even what they might say, based only on our own personal experience.

> I (Isabelle) was visiting Sarah, a sixty-six-year-old white, middle-class woman, in her small stylish flat. Her bookshelves told me of a woman who enjoyed art, theatre, and cooking. Several aspects of her story connected with my own personal experience. Like me, Sarah was one of three sisters, was a single mother to her daughter, Jessica, and had been a professional woman. In this particular session, I had been asking Sarah about the effects of her retirement on her. I was surprised that Sarah, although polite, appeared reticent to engage with my questions. In a later session, I learnt that Sarah "was forced to work after separating from my husband" and always resented this. She was able to let me know that she had initially felt "embarrassed" to admit resenting work, since "you obviously value your career highly".

Focusing on the similarities between us, I had assumed that work would be important to Sarah, as it has been to me in my life. My assumption left Sarah feeling "embarrassed" about her own relationship to work and constrained our earlier conversation. Thus, we can see how perceived similarity can reduce our curiosity with the risk of interfering in our conversations with our clients. Through these sorts of conversations with older people like Sarah, we have learnt to check our assumptions when we begin to feel that we know too well how clients will respond to particular questions.

Talking about difference

Earlier in this chapter, Bob and Beth took the initiative in raising the difference between themselves and us, thus enabling us to further explore the possible implications of our differences. When clients do not name differences that seem to be constraining our work together, we sometimes invite them to bring forth the different contexts informing their perspectives with questions such as, "Where does the idea that . . . come from?", or "Who else sees it that way?" Asking Beth, "Where did the idea come from that I would see sexual encounters with women as wrong?" opened space for her to tell me (Isabelle) more about the judgements and prejudices she had encountered among middle-class people and married women in relation to homosexuality. Introducing the context of time by asking, "Do you think these ideas are the same today as when you were a younger woman, fifty years ago?", opened space for Beth to reflect on what she called "changing values" and to tell me that "people are more open-minded these days." Beth also shared her ideas on the kinds of relationships she assumed were legitimate in middle-class and working-class contexts. Naming Beth's view that "sexual encounters with women is wrong" as "an idea" implicitly suggested that it was only one view, rather than the "truth", and that there may be other, alternative views. Hence, we were able to go on to examine whether or not Beth saw these "ideas" as helpful, or whether there were other perspectives that might help her to go on with her life in a more positive way.

We have also ourselves introduced or named the contexts of difference we consider might be influencing our relationship with clients. For example, we have introduced gender into our conversation by asking, "What difference would it make to our conversations if I were a man/woman? What might I be understanding differently?" And we have introduced the context of age with questions such as "If I were a similar age to you, how do you think our talking together would go?" Recognizing that certain conversations may be more difficult because of power differences, our intention here is to acknowledge the power difference between the client and ourselves, the practitioners, in terms of age, gender, and class as well as to show our interest in the client's views. In doing so, we also invite clients into an expert position about their own context so that we can learn from their experience (Anderson & Goolishian, 1992). We hold the view that differences in power between practitioner and client can never be totally eradicated, but that transparency about our difference, and the stance of seeing the client as the expert, might work towards reducing this. It may also go some way towards acknowledging that therapeutic encounters take place within power imbalances supported by larger, culturally dominant stories about class, sexual orientation, race, and gender.

Talking about discrimination

Esther had been talking with Rajiv, a slim man originally from India, in his late sixties. Rajiv had told Esther that he often felt a "sadness" which was "like a vacuum that you slip into and cannot get out of." Esther was aware of the struggle Rajiv had had since arriving in Britain forty years before. He had come from a wealthy family in India who were respected in their community. Since living in Britain, Rajiv had been unable to secure permanent employment and now depended on his children to support him. Later in the session, mindful of the wide-spread insidious effects of racism, Esther asked Rajiv, "Has discrimination played a part in your sadness?"

While both Bob and Beth, earlier in this chapter, were able to raise differences between themselves and their psychologist, we have found that clients from ethnic minority groups who are different in colour from the practitioner usually do not refer explicitly to racial difference because of concern about the practitioner's reaction to this. Laszloffy and Hardy (2000) emphasize the practitioner's responsibility to raise discrimination and its connection with issues that clients bring. Above, Esther does not only note the racial and cultural difference between herself and Rajiv, she goes further to "name the unnamed" (*ibid*.), "discrimination". In so doing, she indicates to Rajiv her willingness to talk about racism, giving him legitimacy to address discrimination.

As well as talking about difference with older people, we believe it is essential to talk about discrimination with people from marginalized groups. We share Jones' (2002) view that practitioners are powerful within the therapeutic relationship, and that what we choose to address, respond to, or ignore indicates to the client what we view as important or irrelevant. White (1993) saw therapy as a political act, in which we are always taking a position and, therefore, can never be neutral. We also hold the view that it is our responsibility, not the client's, to initiate talk of discrimination, as the client may not feel safe or entitled to do so.

I (Isabelle) had been meeting with a group of staff at a mental health nursing home for some time. On this occasion the small room felt quite full. Four of the five members of staff were black. They wanted to talk about Gladys, who had twice hit out and called black staff "dirty nigger". When I used the term "racial abuse" to inquire about the effects this was having on the two staff, they at first brushed this off with comments like, "Oh, lots of them are like this", and "She doesn't really know what she is doing . . . she has dementia."

I (Isabelle) used the term "racial abuse" to communicate to this staff group that a conversation about discrimination was legitimate. I felt that unless I openly witnessed the racism and directly communicated my willingness and interest to talk about it with this group of staff, they could have assumed that it was not permissible to talk with me about it or that I condoned it. Witnessing racial abuse or discrimination involves certain practices which Weingarten (2005) says are intended to "re-humanize" individuals, to restore dignity and compassion. As a witness to these experiences of discrimination, I was committed first to hearing details of the racial abuse to develop a fuller understanding of the staff's experiences, including the effects on them and meanings they had made of these experiences. I responded by being curious rather than being neutral (Cecchin, 1987), acknowledging that their experiences were difficult, needed to be addressed, and that it was legitimate to talk about them.

> I went on to ask about the kind of support offered to staff following "racial abuse" and about the policies of the nursing home. No one seemed to know what policies might exist. As I asked more about support, I felt more connected with the staff and the group became more animated. In a raised voice, Dolores, a black carer, complained, "I did not come into this job to be treated like this . . . I could not talk to Gladys afterwards because she upset me so much . . . I was angry." I noticed that a timid younger Asian woman, Shamila, seemed to want to talk. With encouragement she talked hesitantly about how she felt differently, that she "did not take those words personally". Another black woman, Margaret, said, "What I would like is if someone just said, 'Are you OK?' afterwards. That would feel good."

The naming of the racial abuse helped to acknowledge the role it played in the work of the staff with their older clients. It also widened the focus of our conversation in the group from not only "how do we deal with the problem of Gladys" to also include "how do we deal with the problem of the racism that we face at work". Widening the focus in this way opened space for different ways of approaching the situation to become available to the staff group.

While it is impossible to know whether this group would have spoken about racial abuse if I, a white practitioner, had not raised the issue myself, Hardy (2001) leads us to consider that they were unlikely to have done so since they may have felt it not safe to talk about these issues with a white woman who they possibly deemed would not understand or might negatively judge them. Or they might have felt it was not legitimate to discuss racism in a case discussion group; that it was a personal issue, or something which just "comes with the job", as Hilda, a support worker, commented.

The staff expressed many different views on how they should respond to Gladys, what they were entitled to feel, and how to understand her behaviour towards them. Sometimes, we find ourselves grappling with competing or contradictory beliefs that we hold either within ourselves or between team members. For example, staff members in this team held all or some of the following views: "Gladys has no right to treat me like this"; "This is not personal, Gladys cannot help it"; "It is my right to be treated with respect", "It is the dementia, I have to let it go". If competing perspectives like these create difficulties for people to the extent that they are unsure how to go on, we find it useful to ask questions such as, "Where does the idea come from that this is part of the job?", or "Where does the discomfort come from in not saying anything, when she says this to you?" These sorts of questions can begin to make visible the different contexts individuals are speaking from.

> When I (Isabelle) asked Gladys's staff team where their different opinions came from, Dolores told me, "My family . . . it is our family duty to take care of the old people." Hilda nodded in agreement when Margaret said, "It is my culture . . . we have a special respect for old people." Louise, the only white carer present, added, "And it is our professional duty to protect people with dementia—they are vulnerable adults." Shamila, the youngest team member, said, "That is why we must just put up with it—it is not their fault", to which Louise insisted, "But we have to stand up to discriminatory practice in the work place. I have been on a course lately and saying nothing is colluding with institutional racism."

Many different contexts informed the viewpoints staff held about how to be with Gladys. When they drew on their family, cultural, and professional contexts, they saw it as their responsibility to "care for and protect" older people with dementia and, hence, their duty to "put up with" the racial abuse. When they focused on the context of "justice" or "antidiscriminatory" policies, they saw it as their duty to "stand up to" racism, a position that Louise, the white staff member, felt obligated to uphold. Therefore, I (Isabelle) faced the challenge of managing these different contexts. How could I enable the staff to fulfil their professional duty and moral commitment towards care and protection of Gladys, whom they saw as a vulnerable old lady with dementia, and also uphold their own rights to be treated with respect and dignity in the workplace? By opening space for them to voice their different perspectives, identifying the contexts informing their different views and inviting them to reflect on the opportunities and constraints of following the different perspectives, the staff were able to come up with new ideas, such as, "I am here to care for Gladys, and I also need to let her and my managers know that it is not OK for anyone to call me insulting names", and "We can also take care of each other, like checking 'Are you OK?' when an abusive incident happens again".

Addressing difference and discrimination in context

Rather than addressing differences such as culture or sexuality in isolation, as if they were in some way problematic in and of themselves, we weave these contexts into our conversations, connecting them with the issues for which the client is seeking help (Laszloffy & Hardy, 2000). The following two examples have been powerful learning experiences for us.

> I (Isabelle) met with James, a sixty-seven-year-old gay man. He told me he had had many experiences of psychotherapy, "all negative" because the psychotherapists "always concentrated on my sexuality as if that was the problem." James told me his "sexuality has never been a problem for me . . . it is the OCD (obsessive compulsive disorder) I have a problem with."

> When I (Isabelle) met with Doris, an eighty-one-year-old white British woman for the first time, she told me that her previous therapist had asked her many times, "What difference would it make if I were a

similar age to you?" Doris wondered whether this therapist had difficulty working with older clients, as she seemed unduly concerned
about it. I was somewhat baffled by this, as I had enormous respect for
this practitioner and would have thought that her questions about age
could be useful and important. I refrained from asking more questions
about age at that time. In a later session, when Doris was talking about
difficulties with her neighbours, I explored the effects of age discrimination on her in relation to this issue. Doris confirmed that she saw age
discrimination as pertinent to her difficulties with her neighbours, but
she said she was concerned that I would have thought she had a "chip
on my shoulder if I had put it like this."

James and Doris, above, show us the importance of connecting
our talk about difference and discrimination to the issue that the
older person has brought for help, rather than raising difference
and discrimination in isolation or in a mechanical fashion. In this
way, the conversation is more likely to be useful to the older person.
Doris's experience with her previous therapist also speaks to us
about the importance of timing. Monitoring the effects of our
conversation can help us notice whether and how clients engage
with the conversation, thereby helping us "tune into" what our
client would see as the most important context informing the
conversation at a particular moment. It seems that Doris's first therapist privileged the context of age without checking what was the
most important agenda for her. Honouring what Doris wanted to
talk about opened space for me (Isabelle) to consider whether age
or ageism were relevant to the issues Doris most wanted to address.

I (Isabelle) went on to ask Doris, "As a woman in her forties, I
haven't yet had first hand experience of age discrimination. Is it OK
for me to ask you a bit more about your experience so I can understand more about the effects this is having on you? Perhaps it will
help us make some more sense of what is happening for you with
your neighbours?"

Here I (Isabelle) raised the age difference between Doris and me
in relation to the experience of age discrimination she had already
acknowledged. I also related my question about discrimination to
her agenda, "upset with the neighbours". By situating ourselves in,
and naming, the context we are acting out of in this way, we are
attempting to reduce the power differential between our clients and
us. We are communicating that, like them, we, too, are people

coming from our personal contexts and not just from our professional contexts. In this way, we try to invite the client to be the "expert on their lives"; we acknowledge the local expertise of both client and professional.

In conclusion

Writing this chapter has reminded us of times we have attempted to attend respectfully and sensitively to difference, and also of the opportunities for this we have missed with clients or colleagues. We hope that our chapter has inspired you to approach difference not as a problem or obstacle, but as a chance to explore and appreciate the diversity that our clients bring, facilitate them in becoming experts in their own lives, and, ideally, begin to bridge the gap between us.

We share a number of ideas here that we have found useful in our conversations with clients about difference. We hope that there may be something in these ideas that might spark new thoughts and conversations for you, and lead you to experiment and enrich your practice in this area. By no means do we always get this right, and we expect occasional "clumsiness" in our practice (Burnham & Harris, 1996). We continue to try things out and to learn from others, particularly from feedback from our clients. We think that by trying things out, which might not be perfect to begin with, and responding to client feedback, we can become more smooth and elegant in our practice.

References

Anderson, H., & Goolishian, H. (1992). The client is the expert: a not-knowing approach to therapy. In: S. McNamee & K. J. Gergen (Eds.), *Therapy as Social Construction* (pp. 30–38). London: Sage.

Berger, R. M. (1984). Realities of gay and lesbian ageing. *Social Work*, *Jan–Feb*: 57–62.

Boyd-Franklin, N. (1989). *Black Families in Therapy: A Multi-Systems Approach*. New York: Guildford Press.

Burnham, J., & Harris, Q. (1996). Emerging ethnicity: a tale of three cultures. In: K. N. Dwivedi & V. P. Varma (Eds.), *Meeting the Needs of Ethnic Minority Children: A Handbook for Professionals* (pp. 130–156). London: Jessica Kingsley.

Cecchin, G. (1987). Hypothesising, circularity and neutrality revisited: an invitation to curiosity. *Family Process, 26*: 404–413.

Cecchin, G., Lane, G., & Ray, W. A. (1994). *The Cybernetics of Prejudices in the Practice of Psychotherapy.* London: Karnac.

Geertz, C. (1973). Thick description: toward an interpretive theory of culture. In: *The Interpretation of Cultures: Selected Essays* (pp. 3–30). New York: Basic Books.

Gergen, M. M. (1990). Finished at 40: women's development within the patriarchy. *Psychology of Women Quarterly, 14*: 471–493.

Hardy, K. V. (2001). African American experience and the healing of relationships. In: D. Denborough (Ed.), *Family Therapy: Exploring the Field's Past, Present and Possible Futures* (pp. 47–56). Adelaide: Dulwich Centre Publications.

Jones, E. (2002). Working with couples. Camden and Islington Mental Health and Social Care Trust Workshop. London.

Kehoe, M. (1986). Lesbians over 65: a triple invisible minority. *Journal of Homosexuality, 12*: 139–152.

Laszloffy, T. A., & Hardy, K. V. (2000). Uncommon strategies for a common problem: addressing racism in family therapy. *Family Process, 39*: 35–50.

O'Brian, C. (1990). Family therapy with black families. *Journal of Family Therapy, 12*(1): 3–16.

Watzlawick, P., Beavin Bavelas, J., & Jackson, D. D. (1967). *Pragmatics of Human Communication: A Study of Interactional Patterns, Pathologies and Paradoxes.* New York: Norton.

Weingarten, K., (2005). Trauma, meaning, witnessing and action: an interview with Kaethe Weingarten by David Denborough. *The International Journal of Narrative Therapy and Community Work, 3 & 4*: 72–76.

White, M. (1993). The politics of therapy. *Human Systems: The Journal of Systemic Consultation & Management, 4*: 19–32.

CHAPTER SEVEN

Moving from problems to possibilities with older people

Alison Milton and Esther Hansen

I n this chapter we explore how we can both listen respectfully to older people's experience of problems *and* invite new conversations about resources, abilities, and hopes for the future in the face of stories that diminish the worth and value of older people. Many of the older people with whom we work have to confront physical, cognitive and social losses. It is not uncommon for our older clients to tell us, "I have lived too long", "This is enough now", "I don't want to have to deal with this at my age", "I would like to die now". An ongoing challenge we face is how to move away from talk that is problem saturated or hopeless to creating space for valuing the older person's skills and abilities and inviting hopes for the future. While this shift can present a challenge with any client, we find that negative stories about old age tend to draw our older clients and us back into problem talk, cloud our hope, and distract us from noticing possibilities.

Negative stories about old age bury abilities and hope

I (Alison) had been meeting for six months with Edgar, seventy-eight, who, with pride, described himself as "a real cockney . . . born within the sound of the Bow Bells". He had originally been referred for help with "depression", which had stopped him going out and taking care of himself. In the past six weeks, Edgar had made considerable progress. He had started visiting the corner shop to buy cigarettes and was taking an interest in others.

As I climbed the stairs in the dark passageway leading to Edgar's flat, I was struck by an acrid smell that seemed unfamiliar and deeply unpleasant. The smell disappeared when I entered Edgar's flat and was overtaken by the more familiar one of stale cigarettes. After half an hour, there was a knock on the door and a tall policeman asked Edgar when he had last seen his ninety-year-old neighbour, who had been found dead in the flat next door. As I was leaving, two policemen at the entrance told me in a matter-of-fact way that the woman had been "lying dead for three weeks and it wasn't pretty". When I next visited Edgar he told me, "That is what is going to happen to me one day."

Since the voice of depression had been absent from Edgar's life for quite some time, I took Edgar's comment, "That is what is going to happen to me one day", to mean that his expectation of the future included being alone, isolated, and of no importance or significance to others, so that even his death might go unnoticed. To clarify, I asked, "Edgar, you said 'that will happen to me one day'. Are you saying this is your expectation of old age?" Edgar replied, "Old age is a bugger . . . nobody wants to be an old man."

This perspective of old age is widely circulated in western cultures and often taken as the "truth". As a consequence, negative stories about old age frequently go unchecked or unnoticed and, because of their hopeless bias, have a powerful effect on the way older people behave and how others behave towards them. We refer to these sorts of stories as "life-diminishing", because we have noticed how they can limit opportunities, diminish abilities, and perpetuate problems by burying accounts and experiences of competency, skills, abilities, and choice, which might otherwise be noticed in an older person's life.

Eileen, eighty-three, a white Irish woman, who had recently been discharged after six weeks on a psychiatric ward for treatment of "depression", was keen to tell me (Esther) about the beginning of her troubles. "One morning last summer my son telephoned to say that Margaret, my daughter, had collapsed and was in hospital. When

I got there, Margaret was lying in bed with all my family around her. I tried to talk to her but she didn't respond. I asked how she could be so ill when she had been fine when I last saw her. I later found out that she had been diagnosed with cancer six months before and that I was the only one not to know. I felt so stupid, like an idiot. She never recovered and died a few days later. They didn't tell me because they thought I would not cope with the news and go to pieces. They must think I am pathetic." I asked Eileen why she thought her family had the idea that she would not cope with the news about the cancer. She replied, "They see me as fragile now and someone who needs protecting."

Eileen's story reflects several life-diminishing discourses about older people, which informed her and her family's view around the time of her daughter's death. These include "older people are fragile", "older people need to be protected", and "older people cannot cope". Eileen, too, had been persuaded by these discourses, and described herself as someone who was "not good for very much these days, as I cannot get about like I used to". The professional system involved in Eileen's care described her as "depressed" and suffering from an "abnormal grief reaction", and these descriptions served further to focus everybody's attention on her problems and difficulties.

Both Eileen and her family had started to live their lives as if these stories of fragility and incompetence were true. For example, she no longer offered advice to her family, nor did they seek it. Eileen withdrew from her grandchildren because she felt she had "no important role in their lives" and she had stopped going out, except to the psychiatric day hospital where she attended on what she referred to as "the day for depressed people". It seemed that Eileen was living her life according to the story that she was "fragile" and no longer had anything to offer to her family. Her life had become dominated by those powerful negative stories about old age that restricted her ability to go on.

Making stories of old age visible

We strive to make these discourses about old age visible to the older person and to others involved, such as family, carers, and practitioners. Our intention is to enable people to see these discourses as just one story among many other possible stories of old age.

> Therefore, when Edgar said, "Old age is a bugger . . . nobody wants to be an old man", I (Alison) asked him, "Who has a different view about old age?" When Edgar replied, "Nobody [has a different view of old age]", I asked, "Have you ever noticed another older person living their life as if old age was not too bad?" After thinking for quite some time, Edgar told me that his neighbour, Jennie, who was in her eighties, always greeted him, always "had a smile for others" and was always "hatching plans". I asked, "What would Jennie make of your ideas about what old age has in store for you?" to which Edgar replied, "She would probably say, 'What load of old nonsense—life is what you make it'."

My questions invited Edgar to become an observer to his own story of old age and ageing. First, I reflected back to him his own words. Then, I went on to invite him to consider alternative stories about ageing, introducing the notion that there is more than one version of old age. Like Edgar, families and carers, too, can be coerced by negative stories about old age. Therefore, I (Esther) went on to invite Eileen to reflect on the stories about old age and protection that were influencing her family's relationship with her.

> Esther: What do you think led Margaret to hold off telling you that she had cancer . . . and for the others to go along with it?
>
> Eileen: She was trying to protect me. They would think I couldn't cope with it, that I'd go to pieces.
>
> Esther: What do you think gave her—them—that idea?
>
> Eileen: I'm old now you know. [A long pause] Or . . . maybe they thought I would fall apart?
>
> Esther: Do you think that one of these views—either that you are old now or that you would fall apart—had more of an influence over the decision not to tell you than the other?
>
> Eileen: No. It was both things. Even before I was depressed, they started treating me differently you know—making decisions without me. Talking about me moving . . . But why would I want to move? I have lived in that house forty-three years.

Esther: When did they start to treat you differently?

Eileen: As soon as I started to show my age. Once I couldn't get around like I used to.

Esther: Where do you think your children might have come across the idea that somehow being older means that you need to be protected or that it becomes harder to cope?

Eileen: Hmmm. I don't know. It has just always been like that for us—in our family.

I (Esther) was intrigued by Eileen's daughter's decision not to tell her about her cancer because, to me, Eileen seemed a wise and stoic woman who had seen a lot of life. Although she was facing some of the physical challenges of ageing, Eileen was managing reasonably well. Wondering what story or view was informing the family's attitude, I asked Eileen, "What do you think might have given Margaret that idea [that you needed protecting]?" My question invited Eileen to become an observer to the discourses informing her family's decision to "protect" her, enabling her to see the effect of these discourses on all of them.

Sometimes we ask where life-diminishing stories come from with questions such as: "Where does the idea (that you wouldn't cope with it) come from?"; "Whose voice do you hear when you/they say that?"; and "What might your age/ethnicity/family say about that?" We have found that inviting people to locate the stories in context in this way opens space for older people and their families to question the validity of these stories and to wonder why they have (unwittingly) allowed themselves to be ruled by them. Because it seemed possible that a number of different contexts, such as Eileen's age or mental health diagnosis, were informing the family's "protection" of Eileen, I asked her which context had "more of an influence". This allowed Eileen and me to reflect on the influence of the family's beliefs about age, and coping in relation to protection.

We do not tell people that they have been influenced by a particular discourse, that their views are wrong, or that their thinking processes are not helpful. Instead, with questions, we invite them to reflect on and evaluate how helpful or unhelpful their stories or beliefs about ageing are to them. Thus, by considering "Where do

you think your children might have come across the idea . . .?",
Eileen was able to reflect, "It has just always been like that for us—
in our family." Locating "protection" of older people within her
family culture enabled Eileen to move away from the view that her
children saw her as "pathetic" to wondering why "It has just
always been like that for us —in our family."

Negative stories about old age bewitch practitioners

We have found that negative stories about ageing influence our
expectations for our work with older people. They particularly
overwhelm us when, as younger, healthier, and more able practitioners, we witness older people suffering loss of physical health or
cognitive abilities. It is difficult to witness our older clients, no
longer able to walk unaided, losing the use of one side of their body
so that they have to rely on carers to wash, or struggling to find the
words to express themselves. Therefore, we try to make our own
discourses about old age visible to ourselves so that we can reflect
on, and stay mindful of, their influence on us.

> I (Esther) was talking with Vera, seventy, in the memory clinic where
> she was being assessed for memory problems and word finding diffi-
> culties that she had been experiencing for the past year. She said, "I've
> lost my girlish laughter . . . There is nothing in life for me any more
> . . . I have always lived life on the crest of the wave . . . now I have noth-
> ing to show for my life . . . it's not going to happen now is it? . . . No
> opportunities to meet someone—not here, not now." Anticipating that
> Vera was about to receive a diagnosis of dementia, I thought sadly to
> myself, "You know. Vera, you are probably right."

I felt that there was nothing I could do or say to help or to
change Vera's situation. This sort of hopelessness tends to overwhelm me most often when the older person has experienced an
enormous life change, such as a stroke or a diagnosis of dementia,
following which they find themselves unable to perform any of the
activities or roles that previously gave their life meaning. Unable to
find "evidence" to counter Vera's negative story of her future, I
joined Vera in her hopelessness. I was "bewitched" (Wittgenstein,
1953, p. 47) by the discourses that devalue the worth of older people

and feed into stories that older people are no longer attractive and have no hope of finding a partner, especially if they have a diagnosis of dementia. Thus, Vera and I had begun to believe that these stories were true and to behave as if they were. As a consequence, I felt unable to talk about a different future with Vera where she might find something in life for her and was tempted to move our conversation away from talking about the future. However, mindful of the strong pull towards hopelessness that a (in Vera's case possible) dementia diagnosis can have on me, I was able to stay with the exploration of Vera's future a bit longer.

Esther (using Vera's own words): If it were "going to happen now" for you, Vera, what would that look like? What would be happening?

Vera: I'd be with someone, share things with someone and grow old with them.

Esther: Where does the idea that "it is not going to happen now" for you come from?

Vera: Well it won't, will it? It just doesn't.

Esther: Believing that it won't happen—or doesn't happen—what effect is that having on you?

Vera: Well, I've stopped trying, stopped looking . . . and stopped taking care of how I look.

Esther: Who has a different way of thinking about this? Who might think that it will still happen?

Vera: I'm not sure . . . nobody I know. No one expects to meet a man at my age.

Esther: What would happen if you were to have a different view on this—or to hope that it might still happen for you?

Vera: Well, I'd do my hair at least.

Chapters Three and Six in this book show how we can unwittingly perpetuate ideas that are diminishing of older people's abilities or opportunities if we allow our assumptions and beliefs to guide us without questioning them. I was aware that I felt anxious about asking Vera about the future for fear that my questions, and her responses, would serve only to consolidate the problem further and convince us further that our story was true and Vera was destined to spend the rest of her life alone. However, questioning my assumptions allowed me to consider that there were still opportunities for Vera and that she might find friendship, intimacy, companionship, and comfort from others in many different ways. We have found it useful to ask ourselves the following sorts of questions to free us from the bewitching effects of our negative stories of ageing: "How would I respond or what would I be interested in asking about if this person were thirty or forty years younger?", or "What would I want to ask about if Vera did not have a diagnosis of dementia?", or "As a younger person, what assumptions do I have about the sorts of relationships that are meaningful/worth pursuing?" This (self) exploration helped me become an observer to my own assumptions and freed me from the previous feeling of paralysis, thereby opening space for a discussion about a more hopeful future.

Resurrecting former stories about ability

As well as making visible the discourses that hide older people's abilities, we try to resurrect former "ability stories" (Lang & McAdam, 1997) to reconnect the older person with their own resources and reignite hope. Therefore, I (Esther) invited Eileen to think beyond or outside of the context of old age when I revisited her family's decision not to tell her about her daughter's cancer diagnosis. I asked Eileen, "What do you imagine might have happened if you weren't—as you put it—'old now'?" to invite her to tell a different story about herself. I hoped she might draw on past stories that gave a version of her competent self before beliefs about age came to dictate that she be seen as "fragile" by her family and "pathetic" by herself. We notice that people often become more engaged and lively when telling us positive or preferred stories about themselves. Eileen immediately brightened in response to my question and defiantly answered, "I'd have been the first to know. I'd have been there. I'd have been the one to look after her." Her certainty and clarity, which were in such contrast to how she had been speaking up to then, pointed me to the significance of the ability to "look after" for Eileen. Therefore, I went on to explore why she would have been the one to look after her daughter and what skills or qualities she had to offer.

Not only do we listen out for abilities hidden by negative stories of the older person, we also create openings for ability stories of the older person to be told. Therefore, I asked Eileen, "Do you think your family knows you can still look after your children—that you could cope with being the first to know?", deliberately implying that she still had the abilities to care for her children and cope with distress. This question stopped Eileen in her tracks somewhat. Until then, our conversation had been problem focused, which was more familiar to her in the psychiatric context in which I was seeing her. I noted that there was surprise in her voice when she replied, "I don't know. I think they have forgotten that I can. They have got all caught up in this me-being-ill-thing", with an intonation that suggested to me that Eileen, too, had forgotten about her abilities. I went on to reconnect Eileen with stories of her abilities and skills.

> Esther: What are they—those abilities—what have your family forgotten that you are capable of?
>
> Eileen: Well, things like being good at taking care of everyone, being a good cook.
>
> Esther: Taking care of everyone, being a good cook . . . who was most aware of those abilities, who appreciated them the most do you think?
>
> Eileen: Margaret—she loved my cooking . . . and my son.

Eileen began to see that she had not actually lost her abilities, but they were being overlooked by her and the family because of the dominant, problem-focused story that was being told about her being both "fragile" and "depressed". This served as a helpful starting point to reconnect Eileen with stories of her abilities and skills.

Separating the person from the problem

For people like Edgar, Eileen, and Vera, negative stories about old age affect the way they see themselves and are seen by others. When older people also have a diagnosis, such as depression or dementia, given to them by experts in positions of power, little space remains for more positive aspects of their identity, such as their values, experience, knowledge, and abilities, to show through. For example, nobody noticed Eileen's ability to make shopping lists for her son and remember bills that needed paying. Vera, previously appreciated for her unique and colourful way of dressing, was described, with concern, as "looking increasingly dishevelled" and "odd" because she was "probably dementing", although her dress style had not changed in years. Therefore, we try to separate the older people we work with from the problems affecting them to enable them, and others, to see that the problems are not an intrinsic part of their make-up or identity, but, rather, something influencing their life at that time. I (Esther) involved Eileen in this sort of externalizing conversation (White, 1988, 2006).

> Eileen: I am so depressed today, I almost didn't come.
>
> Esther: How is it that you did come?
>
> Eileen: I wanted to see the doctor for my review.
>
> Esther: Does *the* depression often try to stop you from doing something you want to do?
>
> Eileen: All the time.

Rather than using Eileen's language, "so depressed", I (Esther) introduced depression as a separate entity, referring to it instead as "the depression", thus beginning the process of externalizing the problem (White, 1988, 2007). With my next question, "Does the depression often try to stop you from doing something you want to do?", I spoke of the depression as if it had a life of its own, not part of, but separate from, Eileen: it was influencing her, affecting her, doing things to her. Eileen's response, "All the time", spoken with considerable defiance, suggested to me that she was beginning to see "the depression" as not part of her make-up or identity, but, rather, an unwelcome interference in her life. Therefore, I went on to "map the effects" (White, 1992, 2006) of the interfering depression on Eileen's life.

> Esther: So the depression tries to stop you from doing things you want to do "all the time", is that right?
>
> Eileen: Yes, I'm so depressed, I cannot really do anything.

Esther: What sort of things does the depression try to stop you from doing?

Eileen: It stops me from going to the shops, playing with my grandchildren, and cooking.

Esther: These things the depression is stopping you from doing, are they things that you miss?

Eileen: Yes, especially the cooking.

Esther: How long has the depression been getting in the way of cooking?

Eileen: Since my daughter died or perhaps a bit before that . . . I'm not sure.

Through mapping the effect of the problem on Eileen's enjoyment of life, I began to hear about other aspects of Eileen's identity that were important to her: for example, that she was a cook, a playful grandmother, and liked to go to the shops. Even though we continued to talk about the problem, I began to get more of a sense of the type of person Eileen was and who she would like to be; someone who was somewhat different from the person sitting in front of me in a psychiatric day hospital. This information enabled me to generate hypotheses about what developments might be of importance to Eileen and I imagined we might explore these further at a later stage. In addition, I hoped that my questions and interest would remind Eileen about other aspects of her identity of which she was proud and with which she wanted to reconnect.

Esther: Has "the depression" that has stopped you doing the things you enjoy been around for some time?

Eileen: Yes.

Esther: And when it first arrived in your life, what did you call it then, did you have a name for it? Or a picture of it in your head?

Eileen: I am not sure, I cannot really remember. That is the trouble.

Esther: What effect does it tend to have on you, when it is around?

Eileen: I feel it has muddled my thinking, I sometimes feel so confused . . .

Esther: So, it gives you a muddled feeling, like being confused?

Eileen: Mmm. . . . It feels like it is too difficult to think, or decide on things . . . or know what to do, so sometimes I end up doing nothing.

Esther: If we talk about it as the "muddle and confusion" does that sum it up? Is that a good description or name for it?

Eileen: Quite good, yes. My son and neighbour call it my "nit wit days".

Esther: And what do you make of that name, do you like it?

Eileen: Not much, no. Although it says it all.

Inviting Eileen to name and characterize (White, 2007) the problem in her own words further enabled her to view the depression as outside of herself rather than as an intrinsic part of her being. Thus, I was able to engage with Eileen's unique knowledge, understanding and experience of the problem, which together we named as "the muddle and confusion". By drawing on her own expertise and experience and using her own language, Eileen was able to draw a distinction between the concerns ("the muddle and confusion", as she named them), the psychiatric diagnosis or label of "depression", and her children's negative attribution of "nitwit days".

As clinical psychologists, we have been trained to ask questions and listen for symptoms that could be given a diagnosis or label. Therefore, deconstructing a problem (White, 1992) in this way is quite different. It can be tempting to revert to a diagnostic framework, particularly as we work in community mental health teams, which require a diagnosis for clients to be eligible to receive a service. When our older clients have suffered physical problems that are visible and irreversible, we particularly find ourselves pulled towards locating the problem inside the older person, for example, "her stroke", or "she has Alzheimer's Disease". Reminding ourselves that the "problem is the problem; the person is not the problem" (White, 1988) has helped us to go on to explore the effects of the problem on the lives of the older people. When I (Esther) found myself pulled by a possible diagnosis of dementia towards a problem saturated view of Vera, I reminded myself "Vera is not the problem; the problem is the problem". Hence, I went on to question my assumption that the memory difficulties or "possible dementia" was the problem for Vera and to learn from Vera that "hopelessness" and "loss of confidence" were her names for the problem, that they stopped her from going out and meeting people, and it was hopelessness and confidence that Vera wanted to focus on in our meetings.

For most of the older people we work with, this process of externalizing and mapping the effect of the problem on the person's life and relationships takes time, since the client usually reverts to internalizing talk such as "I am depressed", "my depression", "I have depression" several times before seeing and experiencing the problem as separate from their selves. This can particularly be the case when the problem has been present in the older person's life for many years and has become intricately involved with their identity and, thereby, bound up with their activity (perhaps attending a day centre), social life (often other people with mental health problems), and support network (such as home carers). If Eileen had replied "All the time" with a sense of defeat at being overwhelmed by the depression, I would have taken care to explore the effect of the problem thoroughly to ensure Eileen felt I had fully understood the extent of her distress while also trying to evoke a sense of hope by enquiring about areas of her life into which the depression had not encroached and so identify a unique outcome (White, 1992; White & Epston, 1990) or exception to the problem (de Shazer, 1985).

Listening for hope and spotting abilities—towards possibilities

I (Alison) was talking with Sofia, a seventy-three-year-old Portuguese woman in her own home. Sofia's breathing was laboured as she talked about the chronic pain from rheumatoid arthritis in her back and the residual left-sided weakness she had been suffering following a stroke a year ago. Sofia had been referred for help with "her low mood" and her GP's concerns that she was "overweight". She told me, "Life is just not how I ever imagined it would be . . . I am always tired . . . in constant pain . . . feeling like I cannot move." I was thinking how terrible this sounded, and asked, "Which areas of your life have been most affected by these problems?" Sofia said, "I no longer care for myself . . . I rely on others for help . . . I can't even get up and get myself a drink or food like I used to," After hearing more about the frustrations Sofia had to endure, I asked, "Which areas of your life are least affected by the problem", to which she replied, "Like I've said, it has ruined everything, there is nothing that hasn't been affected", and went on to reiterate some of the problems she had described earlier. She told me, "The stroke has ruined my life . . . I can't do anything any more." I learnt that in the past she had bought premium bonds for each of her grandchildren when they were born and that she "couldn't even do this now" for her new baby granddaughter. She said, "Not only can I not go to the post office to get the form, but I wouldn't be able to fill the stupid thing in now either. I am a complete failure. What is the point of this?" Then she looked up at me with a wry smile and said, "The only thing I am still good at is moaning about it."

I was aware that I was taking a risk when I asked Sofia, "Which areas of your life are least affected by the problem?", because earlier attempts to move away from the problem had led to her stressing the extent of her difficulties further, as if I needed convincing that her life was so hard. Therefore, I had deliberately asked about the effects of the problem first and spent a considerable amount of time listening respectfully to Sofia's account of her losses. While witnessing Sofia's experience of the problem, I was also listening out for examples in her life, however small, that were unaffected (or less affected) by the problem. Sometimes, older people explicitly mention aspects of their life unaffected by problems, for example, "I still look forward to seeing my friends", or "I can't do anything except watch the TV". When accounts of their life are completely overtaken by problem talk, however, I might explicitly ask, "Which areas of your life are least affected by the problem", as I did with Sofia.

Careful not to assume the meaning of "moaning" for Sofia, I asked, "Is that a good or a bad thing—that you can still moan? Is it something you feel pleased to be able to do?" I was pleased I had checked, since I did not expect Sofia's reply. "Of course! If I couldn't moan I'd go out of my mind. At least I can tell people how it is, how I am, tell them when it hurts. At least I can still talk with people—thank God for that." Evaluating (White, 2007) whether or not "moaning" was a problem for Sofia by asking, "Is it a good thing that you can still moan? Is that something you feel pleased to be able to do?" enabled me to learn how moaning stopped her from "going out of my mind". I also caught a glimpse of what might be important to Sofia, her possible wish to communicate and maintain relationships with others, "At least I can still talk with people—thank God for that."

This encounter with Sofia affected me in two quite different ways. On the one hand, I felt quite choked by her account of her situation. On the other hand, I also felt glimmers of hope, since, embedded in Sofia's comment, I heard something of her values—that generosity towards others and independence were important to her life. "Double listening", both to the problem story and also for abilities, hopes, values, and intentions implicit within the description of the problem, can allow us to bridge the seeming polarity between talking about problems and hearing about abilities (White, 2000). We find this sort of double listening especially useful in our work with older people when the problem story overwhelms our conversations with clients in spite of our efforts to move on from it. Although I was listening to the problem, I was also hearing something about Sofia's preferred self at the same time: that is, who she was and who she would like to be.

As well as listening in a particular way, we also look for actions or events that do not fit with the problem story. When both the older person and ourselves are unable to identify positive developments and we are feeling that all is lost, we appreciate their taken-for-granted skills to which others might not attribute much value. For example we might ask questions such as, "Some people find the depression stops them from even making it to the session—how were you able to make it here today?" We would then go on to explore, "What is it about you that enabled you to come today?" These sorts of question can invite glimpses of abilities that open space for preferred stories of self.

Developing possibility stories

When I next visited Sofia, she had a scarf that she was knitting on her lap. I admired the scarf, to which Sofia replied, "Humph. I hate knitting." Sofia's response made me all the more curious about the scarf and I asked, "Oh—how come you are making it then?" Sofia explained it was for the district nurse because she always complained how cold it was outside when she arrived. Fascinated, I asked, "Sophia, in spite of the pain and the weakness on your left side, you are still doing this?

Why is that?" With a glint in her eye, Sofia said, "It might stop her moaning!" I smiled at this and asked Sofia why she wanted to help the nurse with her moaning. Sofia said, "It is just a thank you because she has been very kind and a real help. I would have liked to do something really nice for her but this will have to do. At least it is something."

I was delighted to find Sofia doing something that definitely did not fit with her story of her "ruined life" in which she was a "complete failure". Therefore, I explored in detail how she was able to knit in spite of the pain, her intentions for undertaking this challenge, and why it was so important to her. Thus, we were able to develop a thicker story that reflected Sofia's abilities and hope.

When older people lose skills, such as their mobility or strength, or resources, such as partners or friends, their participation in activities that they value become more difficult and sometimes impossible. The problem story, "The stroke has ruined my life . . . I can't do anything any more", had distanced Sofia from appreciating that she still was able to be generous to others. Although talking did not change the reality of the physical losses associated with the stroke, it did help her identify other skills (talking with people, knitting, "moaning") that reconnected her to what she valued (generosity) in life.

For all older people, there is a lifetime's wealth of experience from which to draw stories. Therefore, we have access to a considerable time period within which to find problem-free stories from which to learn. When we struggle to find events that do not fit with the problem story from within our ongoing conversation, we try asking about life before the problem. Older people are often more able to talk about their skills and abilities when invited to step outside of diminishing discourses about old age.

In our experience, the interweaving of talking about the problem with fostering the development of preferred ways of being is a process that continues throughout our work with older people. We try to work with our clients towards strengthening skills and abilities to sustain them into the future. Josh Stott and Eleanor Martin discuss in more detail practices such as outsider witnessing (Chapter Three) and spreading the news of positive developments (Chapter Ten) that we, too, have found helpful in this endeavour.

Pacing possibility talk

We sometimes face a dilemma about when to stay with talking about problems and when to move on to talk about developments. We are more likely to feel a pull to stay with the problem when we are swayed by popular discourses that state that we must understand the origins or the cause of the problem in order to be able to solve it.

For me (Alison) the temptation to move too quickly to talking about solutions or developments arises when it is too uncomfortable to hear more about a client's distress, and especially if the older person suggests that life is not worth living. In these cases, I can feel pressured to move things on because I think the client will be safer or more hopeful about life. Similarly, I am aware of steering the conversation away from the problem when I perceive that there has been too little in the way of change and I want to "speed things up", either because I feel under pressure from the client, family, or colleagues, or because I am restricted by the number of sessions my service can offer.

In my earlier meeting with Sofia, I made a judgement that it was not the right time to explore her "preferred self" or previous positive stories of her self as an independent and generous woman. This took considerable restraint on my part because, catching a glimpse of those hidden aspects of Sofia's identity for the first time, I felt almost compelled by enthusiasm to explore them. However, I was aware that my enthusiasm was partly fuelled by my own discomfort with Sofia's distress. I wanted to relieve Sofia of this distress and find solutions that would show her there was a point to life.

From our experience with older people like Sofia, we have learnt that moving on to talk about solutions too quickly might lead to the older person's experiencing us as not appreciating, dismissing, or, at worst, not believing there is a problem. Therefore, we take care to check whether it is time to talk about problems or possibilities. We are sure to take written notes of both the problems and their effects (which we write down in our notes on the right of the page) and all the abilities, resources, hopes, and wishes we hear (which we document on the left of the page) that we might return to when the time is ripe for possibility talk.

Sofia's story of herself as generous and sociable developed in the course of our work together. At a later session, she seemed very pleased when she let me know that the district nurse had been "really pleased" when she received the scarf she had knitted. Just when I thought we were making progress, Sofia said, "What is the point of all this? It doesn't change the fact that I cannot do any of the things I used to do or want to do."

There are times, as with Sofia, when we seem to be making progress, perhaps along one particular line of conversation, and then the whole enormity of the problem threatens to take over again, drawing both ourselves and our clients back to talking about it again. When Sofia queried, "What is the point of all this?", I began to question whether we had developed a story that she did not value, or perhaps it was not "thick" enough to influence the problem story. In this sort of situation, it can feel as if we are to-ing and fro-ing between problem and possibility stories, between respectfully and empathically witnessing the problem and inviting and celebrating developments. Our experience shows us that we need persistence to enable change with older people. This involves staying with the older person as they describe, and we witness, the effects of the problem, and also staying with signs of change.

It is not unusual for us to question whether or not we have done enough or whether further change is possible. It was from this position that I began to question my practice with Sofia and, therefore, took my dilemma about to-ing and fro-ing to supervision. Supervision has helped me identify the times I am liable to move away from problems too quickly, and has also given me confidence to stay with problems. This time, my supervisor gave me some ideas about how to explore with Sofia the path our conversations sometimes took, which offered me new ideas to address the balance.

> The next time Sofia asked "What is the point of all this?", I decided to respond differently and said, "Sofia, I am sorry, because thinking back, I am aware that quite a few times you have asked, 'What is the point of all this?' I don't think I have ever really acknowledged your question. Would it be helpful to talk about whether our conversations here are useful? I would like to make sure that we are talking about what you feel is important."

For me this encounter emphasized the importance of checking with Sofia that our conversation was of use and meaningful to her.

Other questions for evaluating the usefulness of our conversations include: "How are you finding our focusing on the developments you have made?", or "What effect is this way of talking having on you?", or "Would you like to talk more about the developments you have made, how to make progress, or to talk more about what is the point of all this?" Sofia clarified that it was all right to talk about positive aspects of her life, however small, but said that sometimes the problems still overwhelmed her and she had no one else with whom to "get them off my chest". She also clarified that, for her, talking about achievements had never felt comfortable, as she did not like to "come across as bragging", and told me about a strong family belief that "pride comes before a fall". Thus, I was helped to improve my timing with Sofia as our discussion gave us both permission to address the pace at which we talked about developments.

In conclusion

We can often become overwhelmed by dilemmas and problem stories, particularly those that are supported by the negative stories of old age. Writing this chapter has clarified for us the importance of acknowledging the powerful influence that stories about old age can have on our clients, our colleagues, and ourselves. The process of naming and reflecting on these stories has increased our curiosity about them and increased the likelihood that we enquire about and explore them in our work. As we do so, we find ourselves becoming more confident about how to do this and more aware of the importance of doing so. We hope that the chapter provides you, our reader, with similar curiosity and a number of possibilities to explore. We hope that the practices we share in this chapter leave you more optimistic about how to go on in the face of complex problems.

References

de Shazer, S. (1985). *Keys to Solution in Brief Therapy*. London: Norton.
Lang, P., & McAdam, E. (1997). Narrative-ating: future dreams in present living: jottings on an honouring theme. *Human Systems: The Journal of Systemic Consultation & Management*, 8(1): 3–13.

White, M. (1988). The externalising of the problem and the re-authoring of lives and relationships. *Dulwich Centre Newsletter*, Summer: 5–28.

White, M. (1992). Deconstruction and therapy. In: D. Epston & M. White (Eds.), *Experience, Contradiction, Narrative and Imagination. Selected papers of David Epston and Michael White 1989–1991* (pp. 109–152). Adelaide: Dulwich Centre Publications.

White, M. (2000). *Reflections on Narrative Practice: Essays and Interviews.* Adelaide, Australia: Dulwich Centre Publications.

White, M. (2006). Narrative practice with families with children: externalising conversations revisited. In: M. White & A. Morgan (Eds.), *Narrative Therapy with Children and their Families* (pp. –56). Adelaide: Dulwich Centre Publications.

White, M. (2007). *Maps of Narrative Practice.* New York: W. W. Norton.

White, M., & Epston, D. (1990). *Narrative Means to Therapeutic Ends.* Adelaide: Dulwich Centre Publications.

Wittgenstein, L. (1953). *Philosophical Investigations.* Oxford: Blackwell.

CHAPTER EIGHT

Sustaining the ethics of systemic practice in contexts of risk and diagnosis

Glenda Fredman, Sarah Johnson, and Goran Petronic

The sun is streaming into the room. It is hot, as only one window opens and the room is full with seven people. Everyone's attention is riveted on the conversation between Dr L, the psychiatrist, and Joan, aged eighty-two, who is an inpatient on a psychiatric ward. Eleanor, the family therapist, is fascinated. The psychiatrist gently asks Joan a question. Joan says that she must ask Sister Mary before she answers. Everyone is still. Joan listens intently, her head bent. The room is completely silent except for the distant sound of children playing. Joan then says that Sister Mary will allow her to talk to the doctor. The conversation goes on gently and softly in this fashion for the next ten minutes, with Sister Mary consulted each time.

Joan had been living with the voice of Sister Mary intermittently for years. Recently, Sister Mary had strong opinions about what Joan could and should do. Consequently, Joan had stopped eating and was refusing to take medication, which was creating significant concerns for her safety among nursing staff. The psychiatrist's respect, attention, patience, and interest towards both Joan and Sister Mary, enabled Sister Mary to give Joan permission to speak. Eleanor Anderson's memory of this ward round speaks to us of our preferred ways of being with the people with whom we work and resonates with the aesthetics of systemic practice we describe in this book.

The aesthetics of systemic practice

In Chapter One, we identify the assumptions, beliefs, values, and principles, informing the systemic constructionist approach we present in this book. Our ethics and the practices we perform are intricately interwoven into what Lang, Little, and Cronen (1990) call the aesthetics of systemic practice. Working aesthetically, according to a systemic approach, involves joining people in their contexts, locating expertise within the persons seeking help, and working with relationships rather than only with individuals. It "involves maintaining a sense of respect for the people with whom we are engaged in relation to their pains, joy, sufferings and creative potential" (*ibid.*, p. 38). It involves working with people rather than working on people (Fredman, 2004).

Dr L, the psychiatrist, works aesthetically with Joan by joining Joan's context and talking with her and Sister Mary. Rather than discounting Joan's relationship with Sister Mary as a symptom or cause of some other problem, or inviting causal explanations of her behaviour from staff attending the ward round, he instead engages with both Joan and Sister Mary. Attending carefully to Joan's language, he works collaboratively with her. Thus, the psychiatrist adopts a curious therapeutic stance (Cecchin, 1987) through which he asks questions and listens. Instead of positioning himself to immediately diagnose or prescribe for Joan or to instruct or advise the practitioners attending the ward round, he takes time to engage with Joan's ability to interpret for Sister Mary and thus defers to the expertise of Sister Mary and Joan. In this way, he opens space for a greater understanding of Joan's situation for the other practitioners and himself in the ward round.

Requests for help with diagnosis, medication, or risk of harm can position practitioners as experts with the possibility of positioning the patient as incompetent or in need of protection, thereby pulling the practitioner away from collaborative practice. Pressures on resources such as time, beds, and room space can also challenge our ability, as practitioners, to hold onto the aesthetics of our practice. In this chapter, we explore how we can continue to work aesthetically with older people when we experience these sorts of challenges.

Our professional contexts

Throughout this book, the authors have addressed how practitioners working with older people act out of many different contexts. In Chapter Three, for example, Joshua Stott and Eleanor Martin discuss how our personal and professional contexts inform our practice, and in Chapter Six, Isabelle Ekdawi and Esther Hansen address the contexts of our race, culture, gender, age, and sexuality. In this chapter, we focus on how the contexts of our professions, trainings, and the agencies or services within which we work, create opportunities and constraints that can shape our practice with older people.

All three of us bring to our work with older people stories, theories, and ideas from our professional training as clinical psychologists, and from our training in systemic constructionist practice. These stories inform our assumptions, beliefs, and values about how to be with the people with whom we work and about what we deem competent and ethical practice. In this way, then, our contexts inform the judgements we make about what practices are permissible, forbidden, or obligatory, and these judgements inform how we evaluate ourselves as practitioners in terms of competence and ethics. For the three of us to feel competent and ethical clinical psychologists and systemic practitioners, we would need to work in ways that are coherent with the assumptions and values we have described as the "aesthetics of systemic practice" in the introduction to this book.

Our professional contexts also inform the rights, duties, and responsibilities, as well as the abilities, we have to act. Wherever we work, there is usually a predominant approach or model of practice. The three of us all work in public health services, and mainly in hospitals, where the predominant model is medical. People receiving help in our contexts are commonly referred to as "patients", a term that positions them as dependent on professionals for treatment. As psychologists working in multi-disciplinary teams, we have rights to negotiate with the older people with whom we work about how they prefer to be identified, whether or not they want to work with us, and with which psychological approaches they prefer to engage. We also have duties and respon-sibilities to co-ordinate with our multi-disciplinary team and to work within the resources we are allocated. Therefore, in our work with older people and their significant networks of family, carers, and professionals, we always consider: "What context are we (and others) acting out of?"; "What are the stories connected to our different contexts?"; "What do our contexts say about our duties, rights and responsibilities?" You, the reader, may like to think about the contexts informing your work. What does your profession say about your duties, rights, and responsibilities? Does your agency have the same view? Perhaps you are working in a residential home where your duties and responsibilities are informed by ideas about social care and the policies of your agency. Or perhaps you are a social worker who is informed not only by theories of social work but also by the predominant policies of your agency.

The psychiatrist talking with Joan is trained and qualified as a doctor. He, therefore, has responsibilities to diagnose, prescribe medication, and to assess patients' risk of self-harm. Concerned that Joan was "hearing voices" and may come to harm, the nurses, also informed by a medical model, expected the psychiatrist to assess Joan with a view to advising on treatment. Because of his seniority within the medical team, this psychiatrist exercised his right to take time to talk with Joan while she consulted with Sister Mary. By connecting with Sister Mary, he worked collaboratively with Joan and respected her expertise. Learning more from Joan (and Sister Mary) helped him to assess risk and make a useful diag-nosis. Later, he went on to ask Sister Mary for permission to prescribe medication for Joan, which enabled Joan to take the medication. Throughout this process, the psychiatrist created an opportunity for the nurses to witness first-hand the importance of including Joan and Sister Mary in the process of her treatment. The psychiatrist's practice with Joan reflects the systemic ethical posi-tion that informs the approach we present in this book. He was able to honour the diagnostic process integral to his profession *and* approach the symptoms, in this case "the voice" of Sister Mary, as invitations to respond.

Professional discourses informing our practice

Dr Y, a psychiatrist, asked me (Goran) to assess Marlena, as she was "hearing voices". At our first meeting, Marlena told me that the voices "do not bother me". I learnt that, at times, the voices kept her company when she was lonely, "like friends, they can help me to relax". Marlena continued that she used to live in Madrid. "I was young and beautiful . . . when I went out to a shop, local boys would stop their cars to ask me if I would like a lift . . . but now, you know, at seventy-one, I have to live on my own, this is too hard . . ." After our first meeting, I informed the psychiatrist that Marlena was not finding "the voices" a problem and that they helped her to relax. When I next visited Marlena, I was saddened and frustrated to learn from the nurse manager that they had "changed Marlena's diagnosis from depression and personality disorder to psychosis" and they were "referring Marlena to a hearing voices specialist as she needs help."

The pull of our discourses

The nurse manager, psychiatrist, and Goran are each informed by different discourses shaped by the professional and organizational contexts within which they work. By discourse, we mean interrelated ideas, practices, assumptions, rules, and institutional structures that share common values and both reflect and construct a specific worldview (Burr, 1995; Hare Mustin, 1994). Goran, the nurse manager, and the psychiatrist were not necessarily aware of the discourses pulling them towards certain practices and away from others. Yet, these taken-for-granted assumptions shaped their practice with Marlena and their working relationships with each other. Both the nurse manager and the psychiatrist have trained in professions rooted within a medical model. Hence, they were pulled towards discourses that draw attention to problems or dysfunction and position the practitioner as the "expert" who takes responsibility for protection of the patient. Goran, on the other hand, having trained in psychological and systemic models, was pulled towards what Madsen (2007) calls discourses of possibilities, collaboration, and accountability. Each discourse offers both opportunities and constraints, so there are simultaneous openings and accountabilities for each of the people involved.

As a responsible medical officer in this service, the psychiatrist held responsibility for protection of vulnerable patients. Perceiving Marlena as vulnerable, he was, therefore, obligated, according to his professional position, to protect her and saw it as his duty to act on her behalf. Thus informed by discourses of expertise and protection, the psychiatrist, and perhaps the nurse manager, perceived it as their professional responsibility and duty to draw on specialized expertise, their own and that of others, to assess for symptoms of pathology, discover their causes, and develop treatment plans to ameliorate problems. Therefore. they focused on diagnosing Marlena's problem ("psychosis") with a view to identifying appropriate treatment (a "hearing voices specialist") that she "needed".

Pulled towards the discourses of possibilities and collaboration, on the other hand, Goran saw it as his responsibility to build a foundation of competence, connection, and hope with Marlena in the process of addressing the issues described as problematic. He saw it as his duty to work with her collaboratively towards clarifying what she wanted rather than what she "needed". Rather than assuming that Marlena had a problem with the voices, therefore, Goran asked if the voices troubled her and learnt that they were not a problem and sometimes helped. Intending to approach the symptoms she described as "part of the wisdom of the system" (Lang, 2006) rather than part of its dysfunction, Goran listened with curiosity for examples of Marlena's resourcefulness and heard how the voices kept her company in the absence of affirming social contacts. Thus, he explored how Marlena's symptoms, as identified by the psychiatrist, suited Marlena, providing her with company and the opportunity to relax in the face of her loneliness. In this way, Goran opened space for Marlena to tell rich stories, not only of her current difficulties, but also of her preferred earlier self as a young, attractive person, easily able to establish social relationships.

Our professional discourses inform the values and beliefs we have about what we need to do to be a good and ethical practitioner. We might call this our moral order (Pearce, 1989), which includes the rules we have about what we must do, can do, should not do, and also what we are uncertain about doing. Thus, our professional discourses inform or shape our professional identity. According to his training, Goran believes he should engage with people's competence. Therefore, he found the psychiatrist and ward manager's focus on the voices as symptoms of psychosis a challenge to his sense of himself as an ethical practitioner. Hence, Goran did not know how he could stay loyal to his systemic moral order and work with Marlena and the ward team in the context of diagnosis.

Below, we see how a request for risk assessment challenges Josh's attempts to hold on to his ethical position in a similar way. We discuss how clarifying whether we are working in the "domain of production" or "domain of explanation" can help us address this kind of dilemma.

Domains of production and explanation

Josh, a clinical psychologist, and Melanie, a social worker, were standing in front of a battered blue door in a supported living housing unit. The door was slightly ajar and a long thin strip of yellow light marked the door from the wall of the dark passageway. A chain, connecting the door to the wall, broke the beam of light. Just above this chain, Josh saw the upper half of a woman who had very brown eyes and a small head dwarfed by a hat shaped like a tea cosy. In his hand, Josh was carrying a referral letter requesting "an assessment of Olga's mood and mental state" in relation to concerns about her "capacity to safely care for her husband, Emil", who had recently had a stroke. Olga had discharged Emil against hospital advice when he was still very ill and another resident had recently seen him "crawling around the housing unit". Neither Josh nor Melanie could see or hear Emil, so Melanie asked Olga if she could meet with him briefly. Olga replied that she did "not want your sort around" as "I was a nurse and am well able to look after my husband." Josh said, "As a psychologist and a social worker, perhaps we are not the best people to help with your husband's care. What about a nurse coming around for a second opinion? People often get second opinions with health care." Olga said, her voice slowly rising, "Josh, you are a nice boy, but I speak with God and he is telling me that I need no second opinion. He tells me about your lot coming around and meddling. I have been persecuted by this country for long enough and I won't have it any more." With that the door closed, leaving Melanie and Josh standing in the corridor, wondering what to do.

Emil had been identified as a "vulnerable adult". Josh and Melanie were expected to assess Olga's competence and establish the extent of Emil's safety in relation to prescribed objective criteria. These duties were coherent with Melanie's social work responsibilities, which included protection of vulnerable adults (POVA), for which her social services agency laid out clear policies and procedures to follow. Melanie had asked Josh to accompany her because she wanted his psychological opinion on Olga's abilities to care for her husband. Considering Olga's "relationship to help" and anticipating her "emotional postures", along the lines described in Chapter Two, might have helped Melanie and Josh to engage with Olga. For example, recognizing that Olga was unlikely to welcome help, they might have gone on to contemplate, "In what emotional posture is Olga likely to receive us?"; "How is Olga likely to react when we explain why we have been asked to see her?"; "What will help us show our respect for Olga?" Since this referral to Melanie had been framed as "an urgent risk assessment" in the light of concerns about Emil's "safety", however, Melanie's statutory duty to respond immediately gave them little time to prepare for this first visit.

Working in the domain of production

Requests for assessment of risk, safety, and competence can challenge our systemic ethical position, as Josh experienced with Olga, since they require us to work in what Lang, Little, and Cronen (1990) call the "domain of production". When we have no choice about how we act, for example, when we have professional obligations to assess risk to a client or to others, we are working in the domain of production. We are operating in this domain when something has to be achieved and when we are assessing something against specific criteria. Therefore, assessing for risk, administering tests, making diagnoses, implementing legal and service policies, monitoring safety or health, and following protocols are tasks we carry out in the domain of production.

Working in the domain of production, practitioners act and talk as if there is an objective truth and, therefore, tend to ask investigative questions about symptoms to inform diagnoses or to enable them to follow protocols. Consent is considered desirable, but not necessarily essential in this domain, since clients are commonly seen as vulnerable and practitioners as responsible for protecting them, identifying and understanding the cause of their problems, and allocating resources or intervening to ameliorate or cure. In this sense, then, the practitioner may adopt a position of "social controller" or investigator in relation to people's protection, involuntary hospitalization, or allocating them to certain services. Thus, working in the domain of production is coherent with a discourse of expertise, protection, and deficit. Practitioners are expected to adopt a professional distance and position of certainty in order to follow protocols, assess against criteria, and provide "products", results, or outcomes, such as formulations, diagnoses, assessments of risk, test results, reports, and so on.

The request to assess Olga invited Josh into the domain of production, the demands of which were challenging his attempts to join with Olga in a collaborative relationship. Hence, Josh found the responsibility to assess Olga's competence pulling him towards the activities of social controller or investigator and away from his attempts to engage with her aesthetically. Mindful of Olga's experiences of marginalization and oppression, Josh tried to move away from a hierarchical relationship towards connecting with Olga's competence. Therefore, using the language with which she had identified herself, he repositioned her as a "nurse". However, since the meaning of the message is given as much by the receiver as the sender, in retrospect we can see that Josh may have unintentionally contributed to Olga's construction of his response as undermining, meddling, or persecution. Perhaps Olga took his proposal of a second opinion to mean that Josh was suggesting someone more competent than her to help with her husband's care, since she was quick to answer, "I need no second opinion [from] your lot coming around and meddling. I have been persecuted by this country for long enough and I won't have it any more."

Working in the domain of explanation

When the psychiatrist, Dr Y, asked Goran to assess Marlena, as she was hearing voices, the psychiatrist made this request in the domain of production. This was probably with the expectation that Goran, drawing on his expert knowledge, would focus on the symptom (hearing voices) and produce a result, perhaps in the form of a report that could contribute to diagnosis and a treatment plan. Informed by a discourse of possibility, collaboration, and accountability, however, and aware of the potentially disempowering effects on Marlena of working in the domain of production in this way, Goran refrained from "knowing" too quickly. Therefore, he privileged Marlena's knowledge about her situation above his professional knowledge and attended with curiosity to Marlena's meanings. Referring to her expertise on her own experience, Goran assumed Marlena to be the best judge of what was helpful and unhelpful. He also focused on her resourcefulness rather than on problems or weaknesses, intending to work towards building a foundation of competence, connection, and hope that could contribute to resolving difficulties before exploring problems in detail. Thus, Goran was working with Marlena in what Lang, Little, and Cronen (1990) call the "domain of explanation".

The domain of explanation is the domain of therapy in which we foreground creating meaning and understanding. Therefore, we step outside of assessment frameworks and protocols and suspend judgements of cause or accountability. Working instead with the curiosity of an explorer or discoverer, we set out to explore the wisdom of the system, creating maps for others and ourselves as we go along (Lang, 2006). We cannot work in the domain of explanation without consent. Through gaining consent, we address our power in the relationship, viewing the absence of agreement as abusive of our clients' rights.

When we are required to work in the domain of production we ask "orienting questions" (Tomm, 1988) to gather information, which we might check against diagnostic or protocol criteria. We ask investigative questions to generate facts and identify causes, including "what", "when" and causal "why" questions. In the domain of explanation, on the other hand, we explore meaning and we ask about relationships, effects, views, and difference (Fleuridas, Nelson, & Rosenthal, 1986). Rather than assuming we know the answers to our questions, we engage with clients from a genuine position of "not knowing" (Anderson & Goolishian, 1992).

Clarifying which domain we are working in

Above, we see how Goran was invited by the nurse manager and the psychiatrist to assess Marlena in the domain of production, with the expectation that he would provide a report including clarification of her problem and recommendations for a treatment plan. When Goran met with Marlena, he engaged her in conversation in the domain of explanation, asking questions that explored meaning rather than fact, inviting different perspectives, exploring beliefs rather than generating information. Stepping outside of the assessment framework in this way, Goran learnt how "the voices", identified by the psychiatrist and nurse manager as "symptoms", helped Marlena to relax and were a comfort to her during episodes of loneliness. Talking with Marlena in the domain of explanation also opened space for her to tell rich stories of her preferred earlier self. Although Marlena engaged well with Goran as they talked in the domain of explanation, Goran became disengaged from his referring colleagues, since his feedback about Marlena did not fit with their expectations and requirements. Consequently, without involving Goran, they referred Marlena to a hearing voices group outside the service.

Goran's experience points to the importance of clarifying with our colleagues which domain we are working in. We do not, however, always have the space or rights to negotiate or shift domains. As a psychologist junior to the psychiatrist and responsible to the nurse manager, Goran did not have power in the hierarchy to move the work with Marlena from the domain of production to the domain of explanation. However, he could have clarified, with the nurse manager, his intentions to engage Marlena through getting to know her and learning something about her experience of the voices, thereby establishing whether this approach would fit with the expectations of their referral.

In Chapter Four, Joshua Stott and Eleanor Martin discuss how contracting with clients includes clarifying rights, duties, and responsibilities of the practitioner as well as the client. Working in the domain of production calls for different rights, duties, and responsibilities from working in the domain of explanation. Both domains offer opportunities and constraints to what we do. Acting out of the domain of production, the psychiatrist and nurse manager had the duty to assess and diagnose Marlena in terms of prescribed criteria, the responsibility to protect her as a vulnerable adult, to treat her problems, and to allocate resources to her treatment. Working in the domain of explanation, on the other hand, Goran was working with her towards creating meaning and understanding. It can be confusing for clients if we are not clear as to which domain we are working in. Clarity about our respective rights, duties, and responsibilities enables clients to choose what they say and how they talk with us and avoids their experiencing an abuse of the trust that might have developed if we switch from the domain of explanation to the domain of production without being transparent about what we are doing. Therefore, once we have identified the domain we are working in, we can clarify with clients what we are able to offer.

Chapter One outlines the aesthetic principles guiding the systemic approach we describe in this book. These principles inform our practice whether we are working in the domain of explanation or production. In the rest of this chapter we share examples of our practice in which we have identified the domain we were working in, and clarified our rights, duties, and responsibilities in our attempts to work aesthetically with our clients and colleagues. We focus on situations of risk and diagnosis, as these are common challenges to our practice.

Working aesthetically with risk

I (Goran) had been asked to "carry out a full risk assessment" of Mustafa, aged sixty-seven, who had recently cut his wrist. Mustafa made it clear that he did not want to talk about cutting his wrist. He believed that if he decided to attempt suicide again nobody could stop him. I affirmed Mustafa's "right not to talk about cutting your wrist" and agreed that it is difficult to stop people ending their life if they are committed to do so. I explained that, as a health worker, I was "obligated to follow the public health service policies developed to protect people from suicide". Clarifying the policy, I explained that Mustafa had the "right to not answer questions" and I had a "duty to inform (Mustafa's) psychiatrist and doctor" if I were unable to assess risk to Mustafa. I also explained that if I became concerned for Mustafa's safety we would "both need to find a way to proceed whereby I am confident that you (Mustafa) are safe and you feel that your rights are respected".

The request for risk assessment following a suicide attempt invited Goran into the domain of production, in which he had a professional obligation without choice to assess risk of harm to Mustafa according to prescribed suicide risk criteria. Goran, however, was still able to work aesthetically with Mustafa in the domain of production, using the principles for ethical systemic practice to guide his talk. Taking care of how he talked with Mustafa, Goran attended to his language and the meanings they were constructing in their talk. Mindful of their differential power, he talked respectfully with Mustafa, carefully spelling out their respective rights, duties, responsibilities and obligations. Working in the domain of production afforded Goran the right to act on Mustafa's behalf without his consent. Working aesthetically, however, is intended to offer clients more control and choice in their lives. Therefore, Goran invited Mustafa into a more collaborative relationship by making transparent the policies guiding his practice and acknowledging Mustafa's expertise on his own experience. Following this discussion, Mustafa began to tell Goran about his intentions to kill himself and went on to agree to the home treatment crisis team being involved with his care. He thanked Goran at the end of their conversation "for being honest with me".

Whereas the request for risk assessment invited Goran to work with Mustafa in the domain of production from the start, Josh was already engaged with Jean in a therapeutic relationship when he became concerned about her safety.

> Josh was sitting in a square room on a blue chair. To his right was a desk piled high with books about different types of psychotherapy. Behind him was a sash window, held open by a piece of wood nailed to the bottom of the window frame to prevent it from opening more than the foot required to let in fresh air. Josh was reminded of another client's joking, ". . . because we can't be trusted not to jump out" as he talked with Jean, a small woman with bright blue eyes and an oval face with pointed chin, looking a bit like someone in a medieval painting. Jean had just told Josh that she often felt "life is not worth living" and had taken to crossing roads without thinking about or looking for traffic. Josh said, "This concerns me . . . about whether you are safe," and asked whether Jean, herself, was concerned about her safety. Jean echoed Josh's concern.

Josh: When I am concerned about someone's safety, like this, I suggest we think together about what they might be able to do to keep themselves safe. Is it OK if we think about how you can keep safe?

Jean: I think that's a good idea.

Josh: One thing that can keep people safe is going into hospital. What do you think about that?

Jean: That sounds horrid . . . I would rather die than go into a mental institution.

Josh: Mmm . . . I see . . . that's not for everyone . . . I am wondering whether there is something you are already doing to keep yourself safe?

Jean: (thinking for awhile) I'm not sure what you mean?

Josh: Well . . . has there been a time recently when you have crossed the road and been able to think and look for traffic?

Jean: Well, there was, but it was a bit silly.

Josh: I am really curious to hear about it.

Jean: I think it was last Friday—or maybe—was it the Wednesday before? I was standing at that busy junction near the supermarket . . . and then before I crossed I started to sing a song to myself. It was that song I remembered from an advert about following the Green Cross Code.

Josh: Was this something positive—what you did—singing the Green Cross Code song?

Jean: Oh yes—very positive.

Josh: So when you leave here . . . I am worried about your safety . . . is there a way we can use what you have done to increase safety for you?

Jean: It's funny that—I only really remembered singing the song when you asked me about it. I think I could sing it under my breath—when I am crossing the road . . .

Josh and Jean went on to discuss how she might remind herself about singing the Green Cross Code song that kept her mind on the traffic. Together they came up with the idea that she could write the song down and keep a copy in her coat pocket as a reminder.

Josh had been working with Jean in therapy, in the domain of explanation, where working according to his preferred ethical (aesthetic) practice was relatively straightforward. Concerns about Jean's safety pulled him towards the domain of production, when Jean expressed that "life is not worth living" and disclosed that she was crossing roads without due attention. Hence, Josh was professionally obligated to follow his service's risk procedures. Having made transparent the risk and confidentiality policies of his service at the start of their work together (described in Chapter Four), we can see how Josh works aesthetically with Jean in the domain of production. At all times he remains mindful of her safety. However, recognizing that no one story is the final story, Josh also explores initiatives Jean herself has taken to ensure her safety and exceptions to her risky behaviour by asking, "Is there something you are already doing to keep yourself safe? Has there been a time recently when you have crossed the road and been able to think and look for traffic?" Thus Josh focuses on Jean's resourcefulness, rather than problems or weaknesses, towards building a foundation of competence and hope. He goes on to explore with Jean how she can use her competence and abilities to resolve her difficulties, the offer of choice thus enhancing her sense of dignity. At all times, Josh refers to Jean's expertise so that she feels he is working "with" her rather than "on" her.

Working aesthetically with diagnosis

Ruby had received a diagnosis of "endogenous depression" shortly before her eighty-fourth birthday. Talking about this diagnosis at her first meeting with me (Glenda), she said tearfully, "Fancy this at my age . . . Just look at me . . . what have I become . . . a depressed old crow . . . I am no good for anything now . . . am I?"

The diagnosis process can pose a challenge to the practitioner trying to work aesthetically according to the principles outlined at the start of this book. Informed by "expert" and "deficits" discourses, the practice of diagnosis draws us into "objectivity" in our search for the "true" or "correct" definition of the client's problem. Attributing a label or causal description to people's problems can invite blaming or negative self-descriptions. For example, Ruby shows us how the diagnosis of endogenous depression talks to her of her identity not only of who she is, "what have I become . . . a depressed old crow . . .", but also of who she can become, ". . . no good for anything . . .".

The process of diagnosis, in the domain of production, positions people as patients or professionals. As Goran shows in his work with Marlena, above, the expectation that, as professionals, we speak with authority about what patients need can challenge our ability to work collaboratively with older persons according to what they want. Diagnosis, therefore, involves power, attributing different rights, duties, and responsibilities to those involved in the process. The professional has the duty and responsibility to name the problem, prescribe treatment, and monitor the clients' mental state, and the right to allocate resources such as medication, disability living allowance, hospital or residential accommodation. The patient has the right to access certain resources, such as treatments, housing, and financial support with associated obligations to defer to the professional's "expert" advice and adhere to their prescribed treatment. Graham highlighted this balance of power involved with diagnosis when, at couple therapy with his wife, he complained to me (Glenda), "It is all the health minister's fault. How can Dorothy and I find any sort of social life . . . can you imagine going down the pub and saying, 'Hello I am Graham and I'm a schizophrenic, and this is my wife Dot and she is manic depressive' . . . who would want to take us on . . . but then how are we supposed to live without medication and the housing . . . they come with the territory you see . . . don't get me wrong, we like our doctor, we want all the help . . . it's the price we pay, schizophrenic and manic depressive . . ."

On the other hand, Sarah's work with Angelica, a woman in her seventies from Ghana, shows how giving a name or label to a problem can also be useful to the older person.

> Tearfully Angelica told me (Sarah) that she wanted to kill herself. She said that since having a stroke she had been "going mad . . . not able to do basic things like get ready in the morning to keep appointments". Angelica was overwhelmed by sadness. She was frequently tearful, wanted to stay in bed, and had stopped going out or doing activities around the house. She did not want her husband or friends to know about her difficulties for fear they would call her a "madwoman" and shun her. Angelica agreed to a cognitive assessment with me.

Discussing the test results, I explained to Angelica that the experiences she described were related to the effects of the stroke; they did not mean she was "going mad". I showed her a diagram of the brain and the areas that had been affected by the stroke, explaining that I thought the stroke had affected her planning and organizing abilities. I called these "executive functioning" problems, and discussed how she could begin to manage these difficulties. Reassured to hear that she was not "going mad", Angelica went on to talk with me about how we might help her husband and friends understand what was happening.

Sarah's work with Angelica shows how we can have a flexible and creative relationship with diagnosis and labelling problems, using it when and if it fits with the context and relationship with the client and when it can offer the older person a life-enhancing way to go on. In this case, Sarah's attributing the name "executive functioning problems" to Angelica's difficulties helped her to understand her symptoms and reassured her that she was experiencing a recognizable problem that could be helped. The name "executive functions" was able to replace the more pathologizing self-diminishing description of "going mad" and opened space for Angelica to communicate with her helping network. Given a language with which she could account for her difficulties to family and friends enabled Angelica to move forward.

There are times when we have responsibilities to our services to contribute to a process of diagnosis. For example, in Sarah's community mental health team for older people, all professionals are required to complete an assessment form with a section asking for a diagnosis consistent with standardized criteria outlined in the *Diagnostic and Statistical Manual-IV* (*DSM-IV*) (American Psychiatric Association, 1994) or the manual of *International Classification of Mental and Behavioural Disorders-10* (ICD-10) (World Health Organisation, 1992). In Sarah's team, a standardized diagnosis is intended to guide treatment and enable a shared language among the different professions in the team. We have also worked in services where a formal diagnosis is required before patients can have access to any form of psychological treatment. Although the practice of diagnosis pulls us into the domain of production, Sarah's conversation with Matthew shows how we can aesthetically contribute to a mental health diagnosis.

Matthew, a seventy-one-year old man born in Sri Lanka, explained to me (Sarah) that he was "suffering from hallucinations". I asked him, "Is 'hallucinations' the name you prefer to call this difficulty, or is there another name you would prefer to call it?" Matthew thought that "hallucinations" was the correct term, since the psychiatrist had called them hallucinations during a psychiatric hospital inpatient admission fifteen years previously. When I invited Matthew to explain what the meaning of the word "hallucinations" was for him, he said, "Actually, technically they are 'visual distortions', not hallucinations, as whenever I see someone in uniform, such as a policeman or a ticket collector, I get very agitated but 'paranoid' describes how they make me feel." I checked with Matthew, "When we talk about these experiences would you prefer to call them 'paranoia' or 'visual distortions' or 'hallucinations' . . . or something else?" Mathew replied, "Yes—I like 'paranoia'. That's how they make me feel." Since our service required a diagnostic label, I checked later with the team psychiatrist what he thought I should write on the assessment form. He reviewed Matthew's notes and suggested that his symptoms were consistent with a diagnosis of schizophrenia. I wrote "schizophrenia" on the assessment form and alongside it I wrote, "'paranoia' is Matthew's preferred name for his experiences".

I (Sarah) was trying to work aesthetically with the diagnostic practices required by my community mental health team. My intention was to gather information to complete my team's assessment form while building a respectful relationship with Matthew. I began by outlining the assessment process to Matthew, explaining the nature and purpose of the assessment form, clarifying that I would send him a copy of the completed form when he could ask me further questions or amend the details. In the conversation with Matthew, therefore, I weaved between the domains of production and explanation. In the domain of production, I took responsibility for contributing to the team's diagnostic process by exploring in detail what Matthew was experiencing. At all times I tried to work aesthetically to build a therapeutic relationship with Matthew, taking a collaborative stance, being open and transparent about what I was doing, using his language, and checking out with him what he would prefer to call his experiences. Throughout our meeting I engaged with Matthew in an externalizing conversation (White, 1988; see also Chapter Seven) to separate him as a person from the problems he was experiencing. Exploring the effects of the (externalized) problems, for example, I asked, "What effect does the paranoia have on you?"; "Does it interfere with your sleep/ appetite/mood in any ways?"; "Does it get in between you and your brother at any times?"; "Does the 'paranoia' interfere with your thinking at all?" This enabled us to explore Matthew's symptoms without attributing them to his identity.

Above, we see how Sarah was able to co-ordinate the discourses informing her team's diagnostic practices with the collaborative discourse informing her work with Matthew. We are always looking for openings to work aesthetically, whether we are in the domain of explanation or production. We also look for openings to invite colleagues into a relational, collaborative approach when facing the pull of the "deficit", "expert", and "protection" discourses. Eleanor Anderson and Isabelle Ekdawi discuss how they have engaged colleagues with systemic ethics and practices in Chapter Nine. Below, we discuss how we have navigated through seemingly conflicting discourses to enable positive outcomes for older people as well as respectful relationships with colleagues.

Navigating a way through alternative discourses

When Ruby complained "I don't know why I am still alive—what am I here for?" I (Glenda) suggested gently, "That is a really good question . . . I am sure there is a reason—we'll have to work it out." Over our next few meetings, Ruby came up with several reasons that her life was worthwhile, such as "I am the oldest surviving family member, I am the only one who can fill them in on the family"; "They wanted the oldest in the family to bless the baby"; "I need to be here until my first granddaughter gets married—that will be forever!" Ruby also responded well to my invitations to notice and describe moments of pleasure, energy, and enthusiasm for life between our meetings. Together, we noted what helped her reclaim her life back from "the misery" (Ruby's words). She arrived each week with many wonderful examples, such as "I plucked up two courages . . . I took myself off to the hairdressers . . . bought a new outfit to give me a facelift . . .", which were important to Ruby, who wanted to be "interesting and good company". By her third session, Ruby was pleased with how things were going as she had "more of a taste for life", was enjoying visits from her children and grandchildren again, and was thinking of returning to bridge games. She laughed, "My granddaughter says I have a more interesting social life than hers . . . the trouble is finding energy for all my housework . . ." She was also reconnecting with her preferred version of herself as "interesting and good company . . . My daughter says she can see her old mum again." I was, therefore, surprised when, at our fourth meeting, Ruby said she felt "terribly under the weather lately" and feared that "I am getting much worse." She told me that the "hopeless" feelings had returned shortly after her routine psychiatry clinic review, when "The doctor said I have to take more pills for depression . . . I thought I was getting better . . . but obviously I am getting worse . . . I must have been imagining it."

Although I had informed the psychiatrist of the considerable improvements, suggesting Ruby was responding very well to a strength-based approach, the psychiatrist, Dr T, increased the anti-depressant medication. Hence, I was faced with the challenge of continuing to facilitate Ruby's progress towards new possibilities while collaborating respectfully with my psychiatry colleague, whose problem-focused approach was dominating the process of therapy. When faced with dilemmas like these we have caught ourselves using expressions like "undermined", "sabotaged", or "discredited" to describe the effects on us of some of our colleagues' actions, perceiving them as contradictory to, or conflicting with, our practices. However, we have found that using this sort of adversarial language tends to position us in unwanted competitive or blaming relationships with our colleagues, thus potentially interfering with our collaborative working at the expense of our clients' well-being. Lang (2006) reminds us that working aesthetically involves respectful working not only with clients, but also with our colleagues and other practitioners involved. Therefore, we go on below to consider how we can exist alongside models of practice and within professional and agency contexts that have expectations that challenge our ethical positions and strength-based approaches. We reflect on how we might position ourselves to facilitate positive working relationships with colleagues that open space for constructive and creative contributions to the well being of the older people with whom we work.

Becoming reflexive to our discourses and contexts

We have found that reflecting on the discourses that shape our practice enriches our work and professional relationships. We start by "stepping back" to locate our views, prejudices, and practices in the different discourses that organize our practice with older people. We reflect on our own positions, and we try to take the perspectives of our colleagues and other professionals working with the client as well. We ask ourselves how and why they and we are pulled towards one practice or another with questions such as: "What are the different professional/service contexts informing our work with Ruby?"; "Are we acting out of similar or different contexts?"; "What are the taken-for-granted assumptions about what counts as competent and ethical 'professional' behaviour coming from our different professions/work contexts?" (Madsen, 2007); "How do these assumptions affect our decisions/actions with Ruby?"; "What discourses do our contexts pull us towards or away from?"

> I (Glenda) reflected that the junior psychiatrist, Dr T, who had increased Ruby's medication, was probably following prescribed assessment protocols and working according to clear diagnostic criteria, for example, the *DSM-IV* (American Psychiatric Association, 1994). I assumed that he was reporting to the consultant psychiatrist ultimately responsible for his work. Therefore, he would be pulled towards problem-focused, deficit-based and expert practices, the predominant approach in the psychiatry service. I noted that my clinical psychology and systemic psychotherapy trainings pulled me towards different "collaborative" and "possibilities" practices with which Ruby had engaged particularly well. I was also aware that "deficit", "expert", and "protection" discourses are dominant in public mental health services for older people and receive more institutional support than the strength-based, collaborative approach.

Stepping back and examining the values and assumptions informing both my approach and that of my colleagues enabled me to create some distance from my dilemma and from my experience of frustration. Hence, I was able to notice how the different discourses were "pulling" my psychiatry colleague, Dr T, and me towards different practices with Ruby. Thus, I moved towards "externalizing" the respective discourses (Madsen, 2007), whereby

I saw the discourse and not the psychiatrist (or his consultant) as responsible for the dilemma. Appreciating that the psychiatrist and his consultant did not invent the deficit discourse enabled me to move beyond a blaming or critical stance. Hence, I offered to join Ruby at her next meeting with the psychiatrist to explore how we might work together in Ruby's interest while staying loyal to our respective discourses.

Joining with colleagues and clients

Another way to bridge the gap between our discourses is to invite our colleagues to join our work with older people. Including colleagues in our meetings, where they can witness how we work and experience the aesthetic domain first hand, has been powerfully effective in facilitating collaborative working and respectfully shifting colleagues' perspectives. When the client is physically present, practitioners are more able to centre the client (Seikkula & Arnkil, 2006). In Chapter Five, Eleanor Anderson and Sarah Johnson discuss creative ways of calling and holding network meetings with older people, their families, and significant involved practitioners to co-ordinate collaborative working. In this chapter, we discuss how we join with colleagues in the contexts of *their* work with older people. Our intention is to create opportunities for the practitioner to witness the positive developments that the older person and their family have made. We also hope to develop an understanding of the other practitioner's logic in order to help us introduce alternative ideas or practices without compromising their preferred ways of working. So I (Glenda) offered to join Ruby at her next meeting with the psychiatrist, Dr T. Ruby was very keen to have me attend.

Dr T: How are you feeling in yourself today?

Ruby: OK, thank you doctor.

Dr T: Do you feel sad, depressed or empty?

Ruby: Yes doctor.

Dr T: Sometimes people find that they feel more low in the morning than later in the day—is that the case for you?

Ruby: Most definitely. Things get better later in the day.

Dr T: How is your sleep? Do you wake up early?

Ruby: I always wake up before the cock crows . . . not much of a sleeper I'm afraid . . .

Dr T: Your appetite?

Ruby: I don't cook much any more you know. I don't have much appetite.

Dr T: Have you lost weight?

Ruby: My daughter is always trying to fatten me up. She wants me to eat more fat to put some weight on . . . I don't have the taste for it.

Dr T: What about your energy? Do you feel tired?

Ruby: I always had so much energy. Now I can't do half what I did before. It's very upsetting.

Dr T, the junior psychiatrist meeting with Ruby, seemed to be following a prescribed assessment protocol and working in line with the diagnostic criteria of the *DSM-IV* (American Psychiatric Association, 1994). He was asking Ruby orienting and investigative questions designed to help generate clear descriptions of symptoms that he could then match against diagnostic categories or syndromes. In their conversation, we can see how these sorts of question elicit accounts of pathology (Mendez, Coddou, & Maturana, 1988).

In the course of the conversation with the psychiatrist, I (Glenda) noticed Ruby's demeanour change. She was sinking further into her chair. Her increasingly hunched shoulders pulled her head down towards her lap. Ruby's speech began to falter as she lost eye contact with the psychiatrist and her voice grew quieter and quieter. I spoke politely to the doctor.

Glenda: Excuse me, doctor. I am wondering if you can help us. Ruby has a problem finding energy to do her housework.

Dr T: What's the problem?

Glenda: Well doctor, you see, Ruby has rather a busy social life these days. Her daughter says she has more of a social life than she does.

Ruby: (chortles) That was my granddaughter . . .

Glenda: Oh yes-sorry—Ruby's granddaughter—how old is she again Ruby?

Ruby: (sitting up in her chair, her eyes shining) Thirty-three—and still not married!

Dr T: So what's the problem with your energy?

Glenda: Well, Ruby has so much to fit in, doctor. She goes to the hairdresser every week—don't you think this new hair colour suits her . . .

Dr T: (to Ruby) Do you think you are doing too much?

Ruby: I don't know doctor . . .

Glenda: Doctor, Ruby has been updating her wardrobe—she's been shopping for her own clothes again. Is that a new outfit Ruby?

Ruby: (grinning) I got it last week.

Glenda: I think it suits you . . . what do you think Doctor?

Doctor T: (awkwardly) I like it. Very nice.

Glenda: Doctor, Ruby has been asking me about the medication, the antidepressant pills. I said we should discuss them with you. I was not sure if you think she would need so many pills . . . since she has picked up her social life? Can you help us with this?

Dr T: (reading the medical notes and clarifying the current dosage with Ruby). Do you want to cut down your medication?

Ruby: I don't know doctor. I'm feeling a lot better these days. I worry if I stop the pills . . . will I get worse?

Dr T: Well—we could review you earlier next time—say about six weeks—and see how you go. If things are still going so well . . .

Glenda: Are you saying that Ruby is doing well—that all this social life and shopping is a good sign? That in six weeks you will talk about the pills again?

Dr T: Yes. (To Ruby) What is the problem with the housework—why don't you get your granddaughter to help you?

Mindful that this was a psychiatric appointment, I (Glenda) was careful to stay respectful to the psychiatrist's discourse. At all times I deferred to his expertise, informing him not only of Ruby's progress, but also the problems. By joining the psychiatric review meeting, I gained a new perspective on the psychiatrist's decision to increase Ruby's medication. With more of an understanding of his logic, I was able to open space for the psychiatrist to connect with other, more life-enhancing stories concerning Ruby, thereby creating the opportunity for him to witness Ruby's progress.

Psychiatry review clinics can be extremely time pressured. Doctors like Dr T may be able to allocate as little as ten minutes to review a patient. Pressure of time commonly pulls us into the domain of production towards protocols and checklists and away from dialogue. In extreme situations, we risk spending more time talking about patients than with them. Without creating an excessive demand on time, I (Glenda) tried to respectfully involve Dr T in a more relational conversation with Ruby that included systemic practices such as contextualizing her symptoms (loss of energy), connecting Ruby to her family relationships rather than focusing on her as an individual, and bringing forth her competence. Thus, I was able to engage Dr T in dialogue with Ruby that was coherent with the aesthetics of systemic practice without compromising his ability to work according to his medical ethics and standards of competence.

As well as attending colleagues' sessions, we have invited colleagues into our therapy sessions, where they can not only witness clients' progress but also experience first hand how we work (see also Chapter Nine). Inviting professionals to participate in conversations with older people opens space for what Andersen (1992a,b, 1995) calls reflecting processes, whereby each person has the opportunity to hear the different perspectives of the other. Inviting the people present to shift between listening and talking about the same issues moves them between "inner talks" while listening and "outer talks" while talking (Andersen, 1995, 1998). These different positions can offer the people present different perspectives. The juxtaposition of these different perspectives can invite the person to make new connections between these different perspectives, thereby creating opportunities for new stories to emerge. Thus, with the perception of difference, new contexts can evolve, giving new meanings to old ideas (Bateson, 1979).

Highlighting the effects of our different professional contexts

Edward, aged seventy-three, had suffered a stroke leaving him physically dependent on his eighty-year-old wife, Maya. There were plans to discharge Edward from the hospital ward soon. The physiotherapist and occupational therapist working with Edward asked me (Sarah) to help with their concerns that Maya would not be able to support Edward at home. Prior to his stroke, Edward had taken primary responsibility for domestic arrangements. I learnt that Maya, who had avoided coming to the hospital, was unable to go shopping on her own and did not seem to remember information she had been given. The therapists wanted to delay discharge until they could arrange a meeting with the medical team, community services, and Edward and Maya to plan a supported discharge. The ward doctor, on the other hand, wanted to discharge Edward immediately as he was "medically stable" and "the community team can sort out his home care".

I (Sarah) faced the dilemma of how, as a psychologist with less power than the doctor caring for Edward, I could open space for my colleagues to approach Edward and Maya in relationship rather than work with Edward in isolation. I wanted to find a way to introduce a perspective that connected Edward's future health and safety to the couple's well being. In supervision, Glenda invited me to become reflexive to the contexts informing both my practice and the practice of the doctor treating Edward. For example, she asked, "What are the different contexts informing your work with Edward and Maya?"; "Is the doctor treating Edward acting out of similar or different contexts from you?"; "What does your profession/training/team say about how you should work with Edward and Maya?"; "Is this similar or different for Edward's doctor?"; "How do these (assumptions) affect your decisions/actions with Edward and Maya?"

As well as the contexts of our different professions (clinical psychologist and stroke physician) and trainings (psychology and systemic for me, medical for the doctor), I (Sarah) identified two further contexts informing our approaches to Edward and Maya. It became apparent to me that I was acting out of a rehabilitation service context, whereas the doctor was acting out of an acute medical service context. It was clear that these two services, "acute" and "rehabilitation" demanded very different duties and responsibilities of practitioners towards patients. The doctor would be under pressure from the ward manager to free Edward's bed for other patients awaiting acute medical treatment. He would see his duty of care as being to "get the patient medically stable". Working out of a rehabilitation context, on the other hand, I, with my occupational therapy and physiotherapy colleagues, was taking a longer-term perspective with an emphasis on establishing a supportive network of relationships in the community to sustain Edward's future well being.

> I (Sarah) chose to be transparent with the medical team about the different contexts pulling us in different directions. In a ward round discussion about Edward, I therefore asked, "Can I clarify. Are we talking about Edward today with our 'Acute hat' on or with our 'Rehab hat' on? I am aware that there are different demands on us depending on which hat we wear. With the 'Acute hat' we need see only Edward as the patient and focus on getting him medically stable. We have done really well there. Is it possible for us to take a Rehab line now to help us work out how to keep this progress going?"

Thus, I (Sarah) named the different contexts organizing both my medical colleagues and me as "hats" ("Acute" and "Rehab") we were wearing. I also reflected on how the different assumptions embedded in those contexts affected our actions. By sharing these perspectives transparently with my colleagues, we were able to recognize how the highest context organizing our approach to Edward had become the economic context influencing limited bed space. This conversation further opened space for better collaboration and co-ordination between discharge and rehabilitation plans.

Developing a community to sustain aesthetic practice.

We work in the inner city of London, where public services are poorly resourced. The older people using our services are often oppressed by pathologizing discourses because they have been diagnosed with mental health problems and are discriminated against because of their age and health status, and possibly also their race, culture, or physical or intellectual disability. We joined the authors of this book for this project because we wanted to "be with" the people we work with in ways that the systemic constructionist approach makes possible. We wanted to open space for marginalized voices and challenge oppressing practices. We wanted to invite the older people we work with into collaborative relationships with their communities and ourselves rather than isolate them with problems. Many of us writing this book have felt undermined and dominated by "stories of impossibility" (Fredman, 2006), such as "I can't practise like this because I have no power or voice in my service"; "I cannot use this approach because I work in a psychiatric context which favours the medical model"; "There is no time to do this in a busy under-funded service". Therefore, we formed a community of colleagues working to help us challenge these "stories of impossibility". We were careful not to let this develop into a forum for complaint or criticism. Instead, we focused on our visions and hopes for the older people and services with whom we worked. We use this "collaborative community" (meeting monthly) to fuel us with energy to reclaim our passion for ethical, respectful practice, to remind us why we choose to do the work we do, and to reconnect us with and elaborate the values that inform our preferred versions of our selves.

This chapter addresses the challenges to the ethics of systemic practice we present in this book. We hope it offers possibilities to our readers who are dedicated to aesthetic practice with older people using public services, yet may find themselves at times overwhelmed by undermining "stories of impossibility". Perhaps, like us, you, our readers, might like to form similar communities with colleagues to sustain and support your best intentions.

References

American Psychiatric Association (1994). *Diagnostic and Statistical Manual-IV* (*DSM-IV*). New York: American Psychiatric Association.
Andersen, T. (1992a). Reflections on reflecting with families. In: S. McNamee & K. J. Gergen (Eds.), *Therapy as Social Construction* (pp. 54–68). London: Sage.
Andersen, T. (1992b). Relationship, language and pre-understanding in the reflecting processes. *A. N. Z. Journal of Family Therapy*, 13: 87–91.
Andersen, T. (1995). Reflecting processes; acts of informing and forming: You can borrow my eyes, but you must not take them away from me! In: S. Friedman (Ed.), *The Reflecting Team in Action. Collaborative Practice in Family Therapy.* (pp. 11–37). New York: Guilford.

Andersen, T. (1998). One sentence of five lines about creating meaning: in perspective of relationship, prejudice and bewitchment. *Human Systems: The Journal of Systemic Consultation & Management*, 9: 73–80.

Anderson, H., & Goolishian, H. (1992). The client is the expert: a not-knowing approach to therapy. In: S. McNamee & K. J. Gergen (Eds.), *Therapy as Social Construction* (pp. 30–38). London: Sage.

Bateson, G. (1979). *Mind and Nature*. London: Wildwood Press.

Burr, V. (1995). *An Introduction to Social Construction*. London: Routledge.

Cecchin, G. (1987). Hypothesising, circularity and neutrality revisited: an invitation to curiosity. *Family Process*, 26: 404–413.

Fleuridas, C., Nelson, T. S., & Rosenthal, D. M. (1986). The evolution of circular questions, training family therapists. *Journal of Marital and Family Therapy*, 12(2): 113–127.

Fredman, G. (2004). *Transforming Emotion: Conversations in Counselling and Psychotherapy*. London: Whurr/Wiley.

Fredman, G. (2006). Working systemically with intellectual disability: why not? In: S. Baum & H. Lynggaard (Eds.), *Intellectual Disabilities. A Systemic Approach*. (pp. 1–20). London: Karnac.

Hare Mustin, R. T. (1994). Discourses in the mirrored room: a post-modern analysis of therapy. *Family Process*, 33: 19–35.

Lang, P. (2006). Transforming risk towards opportunity. Camden and Islington Mental Health and Social Care Trust Workshop, London.

Lang, P., Little, M., & Cronen, V. E. (1990). The systemic professional domains of action and the question of neutrality. *Human Systems: The Journal of Systemic Consultation & Management*, 1(1): 32–46.

Madsen, W. (2007). Sustaining a collaborative practice in the "real" world. In: *Collaborative Therapy with Multi-Stressed Families*. London: Guilford Press.

Mendez, C. L., Coddou, F., & Maturana, H. R. (1988). The bringing forth of pathology. *Irish Journal of Psychology*, 9: 144–172.

Pearce, W. B. (1989). *Communication and the Human Condition*. Carbondale & Edwardsville, IL: Southern Illinois University Press.

Seikkula, J., & Arnkil, T. E. (2006). *Dialogical Meetings in Social Networks*. London: Karnac.

Tomm, K. (1988). Interventive interviewing. Part III: Intending to ask lineal, circular, strategic or reflexive questions. *Family Process*, 27: 1–15.

White, M. (1988). The externalising of the problem and the re-authoring of lives and relationships. *Dulwich Centre Newsletter*, Summer: 5–28.

World Health Organisation (1992). *The ICD-10 Classification of Mental and Behavioural Disorders: Clinical Descriptions and Diagnostic Guidelines (ICD-10).* New York: WHO.

CHAPTER NINE

Introducing systemic approaches into our services for older people

Eleanor Anderson and Isabelle Ekdawi

Chapter One outlines the beliefs, values, and principles guiding the systemic practices we present in this book. Throughout this book, we authors show that to work systemically does not have to involve seeing families or even more than one person, working with teams, or using a two-way screen. For us, being a "systemic practitioner" means using this systemic approach in all areas of our work, whether that is carrying out a cognitive assessment, care co-ordinating, participating in a multi-disciplinary meeting, or seeing a family for therapy. Although we might draw techniques (the specifics of what we do) from a range of therapeutic models, the methods (the process of what we do) and our overall approach (the philosophical and ethical stance that we take, the aesthetics of our practice) will always be systemic. Therefore, we approach the clients with whom we work, our colleagues, the outside services with whom we connect, and the many people who support our services, such as receptionists, telephonists, and cleaners, in a way that is coherent with our approach.

You may be wondering how you can introduce aspects of the systemic approach presented in this book into your service. In this chapter, we will describe how we have introduced systemic perspectives into our teams and how we have gone on to develop systemic services. The chapter should also be of use if you are a practitioner working on your own who would like to introduce systemic perspectives into your practice.

Introducing systemic perspectives into our teams

Perhaps you are working in a setting where only you or one or two other practitioners are interested in taking a systemic approach to your work. This is how we began. I, Isabelle, was the sole practitioner with a systemic training within a multi-disciplinary team, where I was employed as a clinical psychologist to provide psychological therapy for older people, carry out generic assessments, care co-ordinate, and contribute a "psychological perspective" to the team. I, Eleanor, was the sole systemic family therapist within a multi-disciplinary team in mental health services for older people. My remit was to assess and work therapeutically with older patients and their families, consult and liaise with other disciplines and departments, provide supervision, consultation, and training to other professionals, and develop a family therapy service. Although some of our colleagues were engaged in "family work", there were times when both of us felt like we were lone (systemic) voices in our contexts where the predominant models were medical, psychodynamic, and cognitive behavioural.

Connecting with the team

When we started in our services, we both recognized the importance of developing positive working relationships with the teams we were joining. Therefore, we worked hard to connect with other practitioners in the teams. Taking nothing for granted, we adopted a position of curiosity with respect to what was wanted of us in our new roles.

When I (Eleanor) joined the team, I took care how I positioned myself. I had been introduced to the metaphor of "on the margins", during a timely workshop with Peter Lang (1995) and found the ideas moved me to think about how I felt "on the margins" myself in this new post. I did not yet fully belong to the team, but stood on the margin of it, looking in tentatively and with curiosity for connections and fit between what the team was hoping for from me and the skills that I was bringing. Since a multi-disciplinary team, a mental health setting, and the multi-cultural Inner London context were new to me, I recognized that I needed to learn the "language" of the team.

Positioning myself not as an expert, but rather as curious and open to learning about the team's culture and language, influenced how I began to engage with the team. The initial process was one of finding out about the team and the community it served, learning the "language" and logic of the different professions in the team and community, and checking how team members wanted to use me. In other words, I began to develop the service in the same way that I would begin to work with a family: joining with each member; being curious about the culture; developing a shared language; finding out what they hoped for; and letting them know what I could offer. I did this tentatively, checking and rechecking that I had understood their meanings and intentions. As I took time to ensure that how I worked fitted with the culture and needs of the team and the clients, I was able to acknowledge and respect more and more of what the team could teach me.

Positioning myself in this way was informed by my belief that a systemic approach can be a helpful complement to other therapeutic models and need not replace them. Therefore, I wanted to introduce my colleagues to a systemic approach in ways they might find useful and relevant, rather than in ways that might appear oppositional or threatening to their preferred ways of working.

Opening space for different views

When we work in multi-disciplinary teams, we all have different ways of understanding the clients with whom we work. These understandings come from our different professional trainings and experience and also from our own personal contexts, such as our gender, culture, age, sexuality, and ability. Team cultures vary in the way that different views can be expressed, and the value afforded different perspectives. Most teams allow space for different professional disciplines to present their viewpoint when discussing a client, with the intention of generating a range of ideas or solutions and then reaching a consensus about how to proceed. A consensus, or, as the colloquial saying goes, "singing from the same hymn sheet", is often seen as ultimately desirable. Difficulties can occur when there are strong opinions about whose voice should be privileged.

When we work systemically, we privilege multiple perspectives. We do not name things as "right" or "wrong", but, rather, as "more or less useful" in certain contexts. We welcome different perspectives, therefore, both from our colleagues and from the clients and families with whom we work. In our experience, the ease with which team members can express views different from the predominant perspective within the team varies with a person's experience, profession, age, gender, culture, and confidence as my (Isabelle's) memory illustrates.

> A trainee clinical psychologist, who had just started on placement, asked me how she could best contribute to the multi-disciplinary mental health team meeting that she would be attending with me. Since it is a large team meeting of highly experienced and skilled clinicians, I wondered if individuals with less power might feel too intimidated to speak in the meeting. Therefore, I set myself the task of observing patterns of interaction and communication in the next team meeting to learn how people got their views heard by the team. I observed that people of certain professions, especially psychiatry and psychology, those who were more experienced, white, spoke with a standard English accent, were in positions of power in the team or who had been with the team for a longer time, tended to speak more and be heard. However, I also noted that a female Asian community psychiatric nurse, who did not fall into the above categories, was also successful in gaining the attention of the team. I noted that rather than stating facts, this nurse tended to ask questions of the type that we would call "systemic". For example, she asked, "How would it be different if we put in a carer for Mrs Brown?" Or "I wonder if Mrs Brown's daughter would see it the same way as us, or differently?" When the nurse asked these questions with genuine curiosity she usually managed to engage other team members' interest.

By taking a step back to look at how we were interacting in our team, I (Isabelle) became an observer to my own system and invited my trainee to do the same. Thus, we were able to learn how best to open space to offer our different perspectives in this context.

Asking questions with curiosity

We noticed in that meeting that the community psychiatric nurse was able to invite team members to become observers to our team thinking and practice by asking questions rather than making statements. If the nurse had expressed her view by stating, for example, "I feel uncomfortable about the discharge plans for Mrs Brown", or "You should find out what her daughter thinks about this first", she would have risked positioning herself as oppositional to the team who may have seen her as dismissing their views. Instead, she asked questions which opened space for more possibilities. When she enquired, her genuine curiosity showed, not only in the questions themselves, but non-verbally, too, in her tone of voice, her posture, and her facial expression. When she did make statements about another way to go forward, she offered them in a tentative way, a questioning way, as "one idea", thus creating a context in which different ways of seeing could be talked about. She did not put forward her way of seeing the patient as the only "right" way, but as one of several possibilities.

The use of questions, rather than statements or suggestions, is central to the systemic method (Tomm, 1988). The choice of language and the juxtaposition of certain questions can introduce new information into our conversations and enable clients and practitioners to make new connections. In the process of reflecting on their responses to questions, people become observers to their own thinking, actions, and contexts.

Introducing resources and possibilities

Our team colleagues were trained in professions rooted within medical, psychodynamic, and cognitive models. These models would agree, "our job is to identify problems, discover their causes and intervene to ameliorate problems" (Madsen, 2007b, p. 2). This belief shows itself in case discussions which focus on a client's difficulties. While a systemic model hears about problems and difficulties, we privilege listening for client resourcefulness, focusing on "what *is* and *could be* rather than simply on what *isn't* and *should be*" (Madsen, 2007a, p. 357).

Therefore, when I (Eleanor) started working with my team, I frequently made statements about client resourcefulness or asked questions about competence in meetings. Eventually my colleagues began teasing me about "your Pollyanna viewpoint" of our clients (the children's fictional character, Pollyanna [Porter, 1913], believed that if you looked hard enough, you could always find some good in someone), which alerted me to the risk that I could inadvertently set us up in polarized positions where we were competing about the "correct" view about a client. When we find ourselves "falling in love" (Cecchin, 1987) with "resource" and "possibility" perspectives at the risk of alienating our colleagues, we intentionally become "irreverent" (Cecchin, Lane, & Ray, 1992) to our preferred perspective and reposition ourselves to become more curious about the difficulties that are being talked about. In this way, we genuinely try to develop new understandings of the problem from our colleagues' and clients' perspectives.

> I (Isabelle) was invited to join a ward round of fourteen multi-disciplinary professionals who were squashed around four tables pushed together in the corner of a large dining room. Files containing patients' notes were piled high on the tables and a discussion about Val, sixty-seven, was in full flow. The psychiatrist spoke assuredly, giving his ideas about Val, who was an inpatient on the ward. He stated that she was "splitting" by saying different things to different members of staff. He suggested that she "must be putting it on if she could appear fine one moment and then talk about killing herself the next". He said, "I'm beginning to think she has a personality disorder . . . or it may be her illness."

I felt uncomfortable with the negative identity conclusions that the team was forming about Val. I wanted to defend Val and share the different story I had about this woman: a story about the strength she had shown in overcoming her grief at losing her teenage daughter and the passion she had developed for helping others, before her physical health had failed her. To avoid a polarized discussion, I began by asking questions rather than making statements about Val. I asked, "Who does Val talk about 'doing fine' with?" "What do you think she wants to communicate?", and then, "Who does she talk to about wanting to kill herself?" "What do you think she wants to communicate to them?" I went on to ask about the effect that these communications had on those speaking with her and the effects of her "using us in different ways" on our relationships with each other. Genuinely curious about people's responses, I asked, "What sense can we make that she presents these different versions of herself—the more optimistic side to some of us and the hopeless side to others?"

Introducing a relational perspective

Putting forward my (Isabelle's) positive perspectives about Val risked positioning the psychiatrist as negative and inviting a polarized debate within our team. On the other hand, asking systemic questions about Val invited the team into rich conversation, which enabled us to explore the meanings of Val's different relationships with different members of staff. For example, one nurse suggested that Val "showed her hopeless side when she thinks we might discharge her". The social worker suggested, "She may feel safer to trust some of us with her vulnerability", and the occupational therapist asked, "Do you think she could be holding all these different feelings at the same time?"

I (Isabelle) asked the team a range of systemic questions to introduce a relational perspective into their work with Val. I asked relationship (who) questions; effect questions; difference questions; and I explored possible explanations for the differences and effects on the relationships that the team had described (Selvini Palazzoli, Boscolo, Cecchin, & Prata, 1980; Fleuridas, Nelson, & Rosenthal, 1986).

If, like Isabelle, you are working on your own with more than one person in the room, you could practise asking each person how they see things, saying that you know everyone sees things differently. In this way you will be asking "views" questions, which invite many different perspectives. Then you could go on to acknowledge and summarize the differences you hear, without trying to find one specific answer, which helps to communicate that there is no "right" way of understanding something, no one "truth" to be found, but many different perspectives. Asking "how do you see it?" and "do you have the same view or a different view?" normalizes "seeing differently", whereas asking if people "agree" or "disagree" can risk negatively connoting different perspectives as conflict.

If you usually work with individuals you can "bring people into the room" by asking "who" questions, such as "Whose idea was it that you come today?"; "Who else knows you are here?"; "Who has a view about this?"'; "Who has been of help to you?" (see Chapter Two). You could also ask if the person would like someone else to join them when they meet with you as Josh Stott and Eleanor Martin describe in Chapter Four.

Moving from linear to circular explanations

The authors of this book take the systemic perspective that beliefs and behaviour are understood as connected in a circular relationship. Hence, with a systemic approach we are mindful that attributing a cause, blame, or label to a person is a particular linear punctuation.

> I (Eleanor) was meeting with Tom, seventy-nine, and his wife, Bertha, seventy-two. Tom had a diagnosis of early Alzheimer's disease. His mood was very low and there was a suggestion that he was "clinically depressed". As we talked together, Bertha told me, "I can't be doing with this dementia thing. I never asked to be a carer. Tom does such stupid things. I always have to straighten him out. He's dreadful." As Bertha spoke, Tom's head drooped. He said nothing. My heart sank. I thought, "Bertha, can't you just be kinder to him. No wonder poor Tom is so low."

Problems have the effect of making people look for explanations to understand why they have occurred. Initially, I found myself thinking that Bertha was the cause of Tom's low mood and that all would be well if her personality were different or if she could be kinder to Tom. This is an example of linear thinking (Figure 9.1). I saw Bertha's personality and behaviour as the cause of Tom's problem and Tom's low mood as the effect of Bertha's behaviour. Acting on my linear thinking in our session, I asked Bertha, "What happens if you don't get angry at Tom?" Bertha replied, "He needs to know when he has got things wrong," and continued to list Tom's faults.

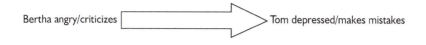

Bertha angry/criticizes ⟶ Tom depressed/makes mistakes

Figure 9.1.   A linear causal explanation of the problem.

The team working with Tom and Bertha had the same linear explanation for the problem, so that the community psychiatric nurse, Annie, told Bertha, "If you could be a bit kinder and gentler with Tom, he would become less rattled and make fewer mistakes", to which Bertha responded, "I am doing just fine, thank you Miss. I know how to be with my husband."

Taking a systemic approach, we acknowledge our responsibility to consider the ethical consequences of any linear punctuation we make. I (Eleanor) recognized that my and the nurse's linear punctuation of the problem had lured us into simply moving the cause of the problem from Tom to Bertha, with the effect that Bertha felt blamed and criticized by us. Hence, I was mindful of the need for us to move from a linear to a circular explanation. Circular explanations address pattern, interrelationship, and interaction rather than cause and effect and systemic approaches pay specific attention to the patterns that connect. Throughout this book, we pay attention to the interrelationship between people's actions and beliefs and to the interdependence of people in relationship. Each person is seen as influencing one another in ongoing recursive relationships, so that looking for a starting point or cause of problems is seen as unproductive.

Mindful that pathologizing, linear punctuations can locate problems within the older person or their family member, thereby inviting blame, criticism, defending, and counter-justifying, I invited Annie, the community psychiatric nurse, to join me in exploring a more circular explanation of the problem with Tom and Bertha at our next meeting. I began by externalizing (White, 1988) "the dementia".

> I asked Bertha, "What was life like for the two of you before the dementia intruded?" Bertha talked at length about their shared post-retirement interests before dementia came into their life. Tom brightened and contributed details of the pleasure they had shared in visiting gardens and flower shows. I went on to explore the effects of the

dementia with questions such as, "How has the dementia affected you, Bertha?", "How has it affected Tom?", and "What has it done to your life together?"

Thus, I acknowledged "the dementia" having effects on both Tom and Bertha, rather than Bertha causing the effect on Tom. I went on to track the effects of the dementia on behaviour and relationships with questions such as, "What does the dementia make Tom do?"; "Does it sometimes get you saying or doing things against your better judgement Bertha? Can you give me an example?"

I learned how the dementia made Bertha irritated and that she expressed this by criticizing Tom and phoning their daughter in Scotland. When I tracked the effects of the phone calls to their daughter, I learnt that the daughter, although sympathetic, told Bertha to "pull yourself together" and "get on with things". This made Bertha feel "no one understands what this is like for me", so when Tom again forgot things, she "took it all out on him even if he can't help it". When I asked how Tom reacted to Bertha's "understandable frustration" I learned that "the frustration" made Tom forget more, so that Bertha became more critical, phoned their daughter, and so on. As this circular pattern (Figure 9.2) was beginning to emerge, Annie, the community psychiatric nurse began to

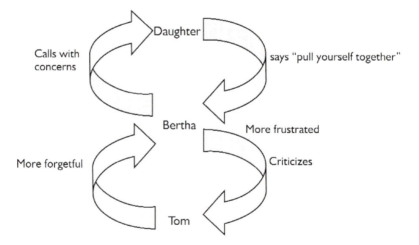

Figure 9.2. A circular pattern emerges.

see the situation from Bertha's perspective, and asked, "Bertha, who gives you support?"

Having only a linear, cause-and-effect view closes down our options to act, as we tend to push for change in what we see as the cause of the difficulty. Allowing ourselves to be curious about patterns, rather than cause, and then asking questions to track these patterns, gives us new options and ways forward.

Introducing context

Attention to context particularly distinguishes the systemic approach. Since context gives meaning, we always make sense of behaviour and beliefs within the contexts in which they arise. Contextualizing older clients' problems can offer new meanings for symptoms, for which practitioners may have previously provided pathologizing, linear explanations.

Above Isabelle invites team members to contextualize Val's behaviour in terms of her relationships with different team members using questions such as, "Who does Val talk about 'doing fine' with?"; "Who does she talk to about wanting to kill herself?"; "What sense can we make that she presents the more optimistic side to some of us and the hopeless side to others?" Contextualizing Val's behaviour in this way opened space for the team to consider the meaning of what Val was doing so that the team moved from attributing negative identity conclusions or intentions to Val like "personality disorder", "putting it on" or "splitting" towards more empowering and fruitful conversations, both with Val and each other.

In Chapter Eight, Glenda joined a psychiatric review with eighty-four-year-old Ruby and her psychiatrist with the intention of introducing a systemic perspective. At the start of the interview, the psychiatrist was using a diagnostic checklist to evaluate Ruby's present state. His questions, designed to generate clear descriptions of symptoms related to mood, sleep, appetite, weight, and energy that he could then match against diagnostic categories or syndromes, did not take context into consideration. As the conversation progressed, these sorts of question increasingly elicited accounts of pathology from Ruby that confirmed the psychiatrist's previous diagnosis of depression. When Glenda drew the psychiatrist's attention to Ruby's "busy social life", she invited the psychiatrist to look at Ruby's symptoms, especially "low energy" in a new context. Hence, the psychiatrist gave the new meaning of "doing too much" instead of "depression" to Ruby's problem once he had located her low energy in the context of her busy social life.

Throughout this book, we show how locating problems within contexts of relationship, family, gender, race, class, culture, physical and cognitive ability, sexuality, and, of course, age gives new meanings to the difficulties older people experience. Asking ourselves and colleagues systemic questions, such as "When does this happen/not happen?"; "Where does she do this/not do this?"; "Who is there when it is better/worse?"; "Who sees it this way?"; "What is the meaning of [the problem] in her culture?"; "If she were a man, what sense would we make of this?" invites us to locate the clients' problem in context, offers practitioners new perspectives, and, thereby, new ways to go on. Locating our perspectives in context can also enhance collaborative working and understanding between colleagues and ourselves.

Introducing systemic perspectives into our services

If you are working in a context where systemic ideas are not the norm, or appear foreign to other practitioners in your service, keeping a systemic approach alive will be a challenge unless you are able to connect with other interested people.

Connecting with others who are interested in our approach

Whether we trained as systemic practitioners or recently developed our interest in the systemic approach, we need to connect with others to sustain and develop our systemic practice. Cecchin (2001) talked about the need to connect with other human beings in order to stay alive. Similarly, we believe that isolation can stifle our preferred way of working. Therefore, to sustain our systemic ethics and practices, we seek out colleagues who share our perspectives. We make efforts to connect with people through presenting the ways we work to colleagues, offering training, workshops, consultation, and supervision. We demonstrate our systemic thinking and practice through the style and content of our written reports and in our communication with professionals, in clinical discussions, and through inviting other professionals to join us in our work.

Inviting others to join our work

Both of us invite care co-ordinators or key professionals to participate in sessions with clients on a regular basis. Inviting others to join our work serves several functions: it facilitates collaborative working; invites different perspectives into our work, and allows our colleagues to gain some experience of what we do. Chapter Eight discusses how inviting our colleagues to join our work with older people can bridge the gap between the different discourses of the practitioners present. When Annie, the community psychiatric nurse, joined me (Eleanor) in Tom and Bertha's session (above), she gained a different perspective of Bertha. Initially, she attributed Bertha's "unkindness" as the cause of Tom's low mood. As my systemic questions explored the complex circular pattern involving Tom, Bertha, the dementia, frustration, and low mood, Annie moved to see the situation from Bertha's perspective and began to wonder about support for Bertha.

When Annie and I (Eleanor) next met with the multi-disciplinary team to discuss Tom and Bertha, we were both able to share our new perspectives with the team. Having drawn out the pattern for the team (Figure 9.2), I was able to engage their curiosity in the effects we, as a team, were having on Bertha. We pointed out that my question, "Bertha, what happens if you don't get angry at Tom?" and Annie's statement, "If you could be a bit kinder and gentler with Tom, he would become less rattled and make fewer mistakes" led Bertha to increase her complaints or respond defensively, for example, "I am doing just fine, thank you Miss. I know how to be with my husband." Annie wondered in this team meeting, "Could Bertha sense our frustration?", and the social worker pointed out that "She may experience us in the same way she experiences her daughter." As we talked, the team began to see the situation from Bertha's point of view as well, and grew more sympathetic, rather than irritated, towards Bertha. Thus, the team began to address how to help Bertha feel more supported, not only in the usual practical ways, but in how we could "be with" her. When the team next met, they spoke optimistically about their ability to work collaboratively with Bertha. Thus, Annie's joining me in the session with Tom and Bertha facilitated our carrying new perspectives into our team.

Reflective practice

Although many of our older clients are isolated from family or community, most of them, because of their vulnerability, are connected with wide networks of carers and practitioners. Therefore, many of our colleagues have seen the value of working systemically with older people and invite us to offer a systemic perspective to their work with these complex systems of relationships through consultation. We are also called upon to consult to agencies or services like residential care homes, day centres, and inpatient wards, on their concerns about older people and/or the practitioners' working relationships (Martin & Milton, 2005). We use a systemic method when we consult or supervise to invite practitioners into reflective practice. Through this process, practitioners get an opportunity both to experience the systemic method and to observe the approach in action, as well as a systemic perspective on the client they bring for consultation.

The team manager asked me (Isabelle) to facilitate a peer supervision group for the community mental health team with whom I work. In our team, it is usual practice in case discussions for a practitioner to present a case, beginning with a brief description of the client, their history, the diagnosis, and interventions so far. Since asking questions of the practitioner presenting the case was a new practice in this team, I asked permission to "begin in a slightly different way".

> I began by asking the social worker who had brought a dilemma for discussion, "Is it all right for me to ask you some questions about this issue while the rest of the team listens?" I went on, "Let's say our discussion today was useful to you; what are you now able to do? What do you feel clearer or differently about?", and "What have we covered by the end of our discussion?" I then went on to create the focus with the social worker, summarizing what he said and asking about connections between his hopes with questions such as, "So, you would like to have some 'different ideas about what to do next' with Donald, and you would also like to feel that you are 'getting somewhere' with him; how

are those two things connected?" I clarified the meaning of his language with him to help me understand, for example, "What would 'getting somewhere' look like?" "What would be different in your sessions with Donald if you felt you were getting somewhere?" I went on to explore the social worker's own resources: "What have you already tried with Donald to help you get somewhere?" "What else have you tried?" This generated a long list of work the social worker had done and services he had put in place for his client. During the course of this conversation, other team members also began to ask questions, and to make suggestions for alternative ways forward. Finally, I explored other resources in the system, with questions such as: "Who else would have a view on what to do next?" "What would this view be?" I asked the other team members if they had further questions.

My usual practice with systemic consultation is to stay more closely to the systemic method to invite reflecting processes (Andersen, 1995): interviewing the presenter; positioning the rest of the team to listen while they keep any ideas they have for the reflecting discussion; requesting that the presenter listen to the reflecting discussion without joining in; and inviting the presenter to have the last word (Martin & Milton, 2005). However, I was aware that using a systemic method involving questions and a reflecting team might feel too different for some of the staff in this team. Holding in mind Bateson's ideas (1972, p. 315) about "the difference that makes a difference" (to introduce enough difference to make change, not so little that it is not noticed, nor so much that it is too unusual and therefore not recognized), I decided to scaffold (Vygotsky, 1978) my approach by starting with methods more familiar to the team and gradually building towards the less familiar.

Therefore, in this initial consultation session, I led a reflecting conversation with the team, inviting members to acknowledge the social worker's dilemmas working with this client, focus on the social worker's resources, list everything he had tried so far, and incorporate some of their own new ideas. Finally, I asked the social worker, "What has been useful from this discussion? What most interested you?"

Following this initial session, the team gradually became used to the format of a consultation session so that we moved towards a systemic consultation model where I interviewed one team member and other members acted as my reflecting team.

Developing systemic services

Surveying what you are already doing

As part of an evaluation of the systemic practice in our Camden and Islington service, members of the systemic family consultation team logged all their clinical activity over a six-week period. This exercise showed us how much systemic practice we were involved in outside of the family consultation sessions that were specifically dedicated to systemic work. Up until this point, we might have described some of this work as "working in pairs", "care planning meetings", or "chairing case discussions". Recognizing that these practices were informed by the systemic approach and involved many of our systemic methods encouraged us to use a systemic language for this work. Identifying this work as systemic practice enabled us to communicate to others more effectively about what our systemic service could offer, and to develop a shared language with other professionals about the work we were doing. Consequently, our colleagues began to request "systemic consultations" or "network meetings".

When we started preparing for this chapter, we hypothesized that whether or not you, the reader, have had systemic training, you might already be approaching some aspects of your work systemically. The fact that you are reading this may mean that you are already interested in trying a different approach. We wonder what you would find if you were to survey your work and log your activity as Isabelle and her colleagues did?

Creating teams

If other colleagues share your interest in the systemic approach, you may want to try working jointly with families together, using one of you as the interviewer and the others as a reflecting team. A reflecting team (Andersen, 1987) can be made up of one other person or several people. Traditionally, the reflecting team was positioned in an adjoining room with a one-way mirror, and a sound system for hearing the conversation in the therapy room. However, as the majority of us do not have these facilities in our working contexts, we work with the team in the same room, sitting a little way apart from the clients and therapist. Thus, we can work in teams in our clinical rooms and in clients' homes. The team listens to the first part of an interview and then team members talk with each other tentatively and respectfully in front of the client and the therapist about aspects of what they have heard to offer different perspectives. The clients and therapist listen to the conversation and have an opportunity to reflect upon what the team said after they have spoken. If there is only one team member, that person and the therapist will talk together, while the client is invited to listen.

The systemic approach privileges multiple perspectives and we use a team, even if it is just one other person, to offer different views and to witness and acknowledge difficulties and achievements. By offering perspectives through verbal descriptions, metaphors, or imagery, team members can give "double descriptions" (Bateson, 1979, p. 231) that not only create opportunities for new meanings but also offer clients the chance to "hear" and "choose" those ideas that fit better for them.

Specialist systemic supervision can enhance our systemic practice. The group of psychologists interested in working systemically in my (Isabelle's) service met together fortnightly in a systemic consultation forum led by a specialist in systemic work to develop our systemic skills. We practised interviewing each other on our work with older people, using systemic methods. Using live supervision, we stopped and started the interview process to reflect on our interview practice. As our systemic interviewing skills developed, the consultation forum progressed to formal, fortnightly systemic clinics that continue to offer systemic therapy and consultation to older people and their networks. Since we are spread out geographically, finding a location and time for us all to meet has been a challenge. To address this, we set appointments at the start and end of the day and met at the venue (client's home, ward, or clinical rooms) so that we had only one journey per session. As well as specifically allocated systemic sessions, we also invite each other to join as team members, especially where there are complex systems involved.

My (Eleanor's) service offered different therapeutic approaches, such as psychodynamic, cognitive analytic, and cognitive behavioural therapies, as well as family therapy. I taught systemic theory and skills to existing team members and trainees, since it was part of my job description, and the training curricula of some professions specifically ask for this. I sought to make training groups as multi-disciplinary as possible, as the different perspectives of the professional disciplines provide a rich training experience and are congruent with the "valuing of difference" integral to the systemic approach that was being taught. Presenting at our "journal club", at the induction programmes for new staff, and also giving short talks to different groups, such as our day hospital staff, engaged people with the approach. I identified key people in the multi-disciplinary network who expressed an interest in learning more about working systemically, gained permission from management for their full attendance, found a suitable date and time, and sent letters to all members of the multi-disciplinary team about the training. Thus, we formed an initial six-week introductory training group. A core group from this training went on to work with me as a team with clients, and continued with ongoing training sessions where we read papers together and practised systemic skills. I continued to offer the introductory course once or twice a year, which provided members for my systemic teams working with families.

While the teaching was on offer for all staff members, it was often difficult for nurses, who worked shifts, to attend. Therefore, I offered specialist training on "working with families" to ward staff. Specialist training not only helped staff to feel more confident about their encounters with family members, but also helped to provide me with practitioners on the ward who could join with my approach when we co-worked with families.

The main challenge to team development was change of staff and short-stay trainees. A core group would build up their experience, begin to work well as a team, and then people would have to move on. We experimented with a systemic clinic, but it was often difficult to co-ordinate a day and time when the team members and the clients could attend. As we were a small hospital, with all our services based in one building, it was easier and more inclusive to be flexible, and meet when interested professionals and clients were available.

Establishing a facilitative network

If you have to work on your own, connecting with people out-side of your service through training, consultation, or specialist supervision can help to sustain your systemic practice. Several of us working in different services with older people across London formed a group, which we called Systemic Therapy with Older People (STOP). Meeting with others who shared our enthusiasm and commitment to work systemically with older people inspired us all to organize a conference in 2003, where we were able to join, and share our work, with an even larger group of multi-disciplinary practitioners. In many ways, this conference inspired us to go on to develop the practice and writing that informs this book.

Continuing Professional Development is another way of main-taining connections with others with similar ideas. Attending systemic workshops or courses can help us keep our practices alive and meet others who work in similar ways. Specialist supervision is another way of nurturing our systemic approach. In our (Camden and Islington) service, we now have both foundation level and intermediate level training courses in systemic practice. Practi-tioners from any discipline in our teams are supported to attend these, which has helped to facilitate the development of a shared way of working among members of our teams.

Evaluating what we do

Since it is increasingly important to be able to justify what we do in public services, we need to show evidence of the effectiveness of our approach. While there have been some major studies eval-uating systemic work compared to other treatment approaches with adult mental health (Asen, 2002; Leff et al., 2000; Shadish & Baldwin, 2003), we know of only a few small scale evaluations done with older adults, and most are unpublished. Richardson (2005) compared family therapy with cognitive behavioural ther-apy and psychodynamic psychotherapy in a mental health older adult service in Lewisham, London, and found that the results were comparable with these other therapies (where referrers are free to choose and the service is free to allocate to the most appropriate service). The fact that such outcomes are achieved in significantly less sessions suggests also that family therapy is a cost-effective intervention. [p. 48]

Her study only evaluated the effect on the older adult, not on the rest of the family members, and she notes that researching the effects of systemic interventions for all family members could also prove interesting.

Our Camden and Islington service has undertaken some projects to evaluate our systemic practice using both qualitative and quantitative methods. We have interviewed in depth a small number of people who used the service to get a detailed qualitative understanding of their experience (Butler, 2003). We have also given all older people attending our service a client satisfaction questionnaire to provide us with a broader, albeit less detailed, picture of older people's experience of, and recommendations for, our service. Alison Milton and Josh Stott also set up a forum for gaining direct feedback from service users about their experience of our service, and their ideas for possible improvements. This group of ex-service users, who initially gave itself the name "Council of the Experienced" and now calls itself "The Advisory Group of Older Patients" (see also Chapter Ten), meets on a regular basis. Ideas or comments generated from the group are fed back to the psychology service, which then has a discussion of these ideas. The outcome of these discussions, and any changes which have been made as a result, are then fed back to the advisory group. Through this feedback loop, the service makes sure that it is accountable to its clients.

Like Epston (2001) we see therapeutic conversations as primary research in which we co-research problems with our older clients, their families, and those involved in the work. Together, then, we can contribute to a wealth of archival documents (*ibid.*) which could take many forms: verbal and visual, such as diaries, letters, transcripts, drawings, photographs, poems, audio or video recordings, and so on. Practitioners and clients can use archival documents as a resource, for example, reading them together, taking them home to share with others. Writing about this, we wonder whether advisory groups of older patients might be interested in helping to build up such archives of accounts and stories which could then be made available to others facing similar difficulties.

In conclusion

Writing this chapter has given us the chance to look back and reflect on our individual journeys from our first, perhaps apprehensive steps into our teams, to the realization of the wealth of systemic practices that now happen in our services. It has helped us to identify the small steps we each took on these journeys. Concluding this chapter is particularly poignant for the two of us, as I (Eleanor) have now retired from the health service, and I (Isabelle) am now working in a different service. Having become aware of those systemic practices that are specifically useful for developing a systemic service, we find ourselves continuing to use them in my (Isabelle's) new service and my (Eleanor's) supervisory and voluntary practice. We hope our journeys will inspire you to reflect on your own work, noticing where you are using systemic practices already and experimenting with developing them further.

References

Andersen, T. (1987). The reflecting team: dialogue and meta-dialogue in clinical work. *Family Process, 26*: 415–428.

Andersen, T. (1995). Reflecting processes; acts of informing and forming: You can borrow my eyes, but you must not take them away from me! In: S. Friedman (Ed.), *The Reflecting Team in Action. Collaborative Practice in Family Therapy*. (pp. 11–37). New York: Guilford.

Asen, E. (2002). Outcome research in family therapy. *Advances in Psychiatric Treatment, 8*: 230–238.

Bateson, G. (1972). *Steps to an Ecology of Mind*. New York: Ballantine. Reprinted London: Paladin, 2000.

Bateson, G. (1979). *Mind and Nature*. London: Wildwood Press.

Butler, C. (2003). What older adult service users say about systemic therapy. *Context, 65*: 15–17.

Cecchin, G. (1987). Hypothesising, circularity and neutrality revisited: an invitation to curiosity. *Family Process, 26*: 404–413.

Cecchin, G. (2001). The drive in life to exist. Kensington Consultation Centre Workshop, London.

Cecchin, G., Lane, G., & Ray, W. A. (1992). *Irreverence. A Strategy for Therapists' Survival.* London: Karnac.

Epston, D. (2001). Anthropology, archives, co-research and narrative therapy. In: D. Denborough (Ed.), *Family Therapy: Exploring the Field's Past, Present and Possible Futures* (pp. 177–182). Adelaide: Dulwich Centre Publications.

Fleuridas, C., Nelson, T. S., & Rosenthal, D. M. (1986). The evolution of circular questions, training family therapists. *Journal of Marital and Family Therapy, 12*(2): 113–127.

Lang, P. (1995). On the margins. Kensington Consultation Centre Workshop, London.

Leff, J., Vearnals, S., Brewin, C. R., Wolff, G., Alexander, B., Asen, E., Dayson, D., Jones, E., Chisholm, D., & Everitt, B. (2000). The London depression intervention trial. Randomised controlled trial of anti-depressants v. couple therapy in the treatment and maintenance of people with depression living with a critical partner: clinical outcome and costs. *British Journal of Psychiatry, 177*: 95–100.

Madsen, W. (2007a). Sustaining a collaborative practice in the "real" world. In: *Collaborative Therapy with Multi-Stressed Families*. London: Guilford Press.

Madsen, W. (2007b). Developing counter practices to sustain narrative practice in traditional settings. Workshop notes, 8th International Narrative Therapy and Community Work Conference, Norway.

Martin, E., & Milton, A. (2005). Working systemically with staff working in a residential home. *Context, The Magazine for Family Therapy and Systemic Practice, Special Edition, Grey Matters: Ageing in the Family, 77*: 37–39.

Porter, E. H. (1913). *Pollyanna*. Boston, MA: L. C. Page.

Richardson, C. (2005). Family therapy outcomes in a specialist psychological therapies service. *Context, The Magazine for Family Therapy and Systemic Practice, Special Edition, Grey Matters: Ageing in the Family, 77*: 46–48.

Selvini Palazzoli, M., Boscolo, L., Cecchin, G., & Prata, G. (1980). Hypothesising, circularity and neutrality: three guidelines for the conductor of the session. *Family Process, 19*: 3–12.

Shadish, W. R., & Baldwin, S. A. (2003). Meta-analysis of MFT interventions. *Journal of Marital and Family Therapy, 29*: 547–570.

Tomm, K. (1988). Interventive interviewing. Part III: Intending to ask lineal, circular, strategic or reflexive questions. *Family Process, 27*: 1–15.

Vygotsky, L. S. (1978). *Mind in Society: The Development of Higher Psychological Processes*. Cambridge, MA: Harvard University Press.

CHAPTER TEN

How do we end? Drawing our work with older people to a close

Joshua Stott and Eleanor Martin

W e began planning for this chapter by wondering where we might start. After spending some time embroiled in a conversation that did not feel productive, Eleanor asked me (Josh) "Imagine we have finished this chapter. You are reading it some years down the line. What do you like about what we have said? What really pleases you about this chapter? Who else appreciates it? What do they say?"

Ending begins from the start

Eleanor was using the sorts of future questions (Lang & McAdam, 1997; Penn, 1985) we might ask our older clients early on in our work. For example, we might say, "Imagine it is the next day after this meeting. Your son is visiting you and you say to him, 'that meeting was so useful. Now everything is sorted and I know what to do'. What have we sorted? What are you able to do?" These sorts of questions help us learn what clients want us to focus on in the session as well as where they would like to reach by the end of our work. When Eleanor invited me to look to the future, I started thinking about what I wanted the chapter to achieve; what would be important to focus on, and what less so; what I would want the reader to take away, and how we could work towards that. Considering the ending at the beginning, in this way, helped me clarify when the chapter might be finished and how to go on writing.

From our conversation, we guessed that you, our reader, might appreciate some explanation of what we are referring to when we talk about "ending". Ending, in this chapter, refers to ceasing our contact with the older client and their system. Ending our contact with older people often means, for them, the end of a close confiding relationship with us. Many of the older people with whom we work have few, if any, close confiding relationships. Because of their life stage, they have often experienced multiple endings, including deaths of significant friends and family members. Their previous experience of endings, including finishing with services, loss of family and friends, and their own journey towards the end of life can inform how they feel and respond to terminating contact with us. Ending our contact can happen for a number of reasons: because we mutually agree with the client that we end; because our service has explicit rules or policies about limiting numbers of sessions; because we or the service recommend referring on elsewhere; because the client chooses to end the work; or because we leave the service. These different types of ending can create various opportunities and constraints for older persons and we hope to illustrate some of these through the stories of the older people we introduce to you throughout this chapter. We also share some of the dilemmas we have experienced when managing endings with older people and our learning from these experiences.

Making sense of endings

In Chapter Three, we address how our stories and discourses from the different contexts of our lives inform our interactions with clients and the sense that we make of those relationships. Hence, how we end therapy and our beliefs about ending are connected with the discourses we act out of and there is a reflexive relationship between our different ending discourses, the sorts of relationship we create with clients, and our approach to termination in therapy (Fredman & Dalal, 1998).

I (Eleanor) was working with Marianne, an eighty-nine-year-old Spanish woman, who attended a local, specialist mental health day centre following a diagnosis of severe depression. She told me that as she was feeling a lot better recently she wanted to reduce her attendance at the day centre. Marianne still wanted some ongoing contact with the day centre because "knowing it is there reassures me and reminds me how well I am doing". She explained, "I don't want this [ending] to be too sudden and quick . . ." as she had found previous abrupt endings with services, practitioners and family or friends the hardest to cope with.

When I approached Marianne's key worker, Janine, about a graded and staged ending for Marianne, she informed me that there was "a centre policy" that older people have "no further contact" with the centre after discharge. This policy was based on the belief that ongoing contact would "encourage dependency". I had really liked Marianne's ideas about a gradual, paced discharge, and felt frustrated with the centre's policy, as there seemed to be little room for negotiation. Anticipating Marianne's difficulty coping with "no further contact", which she would find "too sudden and quick", I was unsure how best to support Marianne's successful discharge from the day centre.

Marianne, Janine, and I (Eleanor) were all coming to this situation with different pre-understandings about what it means to end and the best way to manage the process of ending. We had drawn our different perspectives on ending from our different personal and professional contexts. As an older woman, Marianne was well practised at endings. Drawing on her wealth of experience throughout her long life, she had come to learn that "sudden and quick" endings would feel like a loss for her. For Marianne, ongoing less regular contact with the day centre meant she could be confident "knowing it was there" while she worked on building her life outside the day centre. Informed by the discourses of her profession and the service within which she worked, Janine, the key worker, believed that open-ended contact would foster Marianne's "dependency". Fredman and Dalal (1998) note a particular leaning towards what they called the "ending as loss" discourse, borrowed from psychoanalysis, which sets the context for construing the therapeutic relationship in terms of dependency. They offer a range of different ending discourses and discuss the implications of these discourses for the therapeutic relationship and the therapist's action in therapy. Informed by this sort of "loss" discourse, Janine was trained to focus on rehabilitation to encourage older people to remain independent. A high value on independence is consistent with messages from our modern western capitalist cultures where "virtues" of self sufficiency and independence are valued over those of reciprocal relationships and co-operation. Yet, self-sufficiency in old age, which is often translated into enabling older people to live alone, is not a universal value across all cultures.

My view about ending here seemed closely connected with Marianne's: that ongoing contact with the day centre would be preferable, since it fitted for Marianne. My approach was informed by my systemic and narrative trainings that promote empowering clients and connecting them with valued communities before ceasing contact. This professional discourse that endings need to connect people with communities, rather than disconnect them, informed my proposal that Marianne stay involved with the day centre, without having to attend regularly.

The different ways Marianne, her key worker, Janine, and I made sense of ending influenced our proposed courses of action and therefore affected not only what we did but also our interactions with each other (Fredman & Dalal, 1998). Marianne was asking for reduced, but ongoing, contact with the day centre, in her attempts to change the nature of her relationship with the day centre rather than terminate it. Attempting to facilitate Marianne's connection, rather than disconnection, with community, I supported Marianne's suggestion of ongoing contact with the day centre and felt frustrated about the lack of opportunity to negotiate. My proposal, in turn, frustrated Janine's attempts to encourage Marianne to plan discharge with her so that she was unsuccessful in her efforts to agree a date for a formal discharge meeting. Thus, our different views about ending pointed us towards different courses of action that seemed contradictory and irresolvable.

Co-ordinating and managing meanings of ending

Mindful that the different "ending discourses" informing Janine and my approach to Marianne's request could bring us into conflict, I asked Josh to hypothesize with me about our different ending discourses to help me move from my potentially fixed position. Together, we reflected on the implications of Marianne's, Janine's, and my different discourses, not only for Marianne, but also for the relationships between the three of us. Hypothesizing about ending discourses in this way moved me from a position where I was seeing my view as right and the day centre's as wrong, an "either/or" position, to a position where I saw both our perspectives as understandable in their respective contexts, a "both/and" position. Thus, I was helped to see Janine and I as both acting in Marianne's best interest, which enabled me to talk differently about discharge when I met with Janine and the day centre staff working with Marianne.

> I began by saying, "I can see how far Marianne has come since attending the centre. It would be good at some point to hear your ideas about what has made the difference from her attendance here." The centre staff responded enthusiastically, nodding in agreement. Using the hypotheses Josh and I had generated to guide my talk, I shared my dilemma about discharge. I said, "On the one hand, I have heard how Marianne is concerned about leaving the day centre completely. She has told me that abrupt endings have upset her before. This seems important to her. On the other hand, I can understand that you at the centre might have reservations about Marianne having occasional contact. You have explained that it is not the usual practice here. Also you are concerned that it might pull Marianne back rather than help her to move on."
>
> Janine said, "Put like that, I see what you mean." She went on to explain that the discharge policy was in place to "avoid ambiguity" about who holds responsibility for clients who may be at risk. However, she began to wonder whether Marianne's situation was "slightly different". I asked, "Does the policy make life easier or more difficult for you and your patients?" Janine said, "Well, I thought it helped with clarity, but actually lots of the older people say the same as Marianne . . . they don't like the idea of contact being severed abruptly." Janine went on to talk about her previous job on a psychiatric inpatient ward where the patients could attend a "moving on group" to think about and plan for leaving hospital. She discussed proposing this sort of practice at their next service meeting.

By using the different ending discourses as a resource to guide my conversations with the day centre staff, I was able to co-ordinate our different discourses and thereby manage a coherent ending for all members of the system (Cronen & Pearce, 1982; Fredman & Dalal, 1998). Transparency about my position, sharing my understandings about our different perspectives, and wondering with Janine and the centre staff how to move forward with this, helped us create a collaborative working relationship. My curiosity about Janine's expertise and about the day centre's policy seemed to invite a very different conversation. Before I knew it, Janine was dreaming about the day centre's very own "moving on group" (Janes & Trickery (2005) describe a similar "looking ahead" group). When Janine told Marianne about her plans to set up this group, Marianne said she felt proud that her situation had led to this new initiative.

Hypothesizing about "relationship to ending"

Like Janine, we, too, learnt from this experience with Marianne. We now adopt the practice of hypothesizing about clients', practitioners', and our own "relationship to ending" at the start of our work with older people.

> Grace and Fred, a couple in their seventies, were referred to us by their social worker, who suggested that "their marital disharmony was aggravating Fred's anxiety". The social worker said they had seen a GP practice counsellor for "short term work", but she had found them "difficult to engage" and they did not seem to make any progress. At our first meeting, we heard that it had not been the couple's idea to meet with us and they had felt let down by previous contact as no one had "really listened" or helped them before. They complained that "only six sessions" with the counsellor "could not possibly capture the severity" of their problems. They spoke warmly of Dr Jenkins, who had been their family doctor for thirty-five years, had delivered their two children, knew everything about them, and had "visited night or day". They had "never known a doctor be so committed to his work". Despite the couple's initial reservations, they said they would give meeting with us again "a go", as they were willing to "try anything".

Not wanting to replicate the couple's experience of "feeling let down" by previous practitioners, we prepared for our second meeting by hypothesizing about Grace and Fred's relationship to ending. We noted that the couple engaged well with their former GP, who had offered open ongoing contact as well as long-term committed care. We wondered whether a limited contract of "only six sessions" constrained their engagement with the counsellor. Since our service recommended a maximum of ten sessions for mild problems, based on government guidelines that brief therapy be offered for mild problems (NICE, 2007), we wondered how limiting sessions would fit with Grace and Fred's wish to "capture the severity".

At this point, we noticed that we were focusing on our idea that Grace and Fred would not want to end contact at the proposed time, wanting more than ten sessions. We saw ourselves stuck on this idea and on our assumption that our service's perspective and the couple's relationship to ending were incompatible. To help us move forward, therefore, we tried to create another, different hypothesis about their relationship to ending. We remembered that the couple had spoken so highly of Dr Jenkins, and wondered about their experience of ending with him. We were keen to learn about how they had finished their long and valuable contact with their doctor and what tips it might offer us about finishing.

Hypothesizing about relationship to ending in this way was helpful for us. First, it informed our idea that endings might be a particular and current concern for Fred and Grace, so we decided to enquire about ending in their next session. Second, creating more than one hypothesis about their relationship to ending, and thinking about their previous experience of ending with Dr Jenkins, made us curious about their preferred ways of ending. Hypothesizing about relationship to ending has helped us take a self-reflexive stance in relation to our own relationship to ending. Thus, we have been able to generate an increased repertoire of ideas and stories about endings to inform our exploration of the ending process with clients and practitioners. In this way, we have been able to expand the choices available to our clients and ourselves, as we did with Grace and Fred at our next meeting, where we introduced possibilities of ending.

> I (Josh) began the session with, "It may seem a bit unusual to talk about ending therapy right at the beginning of our work together. It is not that we are intending to end now—unless that is what you want.

But talking about ending can help us think ahead about how we might end our work together when the time comes, so we can make sure we end in a way that suits you. So would it be all right to talk about this now?"

This approach to ending was based on our hypothesis that Fred and Grace might be concerned about finishing. However, not wanting to be wedded to this hypothesis or impose it upon the couple, we tried to "use the idea lightly" (Fredman, 2006). Therefore, we tentatively asked whether Fred and Grace shared our idea that talking about endings would be useful, thus inviting their feedback. By introducing the possibility of ending well before concluding our work, we hoped to open space for useful conversation about the couple's preferred ways of ending.

Exploring preferred ways of ending

Encouraged by Grace and Fred's desire to talk about ending, we began with an exploration of their previous endings. For example, I (Josh) asked questions such as, "How did you decide to end with Dr Jenkins/the practice counsellor?"; "How was that for you—did it suit you?"; "Why/why not?"

> We learnt that Dr Jenkins "left because he retired". He had told Grace and Fred "in good time" that he was leaving. The couple both "missed him terribly . . . he was like family". Although they accepted that "all people have to go some day" we got the impression that Dr Jenkins' departure had left a huge gap in their lives since they were not able to identify any other friend, family member, or practitioner who "can help us like he could". Fred explained, "We see a different doctor every time now—they keep changing—and they don't seem to remember who we are", and Grace added, "The social worker is trying to find someone to replace Dr Jenkins . . . but the counsellor told us only six appointments—so she was going to fob us off as well."

Exploring the meaning of those past endings for the couple invited Grace and Fred to become observers to their own relationship to ending contact with practitioners. Thus, they were able to reflect on questions such as: "[From your previous experiences of ending with . . .] what did you learn about how you like to end contact with practitioners? For example, do you see yourselves as liking lots of warning and planning for ending, or do you prefer to just decide at the end of one session that you are ready to finish? How can we use that learning to help us when we end together?"

> Grace spoke openly about how they were "getting on in life" and "there doesn't seem much point if the doctor is not going to be here in a couple of months", and Fred explained that "it takes years to build a real friendship". They both appreciated that Dr Jenkins had given them "good warning" that he was leaving, but wished he could have "introduced us to another doctor before he went off".

Inviting Fred and Grace's expertise on their preferred ways of ending gave us useful clues about how we might approach ending with this couple to avoid their feeling "fobbed off". We were aware that they liked "good warning", a committed relationship, and, although "all people have to go some day", they would prefer a personal introduction to a new practitioner before their final session. This conversation opened space for further talk about friendship. We learned that, according to Grace, Fred had "been a loner all his life" and he was constraining her attempts to expand her own social network by "making the most ridiculous demands on me". It seemed that visiting their former GP was one place the couple could be a couple, and where Fred felt the sort of "friendship" he only otherwise felt with Grace.

Creating a shared plan for ending

Mindful of the power imbalance between the practitioner and the client, who has less authority to control when we end, we take care to make transparent from the start what aspects of the ending we can and cannot change or negotiate. For example, we could not change the service's limit of ten sessions, but could negotiate the length of time between sessions. Therefore, in our first meeting, we told Grace and Fred that our service allowed us to offer ten sessions and that they could use the ten sessions over a period of six months or a year if they were to space the meetings. I (Josh) went on to ask, "Keeping in mind that this service says we can meet for up to ten sessions, how would you like us to plan for the end?"

Introducing ending early on in the work and using future oriented questions (Penn, 1985) invites older people to project forward to a time when the work is well under way or the ending is near. From this future perspective, we ask questions such as: "How do you know our work is ready to finish?"; "What plans have we made to ensure moving on feels comfortable and safe for you?"; We have found that introducing the possibility of ending and talking about the older person's preferred ways of finishing can help us find language that is meaningful to the client. With this joint language we can go on to create shared plans for ending that fit for the older person and that fit with the demands of our service. For example, we used Grace and Fred's language when I (Josh) asked, "So what sorts of plans can we make to ensure that you are not 'fobbed off' by us? What for each of you is good enough warning? Given that this service says we can meet for a maximum of ten sessions, how can we arrange our work together so you feel confident that we are committed to your well-being?" And "Given that, like Dr Jenkins, we too will 'have to go'—after ten meetings, what should we start to put in place to make sure that you have the sorts of 'friendship' you can depend on in the future?"

Like Grace and Fred, many of the older people with whom we work have little if any contact with people who, they feel, can offer them "real friendship". Loneliness and isolation constantly pose a challenge to our ending contact with our older clients.

Loneliness and isolation challenge ending

I (Josh) was about to meet with Ron, seventy-five, towards the end of our contract of ten sessions. He was living on his own in a small first-floor apartment. Ron had made excellent use of our work together and was pleased with the changes he had made. When we first met he had been telling himself he was "useless" because he "could not enjoy retirement". This sort of self-talk had brought a "heavy depression" upon Ron, further convincing himself of his "uselessness". In the course of our work together, Ron progressed to describing himself as "an intellectual who gave everything" to whatever he was involved in and his mood improved considerably with this new view of himself.

On the one hand, therefore, Ron's progress pointed to a good time to end our work. On the other hand, however, Ron's loneliness and isolation were beginning to challenge my approach to ending. I knew that Ron had very few connections with other people. He had frequently commented that the only time he got to "talk intellectually" was with me and had expressed concern that he did "not know how I will get by" when our contact ended.

> Recognizing that we would have to end our contact before long, I approached our session despondently, not knowing how I might enable this older man to keep his "intellectual" self alive after our work together ended. My shoulders were sagging, my mouth was downturned and I am sure my face reflected what felt to me like the burden of the anticipated ending with Ron. As I had anticipated, Ron turned down my offer to find a befriender with whom he could share intellectual conversations. He did not want to attend a day centre, since it would be "full of old people", reiterating that our meetings were "the only source of my intellectual life".

My dissatisfaction with how the conversation had gone with Ron led me to wonder if there were any other ways I might have prepared for the ending. How might I have created a connecting, rather than disconnecting, experience of ending for him other than offering to set up social contexts for him to meet with others, which clearly did not fit for him? Therefore, I asked Eleanor if she had any memories of ending with older people facing loneliness that might throw light on Ron's and my ending.

Josh's dilemma brought the following memory to my (Eleanor's) mind.

> I was five months pregnant. I had been Martha's care co-ordinator for two years and was very worried about telling her our work would have to end when I went on maternity leave. Martha, seventy-two, had talked often of how lonely she was since her family had moved as she "was never one to mix". In retrospect, I was probably informed by an "ending as loss" discourse (Fredman & Dalal, 1998) since, like Josh, I had concerns, about ending, expecting Martha to be upset, feel let down, or be angry with me. Most importantly, I feared that her mental well-being would suffer when we ended. When I told my supervisor of my concerns about telling Martha about my departure, she asked me, "If you were to see this as an opportunity for Martha, what difference would that make to you?"

Approaching ending as "opportunity" rather than "problem" for Martha gave me a new way of thinking about my leaving and enabled me to raise the topic with her in a different way. I remember feeling more relaxed than I would have imagined and, sitting quite upright when we met, I explained that I was pregnant and in several months would be taking some time out of work. I did not apologize or say "this must be difficult for you", as I initially felt the need to do. I was amazed at Martha's response. She seemed thrilled with my news and told me, "This has made my day." She began to speak differently to me. Now the expert in our conversation, having raised children and helped with numerous grandchildren until they moved abroad, Martha began giving me advice about the pregnancy—what I should be eating, what I should be wearing, and when I should be stopping work. As time went on she asked if she could pass on some of her "tips" for raising a small baby. This became our project together. She had a small notebook, and during each session would write down one of her ideas. She named it the "Mother Book". Her knowledge was outstanding and I asked if I could share her tips with other friends who were pregnant. Our ending was quite memorable, but in a very different way than I had anticipated. I left thinking about Martha as an experienced mother rather than as an older mental health patient, and I suspect it had the same effect on her.

I (Josh) was surprised at how much Eleanor's "Martha and the Mother Book" memory resonated with my experience with Ron. Their story inspired me with hope and a way to go on with Ron.

Connecting to preferred stories of self

Both Martha and Ron were using their sessions with us to counter the effects of loneliness and isolation. It seemed that, over time, loneliness and isolation had disconnected each of these older people from their preferred identities. Without the presence of her children and grandchildren, Martha had lost the contexts within which she could be the wise, warm, nurturing, and experienced mother and grandmother she wanted to be, and her identity as "older mental health patient" seemed to have taken over. Without an interested audience, Ron was unable to show and be "the intellectual who gave everything" and depression and "useless-ness" were taking over his sense of self.

For Martha and Ron, we offered an audience to witness their preferred identities. Eleanor was the audience to Martha's maternal and grandmaternal wisdom. The "Mother Book" Martha created with Eleanor seemed to open space for Martha to express her preferred (mother) self. As Martha offered Eleanor more of her abilities, resources, and values in relation to pregnancy, childbirth and infant care, her "mother" identity began to develop and over-shadow the story of her self as "older mental health patient". Thus, Martha's identity as experienced mother was being constructed through the stories that Eleanor told about her and those that she was telling of her self. During these accounts, Martha started to show confidence in a way she had not shown before. In a similar way, I (Josh) was audience and witness to Ron's intellectual self. Our conversations had created a context within which he could perform the abilities that enabled him not only to engage with his intellectual life but also to feel and be "an intellectual who gave everything".

Inspired by Eleanor and Martha's story, I began to wonder how I might help Ron sustain his "intellectual" sense of himself without requiring my presence to provide the "source". Since Ron was not interested in meeting new people through a day centre or befrien-der scheme, and did not want "strangers" joining our sessions as witnessing audiences (White, 2000; see also Chapter Three), I drew upon White's (2007) re-membering approach to bring in the pers-pectives and voices of other people from Ron's life. I hoped that these voices might offer stories to consolidate Ron's preferred sense of self.

Having checked that "intellectual" and "giving everything" were abilities that Ron valued and saw as important, I asked, "Who from your life currently or in your past would have noticed your intellectual abilities and your commitment to giving everything? Who appreciated these [abilities]? Who would not be surprised that you held on to them? If we were to see your life as being like a member's club, with people you could include from now, from the past, or even from books or television, who would you want in it?" My intention was to identify significant people in Ron's life that could make useful contributions to further develop his preferred story of himself as "intellectual". In this way, I was inviting Ron to approach his life as a "membership club" where he could choose which members would be useful and helpful to him (White, 2007).

Ron was quick to exclude his parents from this club but keen to include his Aunt Lillian, as she was "very special". I asked, "Aunt Lillian sounds an important and special person. What did she offer to your life? Can you describe how she added to your life, what she gave you?"

Having identified Aunt Lillian as a potential member of Ron's club of life I invited him to explore the contribution she had made to his life.

Ron's face seemed to soften and he smiled as he explained to me, "Aunt Lillian offered me respect and seemed to really value me." I went on to ask, "How come she valued and respected you, Ron? What did Aunt Lillian notice about you that others missed? Imagine she was here now and I asked her to tell a story about you that touched on these abilities, what might that story be?" Here, I wanted to invite Ron to take up the position of his Aunt Lillian, to look through Aunt Lillian's "appreciative eyes" at those aspects of his self that he valued.

Ron became increasingly animated as he explained to me that his aunt was interested in his school work and he wondered if she might have told a story about them opening his exams results together and her giving him a book "as a congratulations present". He went on to say, "She made me think that she was proud of what I did. I actually think she really saw me as a little intellectual."

Having encouraged Ron to look at himself through the appreciative eyes of Aunt Lillian, I said, "Ron, you've told me a bit about the difference Lillian made to you. What do you think you contributed to her life?" Thus, I moved on from exploring the effect that Lillian had on Ron's life to considering the impact he had had on her life. I intended to consider with Ron how his actions touched Lillian. I hoped that his gaining a sense of his contribution to her life would further add to his positive sense of self. Indeed, Ron told me that, although having never thought about it before, he now wondered if "perhaps it gave her a sense of achievement or pleasure to see me succeed. She was an extremely bright woman and she had been very good at school, but she could not carry on her education because her mother died young and she had to help out with her three younger sisters. She never got to show her potential and I wonder if she realized it a little through me."

I went on to explore this special relationship further by asking Ron, "If Aunt Lillian were here now, listening to what a great influence she has had on your life, what effect would that have on how she viewed herself?" My intention was to invite Ron to consider the contribution he made to Aunt Lillian's life. Although I was asking complex questions, Ron was very engaged in the process of this conversation. He described how he thought Aunt Lillian "would be proud to hear what an impression she had left on me. I had never really thought about why we were so important to each other and I think we were joined through our shared interest in studying and learning. It was just I could go to school and university and she couldn't. It's good to recognize I was important to someone. I'd never thought in that way before."

Each of the stages of enquiry I followed was intended to thicken and enrich Ron's preferred version of his "intellectual" self. Informed by re-membering practices (White, 2007), I hoped that exploring validating past relationships would enable Ron to reconnect with people who appreciated the same skills and abilities that he valued about himself. Initially, I tried to identify people who Ron would like to include in his "club of life", the people who might make an important contribution to his preferred identity. Through introducing other people's perspectives, Ron was able to elaborate a multi-voiced sense of identity rather than a singular account (White, 2007). A multi-voiced account would be more resilient and less vulnerable to undermining accounts of his identity, such as "useless".

Connecting with past, present, and future community

Ron reflected on how our re-membering conversation reconnected him with Aunt Lillian despite the fact that she had died many years earlier. This reconnection opened space for me to ask again about people who were still alive, people with whom he may have lost contact and might like to get back in touch. Whereas previously Ron had found it difficult to bring anyone to mind, this time he was able to identify several people he might include in his membership club of life. Each new "member" offered a new perspective to Ron's ever growing sense of himself as a "competent, capable thinker" who "gave everything" and was appreciated for his "thoroughness, efficiency and intellectual rigour".

Ron and I also talked about how he wanted to be remembered. I asked what legacy he might like to leave to this world. Thus, we discussed his "ethical will", the values that he would like to bequeath to the world when he was gone (Hedtke & Winslade, 2004) and whom he might want to know about his values. This conversation engaged and energized Ron to reconnect with his desire to write about local history and local issues. In our final session, he told me that he had spoken to a local newspaper and was writing a piece about how the square he lived on had changed over the years. When I asked, "Who else might appreciate your ideas? Who would you like to share them with?", Ron said he had been thinking about people from his past who would have been impressed by his articles and his efforts at further study, particularly his best friend at school, with whom he had lost touch. He had also thought about getting transport and going to the University of the Third Age to enrol in an evening class on short story writing

Our re-membering conversation allowed Ron to connect his preferred view of himself as an intellectual to a community of people, including his aunt, who was dead; people who could become part of his current community, such as the local newspaper, his old school friend, and the University of the Third Age. He also projected forward into a time after his death and thought about what aspects of himself he might like to leave behind. We did not physically invite people into the room, but the questions I (Josh) asked invited Ron to connect with people in his past life, people who might be in his current sphere, and those who might be around after the end of his life. Thus, we were able to create an audience to witness developments in Ron's preferred identity so that his retirement from paid work became a connecting, rather than a disconnecting, experience for him.

We have found that a lot of our work with older clients involves reconnecting them with their desires and values. We see therapy as the start of this process, which can open space for the older person to make further connections with significant people and communities that can affirm their preferred versions of their selves. Talking with Ron about his Aunt Lillian located him in a community instead of in isolation. Having reconnected with his values and desires through Aunt Lillian's appreciative eyes, Ron went on to talk to and remember other people who would appreciate and value his achievements. We also discussed to whom he might want to "spread the news" (Freedman & Combs, 1996) of the journey he had taken to reconnect with his intellectual values and aspirations. Ron identified an old school friend with whom he had lost touch, who he thought might like to hear about his progress, as they shared similar pastimes.

Similarly, Martha and I (Eleanor) considered who might appreciate her hints and tips for motherhood. Between us we came up with an extended potential audience that included practitioners working with Martha and my friends. Thus, I hoped to spread the news of Martha's preferred identity as a mother and share her expertise in the area of parenting. I hoped that circulating the "Mother Book" among other people would strengthen and give further weight to the preferred account of who Martha was. One way we set about spreading this news was through documenting Martha's tips in the "Mother Book" that she hoped I would show other soon-to-be mothers. The more people to witness Martha's abilities and talk about her in the ways that she valued, the more likely she was to resist the diminishing view of herself as an older mental health patient. Recruiting these different audiences to witness Martha's preferred identity was intended to further develop her identity story and, in turn, contribute to an ending where she felt connected to a community rather than isolated and alone. In Chapter Three, we talk about outsiders witnessing older people's stories as one other possible way of recruiting an audience and developing and thickening preferred identities.

Therapeutic documents and letters

Another way of spreading the news of people's journeys and achievements is through the writing of therapeutic documents. During our conversations, Ron and I (Josh) created a letter together. I thought that the most useful type of letter for Ron would be one that reminded him of his abilities as an intellectual and the consequences of these for his future. We had talked together about what might go in this ending letter, and then I wrote it on my own. Although we had discussed much of the content, I was careful to remind Ron that the letter reflected my version of events and it was all right for Ron to have a different view. The letter that I wrote is included below:

Dear Ron,

As we agreed in our last session I am writing to document your developments that we identified as well as some of your ideas about where you want to go from here. This is my understanding of our conversations so it may not capture fully how you make sense of things. My hope is that this letter will serve as a document that you can use however you choose. It may be something you choose to read just once, it may be something you turn to as a reminder of the journey you have taken, possibly when things are going well or maybe when things are getting in the way of you developing your life in the way you wish.

When you first came to see me, Ron, you told me about a dilemma that you were experiencing. On the one hand, you thought that having worked hard throughout your life it was time to enjoy your retirement and "just relax". On the other hand you thought that you had worked so hard that your job had "become your life" and that you now had no role and did not know how to enjoy yourself and relax. This seemed to tell you that in some way "you were useless". You talked about how these "notions of uselessness" had been around for some time, in fact, ever since you were young, when teachers at your school would criticise you because you found it hard to read. The way in which you countered these messages was to work twice as hard as everyone else, and this ability to "give everything" was something we discussed over the course of our work.

I was particularly drawn to how much you had given to your job and how much the people you worked with appreciated your "efficiency" and "thoroughness", and "intellectual rigour". You felt that these qualities were important as they represented someone who was "competent and capable". You dreamt and hoped of being able to both enjoy and relax into retirement whilst keeping alive some of the things that you most valued about how you were at work such as "being a thinker", "being a meticulous planner", "thriving on learning", and "showing your efficiency". We decided that these abilities or qualities were ones that you wanted to reconnect with in your life. These abilities seemed to have something different to say than "uselessness"—indeed they said a lot more about *usefulness*.

Ron, you have come up with many ways to bring efficiency and intellectual rigour to your life. I see many of these as creative and I wonder if you have seen them in that way? They include:

- writing small pieces for the local paper,
- reconnecting with reading,
- engaging with new areas of interest such as finding out more about history and science, which were subjects you gave up early in school.

In our final sessions we talked about how it was sometimes hard to keep going with these activities on your own. You came up with several new ideas to connect them to other people.

- You discussed how you would think about people from your past who would have been impressed by your articles and your efforts at further study, particularly your best friend at school, with whom you have lost touch.
- You have thought about places where you might be able to share your ideas and intellectual side like the University of the Third Age or an evening class on short story writing.
- You have also thought about volunteering.

I wonder who else might appreciate your efforts and how you might share them with others?

I expect that with your many abilities and resources, your journey will be a rich and interesting one, Ron.

Ron, I wish you all the best for the future.

Yours sincerely
Josh

Dr Joshua Stott
Clinical Psychologist

Towards the end of our work with older clients, we usually discuss with them how best to document their developments. We consider who needs to see the document, to whom it should be addressed, and who should receive copies. We consider the context we are working in and sometimes develop several versions of a document to best suit the various audiences. The main intended purpose of this letter was to document the developments for Ron and give him a written account of his preferred way of being to add to the many conversations we had. However, since the service within which I worked also required me to inform the referrer of clients' progress and of the decisions to end therapy, Ron and I agreed that his GP receive a copy of the full document as well as a shorter version containing only basic information about our work and why we were ending.

The stories that our colleagues and we tell about the older people with whom we work construct their identities. Co-creating documents like this allows for the older person to have a say in how they want to be spoken about and thus have a say in the way they are seen, and constructed by others. Therefore, in the final session, I explored how Ron might make use of the letter (Fox, 2003) with the following questions: "Where will you keep the letter so you are likely to make best use of it?"; "When do you anticipate using it?"; "How will you use the letter (for example as a motivator, as a memory aid)?"; "Who would appreciate what the letter says?"; "How might you let them know about the letter?"

There are many other ways of using documents (White & Epston, 1990; Freedman & Combs, 1996). Eleanor and Martha's "Mother Book" is another example. Together, they placed Martha's wisdom and knowledge in the "Mother Book" and this document provided another way of strengthening and enriching her preferred story of her self. By creatively using a document to develop and strengthen Martha's preferred identity, they were also developing an opportunity for "spreading the news" of Martha's developments to other people. Martha was keen for Eleanor to show the book to two members of staff from the day hospital, as she knew they had both recently become new parents.

Reconnecting with clients as consultants

At the beginning of the chapter, we talked about Eleanor's attempts to enable Marianne to stay connected with, rather than to disconnect from, the day centre community she had so valued. Over time, the staff came to appreciate Marianne's views rather than see them as being in conflict with their own. Marianne's hopes and ideas went on to spark new plans for the day centre (the moving-on group) and helped develop the shape of the service. Since then, we have set up more formal opportunities to make use of our older clients' experience, wisdom, and creative ideas through a consultation forum. Initially, we called this forum the "Council of Elders", based on the work of Katz and colleagues (Katz, Conant, Inui, Baron, & Bor, 2000). Over time, our older consultants changed the group's name, first to "The Council of The Experienced", and more recently to "The Advisory Group of Older Patients" (AGOP).

The AGOP is a group of older people who previously were patients using our service. Having been invited back in a different role, as "experience consultants" (Walnum, 2007), they now consult to us about how our service could be improved and changed, or what we should do more or less of. Some members of the AGOP have talked about how helpful it is for them to be able to "give something back", "play a role" or "feel valued and connected" through their contribution to this group. Marianne, too, had spoken of her pride that her views had led to a new group being set up. Thus, asking for their views has provided these older people with a context in which they are able to express preferred aspects of themselves as consultants rather than mental health patients.

The AGOP has advised on many aspects of our service, including how we approach endings. We would like the older people from this group to have the last words in this chapter. Here are some of the views that they expressed and ideas they had for how we might develop our practice:

"When you are thinking about ending your work with clients, try and think about what a strange experience coming to see a professional is for us in the first place. When a professional says things like 'we have no limit on the sessions' or 'we will review after three sessions' it can be difficult to understand. I had no idea what 'a review' meant, until it happened later."

"We want you to be attuned to our concerns about endings, to step inside our shoes and to be interested in what we are thinking."

"Let us end as we like. I gave the psychologist a big hug and kiss. She looked horrified. But that is the way I have always said good-bye to people—I didn't know what the fuss was about."

References

Cronen, V. E., & Pearce, W. B. (1982). The coordinated management of meaning: a theory of communication. In: F. E. X. Dance (Ed.), *Human Communication Theory* (pp. 61–89). New York: Harper & Row.

Fox, H. (2003). Using therapeutic documents: a review. *The International Journal of Narrative Therapy and Community Work*, 4: 26–36.

Fredman, G. (2006). Working systemically with intellectual disability: why not? In: S. Baum & H. Lynggaard (Eds.), *Intellectual Disabilities. A Systemic Approach.* (pp. 1–20). London: Karnac.

Fredman, G., & Dalal, C. (1998). Ending discourses: implications for relationships & action in therapy. *Human Systems: The Journal of Systemic Consultation & Management*, 9(1): 1–13.

Freedman, J., & Combs, G. (1996). *Narrative Therapy and the Social Construction of Preferred Realities*: New York: Norton.

Janes, K., & Trickery, K. (2005). "Looking ahead". Discharge in an older adult psychiatric day hospital. *Context, The Magazine for Family Therapy and Systemic Practice, Special Edition, Grey Matters: Ageing in the Family*, 77: 27–31.

Katz, A. M., Conant, L., Inui, T. S., Baron, D., & Bor, D. (2000). A council of elders: creating a multi-voiced dialogue in a community of care. *Social Science and Medicine*, 50: 851–860.

Lang, P., & McAdam, E. (1997). Narrative-ating: future dreams in present living: jottings on an honouring theme. *Human Systems: The Journal of Systemic Consultation & Management*, 8(1): 3–13.

NICE (2007). *Clinical Guideline 23 (amended) Depression: Management of Depression in Primary and Secondary Care.* London: NICE.

Penn, P. (1985). Feed-forward: future questions, future maps. *Family Process*, 24: 299–310.

Walnum, E. (2007). Sharing stories: the work of an experience consultant. *International Journal of Narrative Therapy and Community Work*, 2: 3–9.

White, M. (2000). *Reflections on Narrative Practice: Essays and interviews.* Adelaide: Dulwich Centre Publications.

White, M. (2007). *Maps of Narrative Practice.* New York: W. W. Norton.

White, M., & Epston, D. (1990). *Narrative Means to Therapeutic Ends.* Adelaide: Dulwich Centre Publications.

Working with elders: inspiring the young

Mary M. Gergen and Kenneth J. Gergen

For those of us engaged in the systemic movement in therapy, these are times of sober reflection. Over the past two decades, as social constructionist thought has been incorporated into the movement, an array of new and exciting practices have blossomed. Practices of narrative therapy, solution oriented therapy, brief therapy, reflecting teams, postmodern therapy, collaborative therapy, and open dialogue, among others, have virtually transformed the contemporary landscape. Yet, in the very recent past, we have also suffered profound losses. Many of the pioneers, Harry Goolishian, Gianfranco Cecchin, Steve de Shazer, Insoo Kim Berg, Michael White, and Tom Andersen among them, are no longer with us. Many others have now retired from the scene. The sobering question now shared by many is whether these losses signify the closing of an era. To be sure, we now have at our disposal a rich and valuable heritage. But do we now simply sustain the existing practices, sharing them with new generations and expanding their application? Or is there reason to anticipate new and innovative developments, possibly a continuous and creative evolution in concepts and practice?

There is certainly reason to hope that we do not become fixed in a set of practices. As anyone familiar with the systemic constructionist orientation is aware, therapeutic outcomes are highly dependent on the collaborative construction of meaning. This means that when any school of therapy becomes institutionalized and its practices become solidified, its capacity to engage in the meaningful conversations of the day diminishes. Not only does its language move from the stale to the banal, but for the potential client, a set of codified practices is alienating. For the client, the therapist is not participating in a genuine dialogue; rather, his or her actions are pre-programmed. Thus, one may conclude, the once robust practices of psychoanalysis, Rogerian therapy, and behaviour modification all lost vitality through codification. There is also reason to believe that the systemic constructionist dialogues will effectively resist the temptation of establishing permanent practices—of life everlasting. For therapists in this domain there is, first, a deep respect for the accounts of the clients. Their discourse is incorporated into the treatment process, thus expanding the resources available to the therapist in subsequent encounters. The possibilities for practice remain flexible and open. There is also the realization that one's premises and practices have no foundations; they are lodged in history and culture, and, thus, ever open to reflective deliberation. In this context, fledgling therapists entering these dialogues may come to realize that their own insights and creative impulses possess validity for their own times. We may indeed revere those courageous beings who opened the spaces of practice in which we currently find ourselves, but this is not an oppressive reverence. Each new voice is a potential resource.

It is with just such hopes that the two of us immersed ourselves in the pages of the present volume. Here is the work of therapists very much engaged in the systemic constructionist dialogues, and whose work is indeed a tribute to those who have gone before. At the same time, these individuals were working with a specialized client population of older people. We were most curious to learn, then, of the extent to which their practices might open up new spaces of deliberation and invention. Would this work make good in the hopes that the systemic constructionist outlook might indeed favour an ongoing process of inspiration and innovation? Our greatest hopes were fulfilled. The work that Glenda Fredman,

Eleanor Anderson, and Joshua Stott have brought together in the present volume represents not only an illuminating contribution to therapeutic practice with this specialized population but they have substantially pressed the systemic constructionist dialogues forward, and in ways that offer rich and exciting possibilities for therapists in all settings. In what follows, we wish to focus on several aspects of the book and the practices it portrays that we found particularly exciting.

Creative adaptation

At the outset, we were most impressed with the ways in which earlier practices were adapted to the new circumstances. The contributors to this work have drawn from the existing toolbox, but without regarding the tools as fixed in their application. Rather, they quite properly realized that if one understands the ideas behind their use, then one can create new but resonating practices more appropriate to the circumstances. For example, the contributors to this volume are fully cognizant of the systemic emphasis on relationships and their importance in generating and sustaining meaning. But they are also aware that not any relationship will do, and that one must be selective in terms of what relationships can actually contribute to the well-being of the client. Family members are invited to join the dialogues with their elderly clients, but the invitations are considered with great care.

Similarly, there is a deep appreciation throughout the volume of the significant role of language in the therapeutic relationship. Yet, pressing beyond such broad-brush concepts as narrative and metaphor, the contributors illuminate the fine details of such interchanges. For example, they shifted conversations from the familiar binary of agree/disagree to the curiosity and appreciation implied in "seeing differently". They avoided the familiar but deadening discourse of "referrals", "demands", and "obligations" in their relationship with colleagues and clients, and introduced an uplifting language of "gracious invitations". Even in the subtleties of addressing the other or referring to their ethnicity, for example, they demonstrated how one might succeed or stumble through subtleties of language use.

Discerning difference

There has been a strong tendency within writings on systemic constructionist practices to focus on positive outcomes. Almost invariably, the cases that are described lead to successful conclusions, and the reader is inspired to incorporate such practices into one's own work. Yet, typically absent from such accounts are instances and contexts in which the practices are ineffective. There is abundant inspiration in the works to date, but little in the way of discernment. Contributors to the present volume pull back the curtain, and allow us to appreciate the struggles of day-to-day practice. They illuminate the ways in which they have been more and less successful. They help us to see the ways in which our suppositions and stereotypes may obstruct the path to productive communication. They use their own foibles and failures to help future practitioners. They reveal their thoughts about the unfolding conversations, what they did, and perhaps should have done. The result is a far more reflexive orientation to one's actions as therapist, and a stimulus to future practitioners.

Self-reference as resource

Therapists typically focus on the life circumstances and history of their clients. From these they draw resources that may be productively used within the ongoing conversation. With the possible exception of relationally oriented psychoanalysis, therapists are far less prone to explore the vicissitudes of their own lives and the way they impinge on the therapeutic process. The participants in the present project see enormous potentials in this resource. In the early stages of the project, they realized that their own histories with the elderly, and their feelings and opinions about aging, could affect— for good or ill—their therapeutic practices. Thus, they met together to tell memory stories. They found themselves deeply moved, and then proceeded to reflect on the themes emerging from these stories. These deliberations were then linked to more general theoretical formulations. The results were salutary. As they put it, ". . . our telling, re-telling, and reflecting on the tellings of our memories enabled us to become observers to our selves and to our discourses, and, thus, to question the ethics of our practice. In this way, we were enabled to find new ways of looking that oriented our future practice so that we found new ways to go on" (p. 13).

Community collaboration

As pointed out, therapists working in a systemic constructionist idiom are usually quite sensitive to the relational context in which their clients live. However, they are far less sensitive to the relational context of their own therapeutic practices. The present work is invaluable in its foregrounding of such relationships and their importance. In particular, the contributors realized the difficulty of working upstream in a society that largely views old age as impending doom. Guided by a constructionist view of meaning as created in relationships, they formed a community of colleagues who helped them to challenge the "stories of impossibility". And, rather than allowing complaint and critique to dominate, they extended a solution oriented approach by focusing on visions and hopes for older people and the services with whom they worked. Further, their "collaborative community" continued to meet monthly, fuelling them with the energy, as they put it, "to reclaim our passion for ethical, respectful practice, to remind us why we choose to do the work we do, and to reconnect us with and elaborate the values that inform our preferred versions of our selves" (p. 208).

Dialogue with diagnostics

Within the systemic constructionist arena, there is a pervasive animus towards diagnostic categories and the reliance on pharmacological "cures". The many critiques of this cultural production of deficit are essential buffers to the cultural movement of the times. However, it is our surmise that such critical work has also functioned to galvanize the resistance of those who are already suspicious of this movement. While effectively preaching to the choir, they have largely failed to penetrate the consciousness of the mainstream professional. Within the pages of the present work, we find a new and possibly more promising orientation to the diagnostic–pharmacological movement. Rather than critique and isolation, contributors to this volume attempted to engage the community in productive dialogue. For example, they offered to accompany the medical doctor to meetings with the client, or invited them to come to join their therapy sessions. Rather than challenging those committed to the medical model, these practitioners took seriously their constructionist view of multiple truths. In this way, they were able to discern certain advantages in diagnosis, while simultaneously offering more congenial alternatives. This kind of both/and orientation can serve as a productive model for the future.

In conclusion

As readers of this work, we were deeply inspired by its ideas, its practices, and its innovations. The contributors draw unceasingly from the past, from each other, from their broader community, and, most importantly, from their work with elderly clients. In drawing all these diverse strands together, they also invite the reader now to join this community. They do not offer a set of marching orders to future generations, but a vision of continuous creativity in the service of serving others. It is indeed a compelling vision.